Praise for *Strong for a Moment Like This*

"These wonderful devotionals were a great source of strength for Hillary during her campaign, and I understood why when she shared some of them with me during the ups and downs of the journey. *Strong for a Moment Like This* is full of wisdom we all need."
—President Bill Clinton

"Seldom are we privileged, and in this case blessed, to witness the direct interaction between fellow pilgrims seeking after the heart of God. The spiritual guidance Rev. Bill Shillady and a cohort of other pastors offered Secretary Hillary Clinton during her contentious presidential campaign is an inspiration and lesson for all who are called by God to mentor and encourage others on the journey of faith."
—Bruce R. Ough, President, Council of Bishops, The United Methodist Church

"Each day during the 2016 presidential campaign, Rev. Bill Shillady and some colleagues sent Hillary Clinton short devotional messages of personal inspiration, professional encouragement, and spiritual reflections on politics, struggle, justice, and leadership. As I read them, I felt I was gaining many things at once: insight into Hillary's spiritual life, insight into challenges I face in my life and we face as a nation, and insight into what good pastoral care looks like. A beautiful read, meaningful on many levels."
—Brian D. McLaren, author of *The Great Spiritual Migration*

"Every disciple of Jesus Christ needs resources to stay rooted and grounded in their primary identity as a child of God. This may be even more true for those who are constantly in the public eye. Dr. Shillady and friends gifted Mrs. Clinton with just such a resource. *Strong for a Moment Like This* devotions gave biblical, theological, and spiritual encouragement to Hillary Rodham Clinton when she was in the crucible. This treasure is now available to all who follow Jesus and seek to 'serve the present age their calling to fulfill.'"
—Gregory Palmer, Bishop, West Ohio Conference of The United Methodist Church

"In sharing with the world these daily devotionals, Rev. Shillady gives readers keen insight into how Secretary Clinton, a warrior who's been battled and scarred, was and continues to be sustained. And, though written expressly for her, each devotional provides clarity and inspiration for all enduring the ups and downs that inevitably come with living with purpose."
—Jennifer Jones Austin, CEO, Federation of Protestant Welfare Agencies

"This collection of devotions provides rich biblical encouragement for the living of these rather extraordinary days. Through sharing some of her correspondence with Pastor Bill Shillady, the book also offers a glimpse into Hillary Rodham Clinton's thoughtful—and daily—engagement with the resources of her faith."
—Ginger Gaines-Cirelli, Pastor, Foundry UMC, Washington DC, and author of *Sacred Resistance*

STRONG

for a MOMENT LIKE THIS

* *

The DAILY DEVOTIONS *of*

HILLARY RODHAM CLINTON

———— * ★ * ————

REV. DR. BILL SHILLADY

ABINGDON PRESS

NASHVILLE

STRONG FOR A MOMENT LIKE THIS
THE DAILY DEVOTIONS OF HILLARY RODHAM CLINTON

* *

Copyright © 2017 by Rev. Dr. William S. Shillady

Library of Congress Cataloging-in-Publication Data has been requested.

ISBN 978-1-5018-5403-3

17 18 19 20 21 22 23 24 25—10 9 8 7 6 5 4 3 2 1

MANUFACTURED IN THE UNITED STATES OF AMERICA

This book is dedicated to
The Clinton-Mezvinsky Family and
Dorothy Rodham, who is dancing with the stars.

------ ★ ★ ★ ------

TABLE OF CONTENTS

* *

FOREWORD

Hillary Rodham Clinton

------ ★ ★ ★ ------

Fifteen years ago, I met Reverend Bill Shillady at a 9/11 commemoration service in Central Park. I enjoyed our brief conversation so much that, a little while later, Chelsea and I attended a service at the church he then pastored, Park Avenue United Methodist Church in Manhattan.

It was, as they say, the start of a beautiful friendship.

Rev. Bill (as we affectionately call him) co-officiated Chelsea's wedding in 2010, presided over my mother's memorial service in 2011, and blessed our newborn grandchildren. On those occasions, his faithful leadership and good-natured presence were a gift to my family.

Then, during the 2016 presidential campaign, Rev. Bill ministered to me in a different way. Every single day of the campaign, he woke up before dawn, sat down at his computer, and wrote me an e-mail message of Scripture and lessons that he or the other writers had written.

Sometimes he wrote about strength and perseverance—qualities the campaign demanded endlessly. Sometimes he wrote about joy—a reminder to seek and savor exhilarating moments, even amid the chaos and intensity of the trail. On triumphant days, he wrote of gratitude and celebration. On dark days, he wrote about grief, but also hope. And every day, he helped me stay focused on the values at the heart of our campaign, which matter not only to me but to our national life: compassion, justice, dignity, love.

There was one day in particular when I needed Rev. Bill's wisdom more than ever: the day after the election. As I write this foreword, I am deep in the writing of a book of my own about lessons I've learned throughout my life, especially on the campaign. It prompted me to go back and read what Rev. Bill wrote to me the day after Election Day—one of the hardest days of my life. His words were a lifeline to me then—something to hold onto while I recaptured my footing. "Sunday is coming," he wrote. He was right.

Rev. Bill believes, like I do, in an active faith. In words attributed to John

Wesley, the founder of our shared Methodist faith, we are called to "do all the good you can, by all the means you can, in all the ways you can, in all the places you can, at all the times you can, to all the people you can, as long as ever you can." It can be hard to figure out how to live those words in daily life. It's really hard in the midst of a political campaign. Some days I did better than others! Rev. Bill helped me find the way.

Many mornings, I would read my daily devotional and think, "This is too good to keep to myself." I forwarded them far and wide. I was especially honored and delighted that he gave the closing prayer at the Democratic National Party Convention that nominated me in Philadelphia, bringing his message of hope and love to the nation.

After the election, we had a long conversation about healing and faith. At the end of it, I said, "You know, you should really write a book. You could reach a lot of people." He laughed at first. But a little while later, he told me he was hard at work turning our private correspondence into this volume. On behalf of all his future readers, I was delighted to hear that. His words have enriched me, enlightened me, lifted me up, and pointed me in the right direction. I know they'll do the same for you.

If you've never read the Bible or if it's been a while, don't worry—he makes it easy. If you've been studying Scripture for years, you'll find insights in these pages that add to your understanding. And whether you've embarked on a long and difficult journey—like a presidential campaign—or just want to lead a more purposeful and spiritual life, this book will be a friendly, energizing guide.

I plan to enthusiastically press this book into the hands of a lot of friends. I'd do that even if I didn't know Reverend Bill, because his work speaks for itself. But as it happens, I do know the man behind these pages. I know how generous and thoughtful he is and how seriously he takes his calling to serve. He currently leads the United Methodist City Society, which supports the church's religious and charitable missions throughout New York City. Indeed, this book supports that mission—another way that it will do good in the world.

Rev. Bill is my friend and my teacher. With this book, he can become your friend and teacher, too.

PREFACE

✳ ✳

It was a beautiful fall day in 2002 when I first met then Senator Hillary Rodham Clinton. We both participated in a 9/11 remembrance ceremony in Central Park It was a wonderful experience to meet one who had seemed so larger than life. I introduced myself, and we soon discovered that we are fellow disciples of Jesus Christ and share so much of our United Methodist tradition.

Over the next decade, our friendship grew, as I was able to be the Clintons' pastor at special times. In 2015, after we celebrated Easter together, Secretary Clinton told me of her plans to run for president. At the urging of the Spirit, I found myself rising at 4 a.m. each morning to write a devotional based on world news, what was happening in the campaign, or a Scripture verse or lesson that I thought would be spritually encouraging. Who knew that the campaign would become one of the most contentious presidential campaigns in American history?

We both love the Word of God, time spent in the Word through study, and our Wesleyan heritage of social justice and doing good. For both of us, this became a worship every morning—a moment of centering for the day ahead. Hillary often would respond with a note of thanks for the encouragement she received or the new insight the devotionals gave her.

A few months into writing, I began to recruit a team to assist me. A number of United Methodist laity and clergy (including two bishops), a Baptist, and a Presbyterian provided wonderful devotionals for me to share with Secretary Clinton. Following my closing prayer at the Democratic National Convention, an online group of 115 young clergy women asked to join the team. They had organized themselves as the "We Pray with Her—Project of Prayer" supporters. I am so grateful to everyone who worked on this project to ensure that Secretary Clinton received uplifting words of spiritual guidance during what was very often a difficult time.

Six hundred and thirty-five devotionals later, after the election, Secretary Clinton encouraged me to collect the pieces as one volume to share with others. It is our hope that these devotionals will be a source of comfort, hope, and inspiration for readers. We would like these words to be a call to action in the continuing love of our nation and an ongoing prayer for our world to be loving, compassionate, caring, and forgiving.

I am honored to have been the "early-rising preacher friend" she sometimes mentioned. At one point, my wife, Judy, told me that my writings were going on too long. That day I wrote to Secretary Clinton, "Judy tells me that my devotionals are too long. It's hard to stop a preacher! I will try to do better." I was happy to receive her quick response, "I don't want to disagree with Judy, but I like the sermonettes!"

I would like to thank Judy for her tireless editing of my work. I confess that she was often right—they read more like sermons than devotionals.

I would also like to thank the United Methodist City Society Board and my staff, which have been wonderfully accommodating of this project.

I would especially like to thank my Administrative Assistant, Daffnie Marinez, who helped in so many aspects of organization.

After our conversations about this book and Secretary Clinton's encouraging thoughts, my royalties will go to the United Methodist City Society to share the transforming love of God in Jesus Christ through its programs and ministries in the metropolitan New York area.

With gratitude to God in whose love, joy, and humor I flourish as a disciple of Christ, I share these words with you.

Rev. Dr. Bill Shillady

SUNDAY IS COMING
NOVEMBER 9, 2016

* *

Psalm 17
Prayer for Deliverance from Persecutors

1 Corinthians 15
The Resurrection of Christ

------- ★ ★ ★ -------

It is Friday, but Sunday is coming. This is not the devotional I had hoped to write. This is not the devotional you wish to receive this day. While Good Friday may be the starkest representation of a Friday that we have, life is filled with a lot of Fridays.

For the disciples and Christ's followers in the first century, Good Friday represented the day that everything fell apart. All was lost. The momentum and hope of a man claiming to be the Son of God, the Messiah who was supposed to change everything, had been executed.

Even though Jesus told his followers three days later the temple would be restored, they had no idea of what that Sunday would be. They betrayed, denied, mourned, fled, and hid. They did just about everything BUT feel good about Friday and their circumstances.

For us, Friday is the phone call from the doctor that the cancer is back. It's the news that you have lost your job. It's the betrayal of a friend, the loss of someone dear. Friday is the day that it all falls apart and all hope is lost. We all have Friday's. But, as the saying goes, "Sunday's coming!"

Today, you are experiencing a Friday. Your Friday is what happened in the last few weeks and last night in the tragic loss. But Sunday is coming!

Jesus completed the excruciating task of giving up his life as a sacrifice for the sins of the world. It was his faith and belief in his heavenly Father, that gave him the grace and peace to submit to Friday. While death had seemingly won, Jesus knew better. When he said, "It is finished" it wasn't meant to be a statement of concession. It was a declaration that a new day was on the way.

Friday is finished. Sunday is coming. Death will be shattered. Hope will be restored. But first, we must live through the darkness and seeming hopelessness of Friday.

You know one of my favorite sayings is "God doesn't close one door without opening another, but it can be hell in the hallway." My sister Hillary. You, our nation, our world is experiencing a dark Friday. Our hope is that Sunday is coming. But it might well be hell for a while.

------ ★ ★ ★ ------

Easter people raise your voices,
  sounds of heaven in earth should ring.
Christ has brought us heaven's choices;
Heavenly music, let it ring.
Alleluia! Alleluia!
Easter people, let us sing.

  "Easter People, Raise Your Voices" by William James

ACCEPT THE CALL

CALLED TO SERVE

Psalm 71

As I have struggled with what to write on this very important day as you declare your candidacy, the words from last Sunday's brunch ring clear. You feel called to enter the chaos and to work for the healing of our nation.

Everyday Americans need a champion. And I want to be that champion. So I'm hitting the road to earn your vote—because it's your time. And I hope you'll join me on this journey.[1]

Hillary Rodham Clinton
April 12, 2015

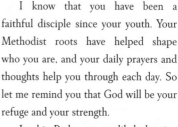

I know that you have been a faithful disciple since your youth. Your Methodist roots have helped shape who you are, and your daily prayers and thoughts help you through each day. So let me remind you that God will be your refuge and your strength.

In this Psalm we are likely hearing from an aged psalmist looking back over his life and faith experiences. From his advanced location in the course of life, this psalmist is able to impart key lessons for the life of faith.

First, a strong faith in and devotion to God is no fail-safe insurance against problems and complications in life. Second, it is God's very nature to provide refuge, deliverance, and rescue to those whom God calls God's own and calls to service in God's name. Third, we learn that we are wholly dependent on God. Finally, a significant aspect of our lives should be the praise of God.

Even though we may experience trouble and even persecution, we should maintain trust and hope in the God we know to be our rock and fortress and who, even in the midst of trouble, is worthy of our continual praise.

------- ★ ★ -------

Gracious God, be the refuge and the source of strength for your child Hillary. Be with her, Bill, Chelsea, Marc, and Charlotte on this important day in their family's journey. Amid life's complexities over these next few months, may they feel your loving presence and your protection. Amen.

THE CALL
Exodus 3:1-6

You have inspired me to write devotionals on the call of Moses and the journey in the wilderness.

In today's Scripture verse, God calls Moses to liberate the children of Israel from Egyptian slavery. I have often thought how strange it is that this great God of creation needs lowly humans to accomplish God's work.

God needs us. Our gracious God is willing, even eager, to have us join in the salvation work of this world, whether we are an excellent plumber or an average minister. No matter our station in life, we are all called as disciples in the name of Christ to minister to others.

God speaks to Moses—not in some religious setting but in everyday work. Moses, tending the flocks, spots the burning bush, and God turns that grazing spot into "holy ground."

Too often, Christians wait for God to speak to them at some religious service. In fact, God more likely speaks to us in our everyday lives. God can transform into "holy ground" our places of business, our kitchens, our schoolrooms, our assembly lines, or virtually any place where people of faith are to be found.

Look today for your "holy ground." May you hear God's call every day in the ordinary aspects of your daily living. God will be there.

------- ★ ★ ★ -------

Lord, we want to hear your word for us. We know you come to us in the ordinary aspects of our lives. Be with us this day, guiding our spirits and opening our hearts to hear your forgiveness and call to us. Give us courage and strength to do your will and help others in need. In Jesus's name, we pray. Amen.

THE STAND
Exodus 3:7-14

Today, as we continue on the call of Moses, we recall that the very reason Moses was out in the wilderness was because he was in trouble with the law in Egypt, having killed an Egyptian guard for mistreating one of the Israelite slaves.

In fact, Moses was so frustrated by the injustices he had seen that he lost his favored status as Pharaoh's adopted grandson and became an outlaw.

I think that God calls us not for our personal transformations but because God is concerned with a greater good. In fact, it seems that God usually calls a person right when that person has, out of genuine concern for others, begun to set aside his or her own personal ambitions.

All Moses did, all of his life, was stand up against wrong and fight for what was right and just. So what was his reward? What did he get for all his trouble?

His reward was the deep and abiding knowledge that he had tried to do what was right. It was the reward of knowing that he had tried to listen hard to the voice of God and to do what God was calling him to do. May it be so for all of us who try to live in the law of love as Jesus has taught us!

------- ⋆ ★ ⋆ -------

Lord, may we do what is right, even when it is difficult for us to do so. Amen.

THE MISSION
Exodus 3:11-14

Today's story is about an encounter between a self-doubting outlaw and a God who's more than up to the challenge of transforming him into an instrument of salvation.

Moses asks what seems an innocuous question after his encounter with God at the burning bush. God promises to deliver his people from bondage, and Moses responds with self-deprecating hesitation, "I can't do this." Then he receives the divine reassurance, "Yes, you can."

And then it comes: "Suppose I go to the Israelites and tell them all this great news and they ask just who this God is who sent me. What shall I tell them?"

God's answer: "I Am Who I Am. So say to the Israelites, 'I Am has sent me to you'" (v. 14).

I have found that I cannot fully know God. I can see aspects of God, but God doesn't have limits. Many people whom God uses are frail, fallible, and ordinary people who manage to do extraordinary things with God as their companion on the journey. As you walk this path, think of Moses, who found the strength and the courage to do mighty things because God was his companion on the journey.

------ ★ ★ ★ ------

God, our life journeys can be difficult and challenging. Journey with us along the way. When the path grows dark and menacing, may the light of Christ shine through others so that we can see the way. Amen.

Former Secretary of State Hillary Clinton announced today that she is seeking the Democratic presidential nomination for the 2016 election.
"I'm running for president," she says in a video posted this afternoon on the website hillaryclinton.com.[2]

NPR
April 12, 2015

THE MOVEMENT
Exodus 14:10-18

Have you ever found yourself in a desperate situation? Ever felt you were painted into a corner or caught between a rock and a hard place? The Israelites, centuries bound and oppressed in Egypt, felt that way when they got cornered at the Red Sea. Their exodus from their old life of slavery was gravely endangered as Pharaoh and his legions of chariots

and horsemen trapped them against the mighty waters. As the specter of capture or annihilation came over them, many were tempted to throw up their hands in surrender. Better to return to slavery than to die by the sword. Though they had begun the faith journey with much enthusiasm, their faith at that time was minimal. What faith they did have lay more in Moses. And so, in fear, they turned to Moses, and Moses, in faith, turned to God.

Sometimes we have the tendency to look backwards when we come to the "Red Sea" in our lives. When times are tough we feel like giving up and going back to comfortable ways, old habits, how things were. There's nothing wrong with memories, but they won't help us to cross our "Red Seas."

------- ★ ★ ★ -------

God, you are my strength and hope. You are my salvation, and I praise you for helping me to overcome the obstacles of my life. Help me not to forget the past, to learn from it, but also to move forward with new convictions and directions. When I meet with obstacles that make me afraid, comfort me with your promises and lead me to step forward courageously. Amen.

THE PRAISE
Exodus 15:1-18

No commentary needs to be said about this beautiful but troubling prayer of Moses celebrating the crossing of the Red Sea. This song of praise to God for deliverance celebrates the power of God, gloriously manifested in the destruction of Pharaoh and his armies. The challenging theological concept of this story is that God is a warrior God.

Let's approach this from Henri Nouwen's perspective:

Perhaps nothing helps us make the movement from our little selves to a larger world than remembering God in gratitude. Such a perspective puts God in view in all of life, not just in the moments we set aside for worship or spiritual disciplines. Not just in the moments when life seems easy.[3]

Hillary Clinton will give extraordinary national and global leadership. Leadership anchored in reason, wisdom, sound judgment, spiritual strength, and moral courage.[4]

Rev. Dr. Otis Moss Jr.
Civil Rights Leader

So let us be grateful to God not for the destruction of the Egyptians but for the newfound freedom of Moses and the Israelites who crossed the sea on dry ground.

------ ★ ★ ★ ------

God of freedom, you brought your people out of slavery with a mighty hand. Deliver us from our captivity of pride and indifference to the needs and gifts of others so that we may be ready to love as you have loved us and to give even as we have received. We remain grateful for your love and grace in Jesus Christ, who taught us the path of peace. Amen.

THE NEED
Exodus 16:31-35

There wasn't much planning as Moses led over two million people out of Egypt. He just knew that God had told him to free the people from slavery in Egypt. Moses obviously stepped out in faith, not knowing how God was going to pull this off.

After crossing the Red Sea and beginning their journey, there was a lot of grumbling by the people. They were hungry and thirsty, and they complained, wanting to go back to the chains of Egypt where they at least knew their daily needs were somewhat met by their masters.

Just imagine what was involved. For two million people to cross the Red Sea in double-file, the line would have had to be eight hundred miles long, and it would have taken thirty-five days and nights. To cross in one night would have meant an opening in the sea that was three miles wide so that five thousand could cross abreast. To feed that many people would have required fifteen hundred tons of food each day—or in modern terms, the contents of two freight trains, each at least a mile long.

Today's Scripture tells of the miraculous action of God through his servant Moses in meeting the needs of the people. Moses believed God, and God provided manna and water. The Israelites began to understand that God cared for them and loved them and wanted to satisfy their hunger.

------ * ★ * ------

Lord, you provide for our every need. Thank you for giving us Jesus, who is the manna that can fill our hungry hearts and souls. Amen.

THE VICTORY
Psalm 13:1-6 NRSV

Hillary, today you will become the presumptive Democratic nominee. Sure, the news sources declared victory for you last night, but today is the day with the primaries at hand.

"How long, O Lord?" (v. 1) is a prayer for patience. It's helpful in situations of crushing boredom: the endless sermon, the pointless meeting, the witless lecture. It's a good prayer for the airplane flight or the department of motor vehicles or any other place that reliably offers maddening frustration.

The Psalm ends with: "I trusted in your steadfast love; my heart shall rejoice in your salvation. I will sing to the LORD, because he has dealt bountifully with me." The in-between, the incomplete, the sense of where God is in all this becomes fulfilled. We have trusted in God's love, and our hearts rejoice.

But today, my sister, you no longer need to ask, "How long?" You are there. One phase is over, and a new one begins. Onward and upward with God's steadfast love!

------ ★ ★ ★ ------

Lord, we trust in your steadfast love and know that in the end the victory is ours through Christ Jesus, our Lord. Help us to trust in your love and be enduring. Amen.

Hillary gave a moving address on the occasion of her historic victory as the first woman in the nation's history to receive the presidential nomination of a major party. It was eight years to the day she gave her famous "18 million cracks in the highest and hardest glass ceiling" speech. History has been written, and beautifully so.[5]

Blue Nation Review
June 7, 2016

THE LIBERATOR
Exodus 20:1-17

In chapters 20 through 23 of Exodus, we have the societal law set before the Israelites beginning with the Ten Commandments. The commandments and the verses that follow frame the most important issues we can address as a society, like the mystery of good and evil, the meaning of living in community, the nature of integrity, the meaning of fidelity, the care of the poor, and the necessity of honesty. In honoring the Law, the Israelites embraced the sanctity of health and life, the power of love, and the need to be bound together in life-affirming community.

At the foundation of the Exodus story is that with the freedom of the coming Promised Land there also comes responsibility as a society, especially to treat people equally and fairly—and to do so in the worshipful atmosphere of a God-given freedom.

Freedom, which has been proven to have been hard won throughout history, is one of the greatest gifts any woman, man, or child can be given. The final paragraph of Nelson Mandela's autobiography, *Long Walk to Freedom*, says: "I have walked that long road to freedom. I have tried not to falter; I have made missteps along the way. But I have discovered the secret that after climbing a great hill, one only finds that there are many more hills to climb. I have taken a moment here to rest, to steal a view of the glorious vista that surrounds me, to look back on the distance I have come. But I can rest only for a moment, for with freedom come responsibilities, and I dare not linger, for my long walk is not yet ended."[6]

The Israelites have a long way to go to the Promised Land, as do we!

------ ★ ★ ★ ------

God, you are the power of liberation, calling your servant Moses to lead your people into freedom and giving him the wisdom to proclaim your holy law. Be our Passover from the land of injustice, be the light that leads us to the perfect rule of love that we may be citizens of your unfettered reign. We ask this through Jesus Christ, the pioneer of our salvation. Amen.

OUR STORY
Luke 1:46-55

Mary's response to the angel Gabriel's news that she will bear a son is most unusual. The young teenager goes from apprehensiveness and curiosity in one moment to joy and exuberance the next. Her song, also known as The Magnificat, delivers to us a poetic recounting of God's story through the ages. It is this story—the story of God—that animates Mary's words and imbues within her a sense of wonder and awe.

All of our lives tell a story, but not all of those stories harmonize with the story of God. When we oppress the weak, trample on the downtrodden, and allow our actions to be controlled by fear, our lives embody a counter-narrative to God's story of justice, deliverance, and peace. But when our lives embrace as kin our neighbors and strangers alike, we find our lives echoing with the cadence of the divine. We, like Mary, have the opportunity to not only proclaim God's story with our lips but with our entire lives. Let each and every day be our own Magnificat to the great things God has done and desires to do in this world.

------ ★ ★ ★ ------

Lord, may I be like Mary and welcome all that you wish to bring into my life. May my life tell your story of peace, justice, and compassion in this world. Amen.

Rev. Kevin K. Wright

FROM: Rev. Bill Shillady
SENT: December 22, 2015
TO: H

Congratulations! You will be a grandmother again. Fantastic news! Will Chelsea and Marc and Charlotte be with you on Christmas Eve? Blessings to you and Bill on being grandparents a second time. I think the following devotional is serendipitous to Chelsea's news.

★ ★ ★

FROM: H
SENT: December 22, 2015
TO: Rev. Bill Shillady

We are so excited!!

Bill and I would love to host you, Judy and Clayton for Christmas Eve dinner, if that works for you. We will be going to church for the 11 p.m. service. Chelsea and Marc will be in the City, and we'll go to their apartment early the next morning. Please let me know if you can be there as our guests. Looking forward to seeing you. H

HERE AND NOW
Matthew 1:28-35

Conventional wisdom tells Joseph that something is up. His fiancée, Mary, is pregnant, and the only thing that Joseph knows about the baby's father is that it isn't him. Joseph, being an honorable man, makes plans to dismiss Mary in secret so as to mitigate the risk of scandal in their small, sleepy town. But before Joseph can carry through with his plan, an angel of the Lord appears and reveals to him what's going on with his fiancée's mysterious pregnancy. Joseph must now choose between believing conventional wisdom and believing God.

Joseph decides to believe God and trust in a reality grounded in a world that he cannot always see clearly—the world of God and God's reign.

God tells us to care for the weak, to visit those in prison, and to treat our enemies as neighbors. This command of God invites us to live into a reality marked by God's grace and love—a reality markedly different than the one we might be used to seeing.

Rev. Kevin K. Wright

------ * ⭐ * ------

Lord, we believe that you have placed us on the planet for your glory. Help us to be instruments of your peace—here and now. Amen.

FROM: Rev. Bill Shillady
SENT: December 22, 2015
TO: H

We would love it. Thank you so much! I will need to leave to go to the church, but Clayton can drive Judy and her mother to the service. The Bishop sends her Christmas greeting to you. See you at Kittle House. Congrats again about being Grandparents!

* ⭐ *

FROM: H
SENT: December 22, 2015
TO: Rev. Bill Shillady

Great. See you there.

AN IMPOSSIBLE DREAM
2 Peter 1:4-5

I t was during Christmastime about fourteen years ago when he knocked on their door to ask if they had any bread. When they invited him inside to give him something to eat and drink, they learned that his entire family was starving. They gave him food to take to his family, and when he left, they got on their knees to ask God for guidance. What was God's yearning for them? They received a clear answer: "Start a church."

Jaime and Hilda Cabrera, in their 70s, had retired in Cochabamba, Bolivia. They planned to rest and to be much less active in the church. But the message from God was clear. They told this story to the members of their little church, and this small congregation knew immediately that God was calling them to be the parent church.

My husband, Jack, and I were privileged to attend the first worship service at La Piedra Viva Methodist Church, the Living Stone. Tears of joy flowed from every eye. The church of the living stone was born. This dream, planted in the hearts of this precious couple, became a reality.

------ ★ ★ ★ ------

Dear God, you plant dreams in our hearts, seemingly impossible dreams, dreams we don't even want to fulfill. And you turn those dreams into reality. May we be bold and courageous to follow those dreams. Amen.

Bishop Jane Allen Middleton

★ ★

FROM: Rev. Bill Shillady
SENT: December 23, 2015
TO: H

Good Morning,
I just spoke to Parker Proust, the lay certified minister who is serving Mt. Kisco. He asked me to ask if you and Bill would be willing to light the Christ Candle at the appropriate time in the service.

★ ★ ★

FROM: H
SENT: December 23, 2015
TO: Rev. Bill Shillady

We would be happy to light the candle.

★ ★

TO GREAT HEIGHTS
Isaiah 40:28-31

Looking outside my office window, I often get a glance of peregrine falcons that live on the steeple of Riverside Church. They soar on the wind right by me. On cold winter days when the Hudson River is frozen farther north, I have watched a huge bald eagle with a marvelous wingspan soar within 20 feet of my window.

Feathered creatures remind us of God's amazing gifts. Throughout the Bible, one reads about the significance of birds. Of course, birds come in all shapes and sizes.

The prophet Isaiah reminds us, "They that wait upon the Lord shall renew their strength; they shall mount up with wings of eagles" (Isaiah 40:31 KJV).

In the New Testament, we find Jesus referring several times to sparrows. "Are not five sparrows sold for two pennies? Yet not one of them is forgotten by God" (Luke 12:7 NIV).

Whether we soar to great heights or find our place closer to the ground, God treasures us and cares for us. *God lasts.* What better news do we need than to know deep down in our souls that, no matter how dire the circumstances or bleak the outlook, the Holy One will be there?

------- ⋆ ★ ⋆ -------

My prayer for you this morning is from the great hymn, "His Eye Is on the Sparrow":

> *Why should I feel discouraged, why should the shadows come,*
> *Why should my heart be lonely, and long for heaven and home,*
> *When Jesus is my portion? My constant friend is he:*
> *His eye is on the sparrow, and I know he watches me;*
> *His eye is on the sparrow, and I know he watches me.*
> *I sing because I'm happy, I sing because I'm free,*
> *For his eye is on the sparrow, And I know he watches me.*

MEANT TO BE
Ruth 2:1-13

Ruth and her mother-in-law, Naomi, received an unexpected blessing. They were both widows with no one to provide for them, so Ruth went to glean grain from a field. The field happened to be owned by Boaz, a distant relative of Naomi's. He noticed Ruth, provided for her needs, and later became her husband. Ruth received a blessing because she was in the right place at the right time.

Have you ever found yourself in exactly the right place at exactly the right time—so much so that you felt it was meant to be? Do you dare to think that God put you there to be of use to somebody else?

I don't think it's such a rare experience. There are many encounters in our lives that, when we look back on them, we realize the awesome grace of God provided for that experience. Sometimes these things feel almost like little miracles.

You and I met at a Cantor Fitzgerald 9/11 remembrance service in Central Park in 2002. You later brought Chelsea to Park Avenue Church, and our relationship has grown ever since. Chance encounter—right place, right time.

Sometimes God uses unexpected encounters to bring unexpected blessings. May you be in the right place at the right time in the days, weeks, and months to come!

------ ★ ★ ★ ------

Dear Lord, help me to go out of my way to be a blessing to others—whether or not I receive anything in return. My heart's desire is to help others along the way to know you through my actions and love. Amen.

Cantor Fitzgerald Relief Fund has provided assistance to the families of World Trade Center victims, as well as victims of natural disasters around the world. For more information, please go to cantorrelief.org.

TRUE LEADERSHIP
Joshua 1:1-9

S omeone has said that a good leader is one who "*knows* the way, *goes* the way, and *shows* the way."

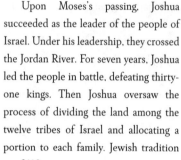
Upon Moses's passing, Joshua succeeded as the leader of the people of Israel. Under his leadership, they crossed the Jordan River. For seven years, Joshua led the people in battle, defeating thirty-one kings. Then Joshua oversaw the process of dividing the land among the twelve tribes of Israel and allocating a portion to each family. Jewish tradition tells us that he passed away at the age of 110 years.

God told Joshua that a true leader was to:

- ➤ Be strong and courageous;
- ➤ Obey all of God's laws for living;
- ➤ Think often about what God has said;
- ➤ Remember that God is with you.

All leaders need to keep these lessons in mind, because people are following our example. If we learn them well, we will *know, go,* and *show* the way that pleases God—and we will be good leaders especially when we remember that God is with us.

------ ★ ★ ★ ------

God, help us to be true leaders in this world for you. Let us remember your Word and live a life worthy of you. Amen.

GOD'S WISDOM
Psalm 51

Throughout the Psalms there are many images of the need for wisdom. In this Psalm, wisdom comes from forgiveness of sin, and it leads to a clean heart and a new and right spirit.

The word *wisdom* is usually synonymous with the Spirit. The true nature of the "wisdom from above" is "pure, and then peaceful, gentle, obedient, filled with mercy and good actions, fair, and genuine" (James 3:17).

But what exactly is wisdom, and where does one find it? The psalmist is clear that wisdom comes from truth that can be found when one acknowledges one's own sin and separation from God. When God's spirit is present in our lives, there is no telling how wise we can become.

What if wisdom is not a state of being or a destination at which one finally arrives? Rather, what if wisdom, like faith, is merely bread for the journey—a companion for one's pilgrim walk? Maybe wisdom is not something we possess, but something that possesses us, coming as it does at crucial moments of life, providing guidance and direction—a serendipitous gift delivered by the grace of God.

If that is so, then perhaps you have been hearing the voice of wisdom at every crossroad you encountered—a voice whose silent murmurings kept you from falling prey to the enticements of competing voices, a voice that kept calling you back to a reverence of God, from which all wisdom originates.

------ ★ ★ ★ ------

Lord, thank you for sending Christ to redeem our world and restore us to your presence. Help me to live in that presence as often as I can, so that wisdom can find me when I most need it. Create in me a clean heart, O God, and put a new and right spirit within me. Amen.

WHAT DO WE *REALLY* NEED?

Galatians 5:22-23

I t goes without saying that we are facing deep divisions in our nation. What kind of leaders do we need to show us the way forward?

William White has become a model for me of the type of leader we desperately need at this moment in history. Born in Philadelphia in 1747, White was a priest in the Church of England. In spite of his ordination vow of loyalty to the king, he supported the Revolution and served as chaplain to the Continental Congress.

I was drawn to White because of the prayer written in his memory that is included in the Episcopal calendar of daily prayers. These words echo my prayer as we continue to make our way through the noisy conflict of this presidential election season:

> O Lord, in a time of turmoil and confusion you raised up your servant William White, and endowed him with wisdom, patience, and a reconciling temper, that he might lead your Church into ways of stability and peace; Hear our prayer, and give us wise and faithful leaders, that through their ministry your people may be blessed and your will be done; through Jesus Christ our Lord, who lives and reigns with you and the Holy Spirit, one God, for ever and ever. Amen.[8]

May God give us in every area of our lives leaders who lead with wisdom, patience, and a reconciling temper so that together we might find ways to stability and peace. Amen.

Rev. James A. Harnish

FROM: Rev. Bill Shillady
SENT: July 23, 2016
TO: H

Hello again,
I hope you are well. Great pick in Senator Tim Kaine. Our friend Jim Harnish, retired pastor from Florida, wrote this blog. He was at your Tampa rally.
Rev. Bill

BREAKING THROUGH
Matthew 14:22-33

When Peter steps out of his boat, he enters the terror of the storm. His motive isn't to escape from threat, for he goes into a situation where the threats will now look different, into a place where Jesus is defying and reordering the assumed boundaries of nature and life. Jungian imagery always portrays water as chaos. Peter steps from fear of the storm into the actual chaos of the storm.

Isn't this what history's most faithful people have demonstrated? Not all of them were great believers, but they knew that if God were to be encountered, it would most likely be in the midst of the storms of life. God must be found in places where the regular delineations and predictable endings don't apply as before. Sometimes incredibly turbulent places are also transcendent spots where God breaks through.

These heroes of faith find and illuminate God in settings where "the way things are" are reconfigured: where the poor receive support, the sick find comfort, and the oppressed enjoy dignity and freedom.

------ ★ ------

Lord, be with your servant. May your hand be a constant to hold us up and keep us steady. Our nation needs us to be bold like Peter and caring of the least, the last, and the lost. Amen.

"We've come so far together, but there is still work to be done," she said as she highlighted the accomplishments of women in far-flung places. But too many women remain marginalized at best and treated like a subhuman species at worst, she said. "This is the great unfinished business of the 21st century."
If there is an issue Hillary Clinton owns, this is it.[9]
The Daily Beast
April 5, 2013

LET US

1 Samuel 8:1-22

S amuel spoke against the request of the elders of Israel for a king. I think the vigorous debate between Samuel and the elders can inform our understanding of our political situation today.

Their debate feels familiar. We're increasingly locked in partisan debates in our country, but do we miss some truth in what the other is saying, just as Samuel and the elders missed what was true because of the intensity of their arguments?

Lost in their debate were the real questions of justice. Who would protect the poor from corrupt judges? Who would protect people from the seizure of their property? Who would protect workers from mistreatment? Who would keep the sons and daughters from conscription in foreign wars?

We take the point of view of Samuel—kings are bad—but I wonder if we ought to pay more attention to the role God plays in the story. What mattered to God was not who would rule but who would speak for justice.

Every election matters. It mattered for the people of Israel that the elders convinced Samuel to appoint Saul king. It matters who wins. But regardless of who rules, we need leaders who will speak up for justice for all God's children.

-------- ⋆ ★ ⋆ --------

God, when you created the world, you said, "Let us . . ." You modeled how to be and who to be—together. You are one; you are many. You are unity. Teach us to value your image of relationship. Teach us the ways of justice. Amen.

TRUE WISDOM
1 Kings 2:10-12; 3:3-14

Most people remember Israel's famous King Solomon for his wisdom, a gift God gave him after he asked not for riches or wealth or long life but for help with governing the people wisely and well.

Today—unlike ancient Israel—our nation claims to be built upon the separation of church and state, but religious beliefs and claims of authority are often brought into the political arena.

We argue vehemently, yet so many of us fail to make sure that all of God's children have the basic goods of life—in other words, we neglect "the least, the last, and the lost." Wasn't this exactly what God expected in both the Old and New Testaments? Aren't justice and compassion the "gospel" values preached and embodied by Jesus, the one whose wisdom we desire?

Tonight, use the wisdom of the heart, your heart of faith. Remember our call as followers of Jesus to care for the marginalized and the "least of Christ's children," and "do good, do no harm, and stay in love with God"—the three general rules of John Wesley.

------- ★ ★ ★ -------

Living God, you are the giver of wisdom and true discernment, guiding those who seek after your ways to choose goodness. Mercifully grant that all of us may seek the wisdom of the heart, a healed heart in which our Lord Jesus resides. Help us to do good and do no harm, and may we stay in love with you. Amen.

* *

FROM: Rev. Bill Shillady
SENT: April 14, 2016
TO: H

Blessings today. I had to write a special devotional for you for tonight. I am very honored to be attending the debate and will be praying for you throughout. Judy and I wish you "wisdom" for this evening.

* *

PUT ME IN, COACH
Isaiah 6:1-8

I f you watch little kids playing basketball, you see a lot of different attitudes from the bench. Some look relieved to be sitting there, glad for a bit of rest. Others seem anxious, wondering when they might get put in. Then there are the enthusiasts, the ones who seem unable to sit still on the bench, ready to spring to their toes and finally blurt out, "Put me in, Coach!" They are dying to get in the game.

Isaiah didn't want to get in the game at first, but when he finally was ready, he didn't say something passive to God, like "Ok, I'll go." He said, "Send me."

You, my sister, are in the game big time. I believe God is calling you. May the angels and seraphs give you what you need to "stay in the game!" And God will give you the strength.

------ ★ ★ ------

God, in you I place my hope and trust. With the Resurrection power as the seed of hope for our world every day, I place my life daily in your game. Lord, renew my strength every morning. Give me the energy and courage to soar like an eagle above the conflict and fray so that I can fulfill your will. Amen.

Mrs. Clinton's 2016 campaign will open a new chapter in the extraordinary life of a public figure who has captivated and polarized the country since her husband, former President Bill Clinton, declared his intention to run for president in 1991. Mrs. Clinton was the co-star of the Clinton administration, the only first lady ever elected to the United States Senate and a globe-trotting diplomat who surprised her party by serving dutifully under the president who defeated her.[10]

The New York Times
April 12, 2015

GOD'S GPS
Proverbs 3:6

In 2006, after winning the Lilly Endowment Clergy Renewal grant, my wife, Judy, and I took a three-month sabbatical traveling throughout Europe following the Reformation trail, enjoying Italy's cathedrals and museums and basically renewing our souls and lives.

It was very easy for us to get lost because the road signs were in different languages, the city maps were somewhat lacking, and the narrow roads and streets challenged my driving concentration. The best thing we did before we left was to purchase a global positioning system for the car we leased. It was a wonderful aid. If I didn't turn when the GPS told me, she never criticized or yelled at me. No, she simply said, "Recalculating" and found another way for me to get to my destination.

I think GPS could also stand for God's Positioning System, because God always knows where we are in our life journey and in which direction we are headed. And when we make a wrong turn, God simply calculates a new route to help us ultimately arrive at our destination. No matter what we do or how we may mess up, God is always watching us.

I like to think of it as John Wesley's idea of prevenient grace: that which goes before us and opens doors for us to make choices. Things are not predetermined, but God provides many choices.

------- ★ ★ -------

Lord, we trust you to direct our paths. Help us listen for your voices through Scripture, tradition, reason, and experience, as well as our family, friends, and mentors. When we make a wrong turn, help us accept the recalculating of our journey and not take too much of a detour. Amen.

NEW LIFE
Matthew 25:34-45

The Catholic social reformer Dorothy Day spent her early years traipsing through Manhattan's West Village without a care in the world. Long nights of booze and cigarettes were followed by afternoon arguments with friends and lovers. One early morning, Dorothy, on a whim, sauntered up the steps of St. Joseph's Church in Greenwich Village. As a stream of bricklayers, factory workers, and shopkeepers paraded down the aisle for mass, she began considering her life in a new way. She would later write of this moment, "Sooner or later I would have to pause in this mad rush of living and consider my first beginning and my last end."[11]

After spending time contemplating her life, Dorothy arose from the pew and began a journey that would take her from being a bohemian writer in the West Village to the magnificent journalist and social reformer we know her as today.

This text from Matthew's Gospel gives us reason to pause and consider the meaning and trajectory of our lives as we enter into a new year. Jesus tells us that our lives are measured not by how much wealth or power we acquire but by the way in which we demonstrate justice and compassion to the "least of these." Like Dorothy, when we pause and consider the words of Christ in the context of our own lives, we might very well find ourselves rising up from where we sit, heading out the door with renewed purpose, and changing the world.

Rev. Kevin K. Wright

———— ⋆ ★ ⋆ ————

Lord, help me to remember that my life is ultimately given to me so that I might give it away on behalf of others. Let your love and peace infiltrate my life and set my heart towards you and those whom you love. Amen.

A GIVEN NAME
2 Kings 2:1-14

I love this story of Elijah and Elisha and the passing of the mantle. The two names are so close that you wonder about their meaning. *Elijah* is derived from two Hebrew names for God: Elohim ("Lord") and Yahweh (God's divine name). Elijah's name is therefore a creedal statement: "The Lord is my God." *Elisha* comes from Elohim and the word *Yasha*, which means "salvation." So, his name is also a statement of faith: "God is my salvation."

So what's in a name? Even if you don't know its etymological origin or have a unique story about its source, I hope you are grateful for it. Like many of life's greatest gifts, it was given with neither your choosing nor your deserving. In those ways, ours names are like the gift of God's grace given to all. Your name, my name—they are who we are, and they remind us to whom we belong.

------- ★ ★ ★ -------

O God, you have graced us when we don't deserve it. You have named us as your children. You have set us free in Jesus Christ with a power greater than all that would keep us captive. Grant that we might live gracefully in our freedom as your children, without selfishness or arrogance, and through love become empowered to share Christ's love with all no matter their name or origin; for the sake of your reign. Amen.

CLOUD OF WITNESSES
Hebrews 12:1-2

When I was the pastor at Park Avenue, one of my great memories is of the New York City Marathon. I loved to shout encouragement to the runners. I hear they love that extra boost of energy and adrenaline that comes from hearing their names shouted by the anonymous bystanders—New Yorkers joining together in positive enthusiasm for the stranger.

The race has already been run by Jesus, the lead runner, the "pioneer." He shows us how to run. We run the race because, like the marathoners, we have a crowd watching and shouting encouragement from the sidelines. This "cloud of witnesses," some of whom have already completed the course in this life, know our names and are encouraging us in their love and memory.

We run because we can't lose with Jesus as our coach. He not only ran the race and finished it but he now offers his assistance to us so that, by faith in him, we too can persevere until the end.

You have thousands of cheerleaders who are shouting those words of encouragement. Remember, if you stumble and fall, Jesus will be there to help you through the pain to the end of the race.

------ ★ ------

Most Holy One, grant that we may be strengthened by the great cloud of witnesses who run the race toward the finish line of justice and compassion. Grant us the massive strength we need for the race we are in. Amen.

"We need strong women to step up and speak out. We need you to dare greatly and lead boldly. So please, set an example for every woman and girl out there who's worried about what the future holds and wonders whether our rights, opportunities and values will endure."[12]

USA Today
February 7, 2017

YOUR GIFT
1 Corinthians 15:50-58

W hen I read the news about your very tight victory in Iowa, the phrase kept coming to me: "Thanks be to God who gives us the victory through our Lord Jesus Christ" (v. 57).

The apostle Paul in this passage tells us that when it comes to our souls, the victory is brought about by the love of God evidenced in the power of the Resurrection. It's Paul's final conclusion regarding the Resurrection that I hope will be helpful for you this morning—"in the Lord your labor is not in vain."

I am honored to stand in the long line of American reformers who make up our minds that the status quo is not good enough, that standing still is not an option, and that brings people together to find ways to improve the lives of Americans.[13]

Hillary Rodham Clinton
February 2, 2016

According to Paul, because Jesus is resurrected, it follows that we should fully give ourselves to our work. This passage helps us understand that what happens daily in our lives does matter.

So here is my thought for you today: give yourself fully to the work that you've been given, keep at it with good spirit and energy, and keep moving onward and upward since your labor is not in vain.

All your hard work is inherently meaningful. It's part of what it means to be made in the image of God. Each child of God has been given something to do, something that he or she is specifically gifted for.

------ ⭐ ------

My sister, you are called and chosen. Your labor is not in vain. Go forth in the power of the Resurrection to do the work that God has given you to do. Be grateful that you have been called in a very special way to be a part of God's great renewal project of the world. Amen.

GOD'S VOICE
1 Kings 19:11-12

In our lives, we hear a variety of voices. We hear voices of family, friends, coworkers, and the media. These outer voices have different purposes. Some offer us information. Others offer us comfort and challenge. Still others ask or demand something.

There are also many inner voices. These voices aren't audible, but we "hear" them nevertheless. There is the inner voice of conscience. There are external voices that we have internalized. Those persons who have shaped us can still "speak" years after their physical presence has gone.

Among the plethora of voices we hear each day, can we also hear God addressing us? How do we discern God's voice from all of the other voices that beckon us to listen and obey? And what does it mean to hear God's voice addressing us?

One way to discern God's voice is to be still and listen. God's voice comes in the midst of sheer silence. Ask yourself, *When can I make times of silence in my life to listen for God's voice?*

------ ★ ★ ------

Eternal One, you speak to us in many and various ways. Yet too often we do not hear your voice. Sometimes we are too distracted. Other times we are too busy talking. Help us to find spaces of silence in our daily life to listen for your voice that comes as a whisper. Amen.

Robert Martin Walker

GOD'S GUIDANCE
Psalm 150:1-6

S omeone once meditated on the word *guidance* and made this observation: It is spelled G-U-I and then the word *dance*. The author said the G stood for God, the U stood for you, and the I stood for each one of us. That way, the word would mean "God, you and I dance."[14]

In dance, one person takes the lead and the other follows. Now the leader isn't pushing the other around or forcing the other to go in one direction or another but is instead giving gentle nudges and hints of the directions in which to move.

In a similar way I believe God, as the Holy Spirit, is dancing with each of us and leading us in the dance of life—not by pushing us around and ordering us to do things but by giving gentle nudges and hints of the directions in which we should move.

------- ＊ ★ ＊ -------

Lord, you are my dancing partner in this life. I want you to take the lead and direct my path in this dance. Nudge me in the paths of righteousness, love, and peace. Amen.

＊ ＊

FROM: Rev. Bill Shillady
SENT: May 11, 2015
TO: H

Good Morning! Judy tells me my devotionals have gotten way too long. It is hard to stop a preacher! I will try to do better.

＊ ★ ＊

FROM: H
SENT: May 11, 2015
TO: Rev. Bill Shillady

I don't want to disagree with Judy, but I like the sermonettes! - H

＊ ＊

GOD'S GOODNESS
Romans 8:28

We, as people of faith, believe there is a God who is our co-pilot. When life goes smoothly for us and God's blessings are evident, we are tempted to believe we are in control. We may even think we do not need God. When the bottom falls out and the trials of life seem to be swallowing us up so that we seem to lose control, we may be tempted to wonder what is happening.

In this passage, Paul proclaims that God is present in the matters of this life. This is true as God is the God of all creation and has brought the world into relationship because of his Son.

I do not think that God controls everything. We have our human choices, but it is wonderful to know that God has "goodness" as the ultimate destination in our process of faith.

I love what Henri Nouwen says about this matter:

> A man with hope does not get tangled up with concerns for how his wishes will be fulfilled. . . . His prayer might still contain just as many desires, but ultimately it is not a question of having a wish come true but of expressing an unlimited faith in the giver of all good things. . . . For the prayer of hope, it is essential that there are no guarantees asked, no conditions posed, and no proofs demanded, only that you expect everything from the other without binding him in any way. Hope is based on the premise that the other gives only what is good. Hope includes an openness by which you wait for the other to make his loving promise come true, even though you never know when, where, or how this might happen.[15]

In our freedom of choice, as people of faith, God's gentle hand of prevenient grace goes before, providing myriad opportunities that all lead eventually to the good, even when we make bad choices.

------ ★ ★ ------

Thanks be to God for the love that guides us onward and upward. Amen.

GOD'S HIGH CALLING
Ephesians 4:1-10

Your calling is to be a living member of the living body of Christ. Christ lives in you through grace—and you live in Christ. How does your life reflect this reality?

You are not alone as you dwell in Christ. Where or how do you struggle to be humble, gentle, and patient with others in the church? What are you doing in your life to bring unity and peace into the Body?

------ ★ ------

Generous God, I give you thanks for the high calling you have placed on my life. I give you thanks for the gift of grace that strengthens me to be ever more humble, patient, and understanding of others in the church, especially with the ones who challenge me most. I give you thanks that you fill all things with your love, a love that can bring unity even in the midst of deep difference. You are my all in all, and I give you thanks. Amen.

Rev. Ginger E. Gaines-Cirelli

[Clinton] has made the status of women and girls a centerpiece of her life, and as secretary of State, she elevated it to a focal point of U.S. foreign policy. "I have always believed women are not victims," Clinton told the sold-out David H. Koch Theater at the Women in the World Summit at Lincoln Center. "We are agents of change. We are drivers of progress. We are makers of peace. All we need is a fighting chance."[16]

The Daily Beast
April 5, 2015

HELD TOGETHER

"Take the hand of the person next to you; hold hands this evening, friends. Hold the hand of someone next to you. Hold the hand of your neighbor as a symbol of us being stronger together!

Let us pray.

O God of many names, we know that you call us to work hard to bring people together.

To build bridges of hope for the future, we reach out tonight to our neighbors, no matter their race, creed, sexual orientation, or color. Lord, we hold hands together for the healing of the pain and grief from violence and death. Lord, we allow your love to overcome our fears as we learn to respect the "other" and to treat the most vulnerable of our society just as we do our friends. Help us, O God, to become the loving children you want us to be.

Lord, we ask you to open our minds to discern the complex issues of our communities, our nation, and our world. Lord, open our hearts to your Spirit and to the teaching to love our neighbors as ourselves. Help us to open our doors with radical hospitality to all our neighbors, seeking both conversation and civic actions as we work together to end discrimination in all forms—and to solve all communities' problems together.

Lord, you have spoken through your prophets and teachers throughout history. They have taught us that we must not demonize individuals or groups or peoples of other faiths as a response to perceived threats. They have challenged us to tear down the walls of fear and hatred so that we can be stronger together. They have called us to love others as we love you—and to treat others as we wish to be treated.

Lord, as we hold hands right now, we are reminded that together we can transform the world for good.

Lord God, give us the courage—the courage to leave this convention with determination and fortitude to move onward and upward to become a better nation, one that can solve our many problems TOGETHER, not apart. And Lord, help our world to see our nation as a shining lamp on a hill. Be with our sister, Hillary, and our brother, Tim. Give them courage, strength, and stamina for the next 102 days ahead and then to lead our nation.

Great God of the Universe, may we, as the founder of Methodism, John Wesley, taught: "Do all the good we can. By all the means we can. In all the ways we can. In all the places we can. At all the times we can. To all the people we can. As long as ever we can. Amen."

Rev. Dr. William Shillady
Democratic National Convention Prayer
Philadelphia, Pennsylvania
July 28, 2016

HAVE COURAGE

RENEW OUR SOULS

Isaiah 40:28-31

To the dispirited and hopeless community of exiles in Babylon, the prophet (Second Isaiah) speaks a message of long-term hope. The verse stresses the inadequacy of human power for the long distances of history and the circumstances of life. The listeners are called to wait upon the Lord and not to trust in Babylonian deities or fully in their own human capacity—but in God's everlasting processes in order to experience transformation.

Wings like eagles, boundless energy, stamina, and unwearied, running, happy feet will be given to those who have endured the long span of captivity and have remained faithful in the midst of human and Babylonian alternatives.

The weak, the faint, the despairing, and the doubting get a do-over and perhaps also a makeover. God's creating power can transform human ability to deal with the terrain of their new circumstances in Babylon.

------- ★ ★ ★ -------

Lord, help us to wait upon your presence and strength. Our human capabilities can take us so far, but when we are tired, exhausted, and weary, we will wait for you to renew our souls. Re-energize our spirits in those times. Amen.

FROM: H
SENT: April 5, 2015
TO: Rev. Bill Shillady

Thanks so much for the lovely brunch and lively conversation today, and what a treat to be with the Bishop. And I look forward to your e-mail support as the craziness begins.

Chelsea and Marc (and, of course, Charlotte) send their warmest greetings to you and Judy.

★ ★ ★

FROM: Rev. Bill Shillady
SENT: April 6, 2015
TO: H

You are welcome.

You and Bill, Chelsea, Marc, and Charlotte are in my prayers daily.

I will, to the best of my ability, send you a verse, thought, and prayer each morning to remind you that you are in my prayers.

It was great to be with you yesterday. I know the Bishop really enjoyed meeting you and the president. She was totally "blown away" by your knowledge and concern for our church.

FACING THE STORMS
Mark 4:35-41

One of the most famous paintings of this scene from Scripture was done by the Dutch painter Rembrandt in the seventeenth century. It is called *The Storm on the Sea of Galilee*. Sadly, it was stolen from a museum in Boston a few years ago and has never been recovered.

It depicts Jesus calming the waves of the sea, saving the lives of the fourteen men aboard the vessel. One can see the storm of wind and waves and Jesus awakening at the back of the boat. You can also see that Rembrandt painted himself into the picture with all the fearful disciples. There is Rembrandt, looking as anxious and afraid as all the others.

Rembrandt explained that he was just like one of the disciples. When things were going well, he loved, trusted, and had great faith in God. But when the storms of life arose, he was just as fearful and anxious as the disciples and needed Christ to come and give him peace and assurance.

I have seen my mom do some pretty remarkable things—and, yes, I am biased. . . . I don't think it ever occurred to her to stop fighting, because she never forgot what's at stake.[1]

Chelsea Clinton
November 3, 2016

We are all like Rembrandt. When life is good and we are doing well in our relationships, in our work, in our emotions, when everyone in our family is healthy and well, it is easy to be a person of faith. It is easy to be thankful to God for all the blessings in our lives and to trust God.

But when storms arise in our lives, when we lose a loved one, lose a job, or face other disappointments in life, then it is a challenge to be a person of faith.

Lord, come to me and help me have faith during the storms of life. Amen.

WORRY NOT
Matthew 6:22-34

Permit me to give you the practical reasons not to worry. It doesn't help. It wastes time. It blocks positive energy. It goes quickly to sounding off and whining.

Permit me to give you all my excuses for worrying: I can't find my car keys. I can't remember my passwords. I'm not sure I have done everything I was supposed to do. My car is making a funny noise. The air conditioner doesn't seem to be working. Climate change may cause me to buy more air conditioners, which only causes more global warming as I increase my carbon footprint. These are perfectly good reasons to worry, and I hope you will join me in legitimizing them.

So how dare Jesus tell us not to worry. Does he not understand all of the pressures of life?

We love to waste time and energy, and we have good reasons to do so. The problem is that we feel we are way more important than we really are. This self-importance is the source of most of our delusional worry. Perhaps a quotation attributed to the Dalai Lama says it best: "People were created to be loved. Things were created to be used. The reason why the world is in chaos is because things are being loved and people are being used." This is what we should worry about, our concentration on things.

Jesus helps us to see in our parable that the heart should be focused on God, and not on things. That our worry should be focused on others and their health, their well-being, and their souls. Our worry should not be self-centered but other-centered.

------- ✶ ★ ✶ -------

O God, help us to concentrate on your kingdom and then we need not worry, but all the things we need for building that kingdom will be given to us. Help us move beyond ourselves toward others, so that we may move beyond worry. Amen.

WHAT MORE?
Romans 8:28-39

W hat more do we need?

These words of the apostle Paul echo across the ages and resonate in the hearts of those of us who cling to the promises of God. Today, our very existence as human beings feels as though it is under constant assault. From acts of terror to demagogues sowing unrest to ongoing environmental degradation, the way can seem bleak and without hope. But we live and lead with a faith in God that God will never forsake or abandon us.

What more do we need?

Paul writes that in all of these things we are more than conquerors. When our burdens seem too heavy, our responsibilities too unrealistic, and our challenges insurmountable, we persevere, trusting God in all things, standing steadfast in our faith, and believing always that all will be well with our souls. Nothing can separate any of us from the love of God. Nothing.

What more do we need?

If God is for us, who or what can be against us?

------- ⋆ ★ ⋆ -------

Gracious God, it is only your unwavering presence in our lives as we look to you and your eternal light of love and joy that keep us on the paths of righteous with courage. We pray, gracious Creator, though we may get tired from time to time, that we remain fortified by the knowledge that neither death nor life nor things present nor things to come nor anything in all creation can separate us from you. Amen.

Rev. Frederick A. Davie

AN ONGOING PROCESS

John 12:20

One of my favorite pastimes is baking, primarily because I like sweets. There is also a sense of accomplishment whenever one takes the time to make something from scratch and share it with others. Most bakers are not looking for a short cut; they are extending themselves, giving up their time and their resources so others can experience a slice of joy.

Therefore, I was not surprised to read that Betty Crocker's cake mix—a box that only required that you add water—did not do well. A survey showed that people didn't buy that particular mix because it was too easy. They wanted to be a part of the process.

Unfortunately, many people make the same mistake when it comes to sharing what it means to be a Christian. We try to make it easy; just be baptized as an infant or an adult and—presto!— you are a perfect Christian.

The life of a Christian is an ongoing process of seeking direction, asking for forgiveness, forgiving others, and faithfully serving God's people wherever they may be found. We need more believers who are willing to be a part of this ongoing process of transforming the world for the sake of Jesus Christ.

> *Church really opened my eyes, my mind, and my heart—especially my youth minister, who forced us out of our comfort zone, who made us have to really live in what John Wesley called "his parish," meaning the world, in ways that were a little bit discomforting, to be fair. This was a youth minister who said no, you can't just be sitting satisfied in your own church in a suburb of Chicago that was all white. We're going into the inner city of Chicago. We're going to go into church basements and have fellowship with youth from African American churches and Hispanic churches. We're going to sit and we're going to talk about our lives. And we did.[2]*
>
> **Hillary Rodham Clinton**
> September 13, 2015

In other words, if we want to get something out of our relationship with God, we have to invest our hearts, our time, and our energy. We can't give ourselves freely to the transformation of the Holy Spirit and still hold onto everything that keeps us from experiencing real change.

Rev. Dr. Denise Smartt Sears

------ ★ ------

Father, help us to keep being courageous and follow the process. God direct our path along the journey. Amen.

FACING OUR CHALLENGES
2 Timothy 2:8-15

Recently more than a hundred faith leaders from around the country—Christians, Muslims, Jews—gathered here at The Riverside Church to have a serious conversation about gun violence in our nation and the role of the faith community in addressing that violence and changing a culture of death in America.

We as faith leaders and people of faith can heed the call to step up and begin applying our efforts to the work of changing hearts and minds, of divorcing the American love affair with guns from the framework of Christian faith, of speaking boldly to say that death and violence are unacceptable in our churches, in our communities, in our countries.

But proclaiming that message is going to invite criticism, resistance, and consequences. How can we, faith leaders and followers of Jesus, face all of that and keep going?

We can do it by enduring. By revisiting what lies within—the conviction that it's love that can change our world, that even when change seems so far off it doesn't even seem like a realistic option, we endure. We keep going. We put one foot in front of the other, over and over again, until we make it all the way to the finish line.

------- ⋆ ★ ⋆ -------

Lord, help me to remember today what I believe—the deep convictions that fire my resolve—and help me draw on the strength of those convictions to face the challenges that confront me this day. Amen.

Rev. Dr. Amy K. Butler

Hillary Clinton's campaign is releasing a new ad . . . that focuses on the effort to reduce gun violence, an issue the Democratic frontrunner has made central to the nominating contest....

"This epidemic of gun violence knows no boundaries. Between 88 and 92 people a day are killed by guns," Clinton says in the ad. "We need to close the loopholes and support universal background checks. How many people have to die before we actually act?"[3]

Time
November 3, 2015

CLOSE AT HAND
Luke 21:25-36

Stand up straight, Luke says! I definitely recall that admonition from my parents, my gym class instructor, and other adults when my teenage slumping posture was a hindrance to my well-being or activity.

But I don't think correct posture is what Jesus had in mind. I think he was speaking to the man by the pool of Bethsaida, or the woman who had been sick for eighteen years, or the paralyzed man whose friends lowered him through the hole in the roof of the house so that Jesus could forgive his sins and he could stand up straight and walk.

Jesus tells us that our redemption is close at hand. He uses a word that designates the act of purchasing the freedom of a slave or captive. He gives us crucial instructions in this passage while we await the freedom of God's coming kingdom, a season of waiting that will likely last our whole life long.

> *Let's ask ourselves, what can I do? What can I personally do to stop violence and promote justice? How can I show that your life matters to me? That I have a stake in your safety and wellbeing?*[4]
>
> **Hillary Rodham Clinton**
> July 8, 2016

Jesus tells us not to let our hearts be "weighed down with . . . the worries" that come with everyday living (v. 34 NRSV). Be careful! Be Alert! The Scripture tells us not to waste our time or our energy or our attention on the yearnings of the heart or for things that society holds to be important. Those desires will dull our hearts and desensitize our spiritual focus for the signs, great and small, that God's sovereignty is indeed breaking into our world.

------- ＊ ★ ＊ -------

God of surprises, open our hearts and minds to see your presence in this world. Help us stand tall, as agents of freedom and redemption, while we wait for your reign to come to fulfillment. Amen.

ESSENTIALS OF FAITH

1 Corinthians 16:13-14

The apostle Paul reminds us of the essentials of our faith. How often do we think of the courage required to be a Christian?

Does the name Miep Gies ring a bell? She was the secretary of Anne Frank's father and one of the four people who helped the Frank family and the others hiding in the attic at Otto Frank's business. She saw the truckloads of Jews being taken every day from Amsterdam and was convicted in her soul to do whatever she could to help them.

With her husband, Jan Gies, and the other Opekta employees, Miep helped hide Otto and Edith Frank, their daughters Margot and Anne, and several friends from July 1942 to August 1944.

Miep entered the secret room every day, bringing food she bought from various vendors with forged ration books and didn't carry more than one bag so as not to raise suspicion to the attic dwellers. She put herself in harm's way to save the lives of those hiding in the attic.

When the Franks were captured, they were taken to Gestapo headquarters and held there until they were placed in railroad cattle cars to Auschwitz. Miep, the young secretary, went to Gestapo headquarters to try one last time to save the Franks. What courage!

Being a person of faith requires great courage. Stand firm with courage and do everything with love (vv. 13-14). What essentials to live by!

------ ★ ★ ------

Lord, we pray for the courage required to do everything in love, with conviction and hope. Help me love even those who are most difficult to love, and give me the courage to stand firm in the love of Christ every day. Amen.

The American Jewish Congress has bestowed its annual lifetime achievement award on Hillary Rodham Clinton. The former U.S. first lady and secretary of state spoke at the group's gala Wednesday night in New York City. Clinton emphasized the longstanding relationship between the United States and Israel. . . . The Stephen S. Wise Award for Lifetime Achievement also has been given to President Harry Truman and U.S. Supreme Court Justice Earl Warren among others.[5]

Haaretz
March 20, 2014

A PRAYER FOR COURAGE

Joshua 1:9

Awesome Creator of all that is and is to be,
We come to you as those in need of the love and grace only you can give.

You know us better than we know ourselves,
You know our fears and our worries, our dreams and our desires, our hopes
and our distresses, our faults and our failures.

You know everything about us and yet love us unconditionally.
Too often, we allow ourselves to be governed by our fears.
We fear for our safety and the well-being of those we love.
We fear failure and rejection.
We fear conflict and anger.

Such fears diminish our lives and limit us. They encircle and imprison us, not
allowing us to live fully and freely. They cause us to avoid risks and play it safe.

Yet, you have said again and again, "Do not be afraid." You call us to live
by faith and not by fear. You call us out of the darkness of fear and into the light
of your love.

In Jesus Christ, you have pointed the way to a fearless, courageous way
of living. He didn't fear those who wanted to harm him. He didn't shrink from
conflict or argument. He didn't even fear a cross of suffering and death. He
knew you were with him in every difficult and distressing circumstance. And this
knowledge was enough.

So let us crucify our fears with Christ. Let us nail our insecurities and our
anxieties to the cross. In so doing, may we experience the resurrection and new
life you offer us as a gift in each moment.

Give us the strength to live by faith rather than by fear. May we be bold in
our loving and courageous in our living. May we not allow our fears to prevent us
from taking the risks of self-giving love. And allow us to fulfill your calling to be
wounded healers as we calm the fears of those who are afraid. Amen.

Robert Martin Walker

OUR FUTURE
Psalm 91:1-2

Many years ago, my husband and children and I were members of a small, struggling congregation in New Haven, Connecticut. We had a tradition of honoring each person's birthday by asking another member to offer a blessing to the celebrant, speaking a word of affirmation and sending them into their next year of life.

One Sunday, the pastor said to Essie (truly a benevolent church matriarch), "Essie, your birthday isn't until next week. Shall we observe it today or wait?" She said words I've never forgotten (and it's been almost 40 years!), "Do it now. Tomorrow is not promised."

Today is indeed the day the Lord has made, and we need to live in this present moment, fully and faithfully. We cannot know what the future holds, but we can trust that God is with us now and that we are empowered to serve God today.

If we are serious about building a better, stronger and fairer America, we need to be serious about supporting and nurturing our girls. Our country can only fulfill its potential when every single child—particularly, every girl—can fulfill hers.[6]

Hillary Rodham Clinton
March 7, 2017

★

Lord, allow us to live under your protection and stay in the shadow of you. Amen.

Bishop Jane Allen Middleton

THE ARMOR OF GOD
Ephesians 6:10-18

The extraordinary promise of Scripture is that God ultimately will protect us from harm. But we are required to participate in this protection. In fact, it is our righteous living that will save us. There indeed are dark forces in this world, but as Christians, we claim the promise that the power of love and truth in Jesus Christ will overcome all evil.

So what is required? First, the belt of truth, the mandate to be as truthful as possible. Second is righteousness, living the Golden Rule and the law to love God with all one's heart and soul and mind and strength and to love one's neighbor as one's self, with a humble spirit.

Next is to walk in peace, to have peace as one's companion. Holistic peace brings justice to all people, and to live with this as such a companion every day leads to that goal.

Faith is described as a shield, which is an apt metaphor for the power of faith to protect us from evil, vicious lies, doubt, and accusations. Upon our heads we wear salvation, the promise of God's holiness bathing us at all times, perhaps as a halo. Our "weapon" is the Spirit, the power given to us through the words and truth of Scripture. And finally, praying at all times in the Spirit.

------ * ⭑ * ------

Father, hear our prayers. Clothe us with your righteousness. Amen.

Bishop Jane Allen Middleton

Hillary Clinton today said Donald Trump owes President Obama and the American people "an apology" for pushing the notion that President Obama was not born in the U.S, and that even if he flip-flops on his position now, "there is no erasing it in history."

"For five years, he has led the birther movement to delegitimize our first black president. His campaign was founded on this outrageous lie. There is no erasing it in history," the Democratic presidential nominee said during remarks at the Black Women's Agenda symposium in Washington, D.C.[7]

ABC News
September 16, 2016

A WAY TOGETHER
Mark 10:27

One of the most important reminders on the journey to discovering what matters most is that God can use all of us in ways that we cannot even begin to imagine. Miracles happen that we cannot explain. Unlikely people rise up to do extraordinary things when we least expect it. It is so important to remember that with God, nothing is impossible.

In Lewis Carroll's *Through the Looking Glass*, there is a wonderful exchange between Alice and the Red Queen. Alice says, "There's no use trying, one *can't* believe impossible things." The Queen responds, "I daresay you haven't had much practice. When I was your age, I always did it for half-an-hour a day. Why, sometimes I've believed as many as six impossible things before breakfast."[8]

We all have points in the journey when we struggle with faith. When we do, we are not unlike most of the people described in the Bible. Whether it was how to get across the Red Sea, how to convert the residents of Nineveh, or how to spread

the word to the Gentiles, there has always been someone who has struggled to trust God. When someone says, "We can't," seeds of doubt are planted. When someone says, "Yes we can," faith has been demonstrated.

Remember today that God is in charge, and with that assurance we can find a way through the storm together. We may not know the future, but we do know who holds our hands. Thanks be to God!

------ ⋆ ☆ ⋆ ------

God, help me to put aside my doubts and believe more fully in you. Amen.

Bishop Thomas J. Bickerton

GOD'S UNFOLDING VISION
Habakkuk 3:17-19

The Scriptures remind us that in the face of all the complexities and confusion and suffering and banality and injustices of human life, we are called to live by faith, trusting and rejoicing in God's vision. We are called to see ourselves as participants in God's unfolding vision—and through that, to be strengthened and transformed.

That's what we're here for. We're here, in all the circumstances of our lives, to rejoice in God who is surely at work in the world and to seek to live faithfully as participants in God's loving, saving work. We are called to be servants of God's vision and God's mission: *shalom*, wholeness for all creation and peoples together. You really are called to make a difference, regardless of your circumstances, and perhaps even more powerfully *because* of your circumstances.

Living with that kind of faith, even as falteringly as we do from day to day, allows us to live our lives with patience, joy, and hope, even when "the fields yield no food"—because we're not there yet—because we trust that whether we see it or not, God's vision will surely come and maybe, even in some small way, will appear today. Maybe it will even appear through you.

------ ★ ★ ★ ------

Powerful God, I am part of your unfolding vision in this world. In the midst of challenge and uncertainty, you are my strength. I rejoice in your presence and in your call upon my life. Amen.

Rev. Ginger E. Gaines-Cirelli

★ ★

FROM: Rev. Bill Shillady
SENT: July 17, 2016
TO: H

Dear Hillary,
Good Sabbath Morning,
I am so honored and thrilled by your invitation to the Democratic Convention. I will deliver the most important prayer of my life, and I will do my best. I will base it on the theme of the night—"Stronger Together."
Be Blessed. You are in my prayers.
This is the day the Lord has made. Let us rejoice and be glad in it. Let us make the best use of this day, a gift from our creating and loving God.
Rev. Bill

★ ★

HYMN OF PRAISE
Colossians 3:16

S aint Augustine said that anyone who sings to the Lord "prays twice"—praising God in both word and music.

God is the great music lover, having created not one bird to sing, but millions. The music of the waves beating ceaselessly upon the shore, the wind rustling the leaves of the trees on summer evenings, and the thunder of the waterfall. Psalms speak of trees clapping their hands for God, and the whole world alive with acclamation. When we worship, that's us joining our voices to the praise that permeates a doxological planet.

In Alex Haley's *Roots*, Kunta Kinte lies on the dirt floor of his slave cabin in the New World where he has been brought from Africa. The horrors of slavery have about obliterated any infantile memory of his native land, until that night when he hears a woman singing a song in a tune strangely familiar to him. It was a song from Africa, and its tune awakened long suppressed memories. He remembered that he once had a home. He remembered who he was.

Sometimes, as I am singing certain hymns, my soul is stirred. I remember whose I am—God's child. When Paul urges the church at Colossae to let God's Word "dwell among you richly" (KJV) he lists not only preaching and teaching, but also music. When we sing the words of the great hymns, the Word of God burrows down deep in our being.

------- ⋆ ★ ⋆ -------

God who created music, may our lives flow in endless song, and when we need to be reminded of your love, may the tune and words of a favorite hymn rise up from our soul to remind us that we are children of God. Amen.

LOVE AND DEVOTION
Proverbs 23:24-26

I had a pre-set devotional for you today, but I wanted to send something different based on what your day holds.

I believe that the spirit and love of those saints who have gone on to glory are with us, around us, and in us all the time. Today especially, I know that your mother Dorothy's spirit and love will be with you as you remember her life story. She will take a break from dancing in the stars and will look down on you with pride and joy. Her love and her indomitable spirit will surround you today.

------ ⋆ ★ ⋆ ------

My prayer for you today:

Lord God, we give you thanks for those whom we love but see no more. For all that Dorothy has given her daughter, for all the love and devotion, for all the joy, and for all her sacrifice throughout her life that made Dorothy the beloved child of God that she became, we are grateful that she now rests from her labors in your loving presence.

I pray today that you will be with your beloved child, Hillary, and that your spirit will give her the words, the courage, and the strength to guide our nation into a promised land for all and not just for a few.

Bless her, Bill, Chelsea, Marc, and Charlotte, all her family and friends and her faithful staff as they embark upon this significant day in the journey toward the goal of leadership of our great nation and peace for the world. May all the saints who have worked for the betterment of our society surround her and inspire her this day; in the name of Jesus Christ. Amen.

------ ⋆ ★ ⋆ ------

Blessings on this day, and I will look forward to hearing your words for our nation.

Dorothy Rodham, who overcame years of struggle to become a powerful influence on the life and career of her daughter, Hillary Rodham Clinton, the first lady, senator from New York, presidential candidate, and now secretary of state, died on Tuesday in Washington. She was 92.[9]
The New York Times
November 1, 2011

GOD IS GOOD
2 Corinthians 4:7-16

Paul reminds us in this passage that in God's mercy, as we engage in ministry in the name and light of Christ, we do not lose heart. As people of hope and faith we have the ability to see the invisible in the visible, the eternal in the earthly.

Nothing—death, life, principalities, powers, height, depth, nor anything in all creation—can separate us from the love of God in Christ Jesus. Life is difficult, but God's goodness wins even when we can't see it.

Hope is the power that keeps the vision of good in our hearts and minds. Faith is the attitude that says, even though life is unfair and we have no control, deep in our hearts and consciences, we know that God is in control but not controlling, that God's kingdom will be a reality, and we must try to live in it here and now.

In his letter to the church at Corinth, a church that was testing his patience and showing just how difficult a church could be, Paul challenged the church leaders to "not lose heart." I love the litany that puts both halves of the one truth together.

> We are inflicted in every way [life is difficult].
> But we are not crushed [God is good].
> perplexed [life is difficult].
> but not at our wits' end [God is good].
> Persecuted [life is difficult].
> We are never forsaken [God is good].
> Struck down [life is difficult].
> But not destroyed [God is good].
> Life is difficult, but God is good!

------ ✦ ------

Lord God, help us not lose heart in our daily living. Remind us of your love and grace that gives us hope that all things will work together for good to those who are in love with you. Amen.

AMAZING GRACE
Romans 5:1-5

John Wesley, the founder of Methodism, laid out a unique theology. He called it "practical divinity." Wesley shows us that God's prevenient grace, the grace that is working in our lives before we realize it, is a part of God's plan of salvation. It is the first step of God's grace that moves us toward reconciliation and transformation.

When something shifts our perspective and we acknowledge our need for Christ, in that we want to change, then justifying grace enters the picture and convinces and convicts us to that transformative moment that some call being "born again." For some, this is a single powerful moment. For others, it can be a series of events in our lives that cause this full realization of a new relationship with God.

The next grace Wesley called sanctifying. It moves us on in our relationship with God and neighbor and deepens our love of Christ; it helps us do the work of transformation to become more like Christ in our living and breathing.

Finally, Wesley referred to perfecting grace. It is that presence of God in Christ that moves us toward being a perfect disciple of Jesus Christ. Wesley proclaimed he met only two people who ever achieved this perfecting place.

No matter our station or status in life, no matter how bad we feel about ourselves, no matter how much of a "wretch I am," it is God's amazing grace that abounds even more. God works to bring us to the moment where we receive that grace, knowing we are forgiven and made whole before God through Christ.

---- ★ ★ ★ ----

Thank you, Lord, for the amazing grace that you share with us. May it continue to provide your presence to me, and may it lead me to be a faithful disciple of Jesus Christ for the transformation of the world. Amen.

ON EAGLES' WINGS
Isaiah 40:31; Matthew 5:3

Do we have the courage to fling ourselves off the edge of our insecurities and freefall into the Creator's all-sufficient grace?

That is what the Bible means when it says, "blessed are the poor in spirit for theirs is the kingdom of heaven."

We can run and not be weary; walk and not faint. We can do all things, not of our own accord, but through the power of this great universe that catches us, lifts us, and sustains us on wings as eagles.

What freedom! What security! What joy!

------- ⋆ ★ ⋆ -------

Teach us, O God, to lean not on our own understanding, but to put our trust in you. Not in the might of humans, nor the strength of horses, but in you, and you alone. Amen.

Rev. Frederick A. Davie

As Hillary Clinton delivered her victory speech Tuesday night marking a milestone for women, she looked to one woman in particular for inspiration: her late mother. . . . Clinton said she wished her mother were still alive to witness Tuesday's celebration.

"I wish she could see what a wonderful mother Chelsea has become and could meet our beautiful granddaughter, Charlotte," Clinton said. "And, of course, I wish she could see her daughter become the Democratic Party's nominee."[10]

CNN
June 8, 2016

BRING ABOUT TRANSFORMATION
Proverbs 3:5-6

There is an old saying, "To your own heart be true," which probably is an erroneous quote of the great line in Hamlet, "to thine own self be true." Nonetheless, it's a great line of wisdom when you think of trusting in God with all your heart and being truthful to that heart.

Henri Nouwen writes,

"Have courage," we often say to one another. Courage is a spiritual virtue. The word *courage* comes from the Latin word *cor*, which means "heart." A courageous act is an act coming from the heart. A courageous word is a word arising from the heart. The heart, however, is not just the place where our emotions are located. The heart is the centre of our being, the centre of all thoughts, feelings, passions, and decisions.[11]

Jesus was asked, "Of all the commandments, which is the most important?" He replied, " 'Love the Lord your God with all your heart and with all your soul and with all your mind and with all your strength.' The second is this: 'Love your neighbor as yourself.' There is no commandment greater than these" (Mark 12:28-31 NIV).

Here we have the foundational meaning of trusting in God and being truthful to our hearts and selves. Our love for God, which stems from the heart then causes us to desire to love our neighbor and even our own selves.

May we have the courage to live as disciples of Jesus Christ to bring transformation to our world.

------ ⋆ ★ ⋆ ------

Gracious God, help all of us to put our hearts and souls into loving you more deeply and trusting in your love for us. As you become the center of our hearts, then we know that all our actions will lead us in the path of righteousness and service; in Christ's name. Amen.

GOD IS WITH YOU
2 Samuel 6:12-23

As a pastor, I regularly sit down with people who have lost their jobs. We speak of grief, of anger, but mostly we speak of what's next. Let's begin by taking ourselves out of the history books; don't let the weight of the lost presidency keep you unable to move. We are no longer your responsibility.

The Bible is full of people who have lost everything—some, like Job, for no reason and some, like Michal, for following what she saw was her right path. After scolding her husband, not understanding his worship, she lost everything.

What do we do when we seem to have lost it all?

Do we, like Aaron Burr, blame others for our loss? Do we, like Michal, fade into the background, known only for what we lost? Or do we, like millions of men and women before us, choose to acknowledge that God has called you to something more? Today we ask the difficult question we aren't yet ready to wrestle with but are still silently wondering, What's next?

May God give you strength and courage to make space to mourn, to worship, and to seek clarity and renewal of a vision of hope for what lies ahead. And may you know that through it all: God is with you.

------- ★ ★ ★ -------

God, sometimes all I want to do is scream at you. I want to wallow in my grief and my anger. I swear. I throw every tear-filled question at you. But God, I know you are listening. I know you sit beside me. Amen.

Rev. Sara McManus

FROM: Rev. Bill Shillady
SENT: November 11, 2016
TO: H

Good morning my sister Hillary,

I have received countless messages of love and support for you. I have gotten emails and text messages across the globe [from people] who are telling me they are praying for you, thankful for all you have done, grateful that you put yourself on the line, and disappointed and devastated by the outcome.
Rev. Bill

OPEN HANDS
Mark 16:1-8

A stained-glass window above the altar at my church contains the image of Christ with outstretched hands above the words, "Come unto me." It invites us to meet Jesus in the bread and cup at the Communion table.

But prior to the renovation of the chapel, that window was above the entrance door where the open hands of Jesus invited people in from the street. After worship, people saw it as they left the chapel and stepped out onto the sidewalk along a busy street leading into the heart of the city.

I often wondered if the designers' original intent might have been to remind those of us who had been in worship that the risen Christ is already out there ahead of us saying, "Come, follow me into the world beyond these doors."

Both interpretations are correct. Jesus calls us into the place where we hear the word preached, are baptized into the body of Christ, receive the bread and cup, and are bound together in Christian community. But the other way of seeing it is equally true. Christ also calls us out of the church and into the world. By the power of the Spirit, we are sent as the agents of his healing, forgiveness, justice, and peace in the community beyond the church walls.

------ ★ ★ ★ ------

O God, give us courage to follow the risen Christ into the world where he promised to meet us. Amen.

Rev. James A. Harnish

[Bill] Clinton said Hillary Clinton is the only candidate with a plan to help repair the Appalachian economy, offering tax incentives to companies willing to build where jobs are badly needed and willing to share their success—profits—with employees.

"She wants to fix your wounds, sew them up, stand you up, tear down the totem poles (of social standing) so we can all go forward together," Clinton said.[12]

The Columbus Dispatch
October 4, 2016

STEADFAST
Ecclesiastes 1:1-10

There is no doubt that much hung in the balance this presidential election. The next months and years will require much vigilant and persistent advocacy for the marginalized and for reconciliation in our broken body. As your own personal healing process begins, hear the voice of the Teacher in this passage calling for hearers to gain perspective.

In a moment such as this, likely the last thing you want to hear is a call to gain perspective. Without trivializing the magnitude of your loss (and ours) in this election, the writer calls us to consider this dark moment in the context of the fullness of human history and to remember that there is nothing new under the sun; yet God's presence and power remain steadfast. The shift of the public toward embracing an ideology of fear is nothing new; it is simply history repeating itself.

The darkness of this world has always threatened to blot out the light, yet in Jesus Christ we know that even in the darkest night, the spark of hope still burns. Know in the midst of this, the darkest night, the sun will rise and hurry to the place where it will rise again tomorrow. The fire of hope will be kindled again, and the darkness will not overcome it. The work of God's justice will continue, just as God will bind up your wounded heart and call you ever forward. May these gifts find you in abundance on this day and in the weeks and months to come.

------ ★ ★ ★ ------

God of healing and hope, give me the courage to gain perspective in this moment of devastating heartbreak. Give me strength to heal, to hope, and to gain perspective in the weeks and months ahead. I pray in the name of Jesus—the light shining in the darkest night. Amen.

Rev. Colleen Hallagan Preuninger

LIVING A GOOD LIFE
Luke 1:37

A 2012 essay by Steven Petrow in the *New York Times* was titled "New Cancer Threat Lurks Long After Cure" and dealt with secondary cancers. These cancers are caused by the radiation and chemotherapy treatments for an initial cancer.

Mr. Petrow contended that cancer survivors go in one of two directions. Some are stalked by anxiety, depression, or post-traumatic stress disorder. Others experience higher self-esteem, a greater appreciation for life, or a deepened spirituality.

He cites the late Senator Frank Church, a cancer survivor who wrote that survival led him to live life more fully: "Life itself is such a chancy proposition that the only way to live is by taking great chances."[13]

Taking risks in life can lead to more fulfillment and satisfaction. However, not all risks need to be great. Taking even small risks like speaking to a stranger or doing an unexpected kindness for someone can lead to a more satisfying life.

Another way of saying this is that we need to get outside of our comfort zones. Trying new things and doing things that are unfamiliar often require us to go beyond what is safe and comfortable. Doing this leads to growth, and growth seldom happens without risk or difficulty.

Ask yourself: What risk do I need to take in order to grow?

------- ★ ★ ★ -------

Amazing God, you have taken the risk of creating us and endowing us with freedom. Give us the wisdom to discern which risks to take and which to forego. Amen.

Robert Martin Walker

WHAT LIES AHEAD

2 Timothy 4:6-8, 16-18

"What lies ahead" may seem like overly optimistic language, as today's passage seems to be something of an epitaph, an ending. The writer of 2 Timothy is tired, beleaguered, and, in short, finished. The writer is discouraged by the resistance he's met warning of folks who claim to be part of the Christian witness but behave in destructive ways, and he's just plain tired.

While we read these verses often in the liturgy of a funeral, nobody in this passage is dead. The writer of 2 Timothy may have felt like giving up, but he is not at the end of his life just yet. And when you're not dead yet, then the question is, What lies ahead, and how can I flex my muscles just enough to take on the immediate challenge with which I'm being presented?

This is the question the text offers us Christ-followers, too. When we feel like we're at the end, the discipline of the Christian life invites us to ask instead, What lies ahead?

That's really a fundamental challenge of the Christian life, isn't it? We run the race of faith because, like the beleaguered writer of 2 Timothy, we believe with all of our hearts that we each are part of something bigger than just our one little life.

After all, the end doesn't belong to us. It belongs to God. What is in our purview is what lies immediately ahead: the next step, the next task, the next challenge.

------ * ⭐ * ------

Lord, lend me strength for the work of this day, skill for the difficult tasks that need my attention, and courage to stay the course, one more step, until I reach what lies ahead. Amen.

Rev. Dr. Amy K. Butler

READY TO SOAR

Isaiah 40:31

One of the joys of our vacation rental is an osprey nest across the pond from our deck. There is a young osprey and its parents who are in constant action. The young bird is just beginning to fly and often calls to its parents from the nest. It still seems fearful of flying.

In America, the place of your birth should never be a barrier that stops you from reaching your God-given potential—that's what makes our country great, and that's the promise I'm going to fight to fulfill.[14]

Hillary Rodham Clinton
August 15, 2016

I've watched this bird try to fly. First it hops around in its nest, then cautiously jumps and flies short distances from branch to branch. In just a few days of watching, it has gone from hopping and jumping to soaring with the wind. It's on its way.

My sister, continue to wait on the Lord, because I know how exhausted in every way you must be. But you can soar! Rely on the faith that took root in you long ago. Continue to reflect on each day and remember to do all the good you can. Share your faith and soar! Feel the strength of all the prayers beneath your wings. Find hope for today and for tomorrow!

Lord, give me strength today to conquer that which falls before me. Help me not to grow weary but have the courage to accomplish what needs to be accomplished. Amen.

RISE UP
Ruth 1:1-5

I love the story of Ruth. It depicts two of the most resilient characters in the Bible. First, there is a famine that knocks Ruth and Naomi and their family down to the ground. They get back up. Then Naomi's husband died, leaving her with two children on her own. She got back up. Her sons married, but then they died. Ruth dusted herself off and got back up. Ruth and Naomi had to travel a great distance in hopes of food. Still, they persevered. They stuck together, they worked together, and every time they were knocked down, they got up together.

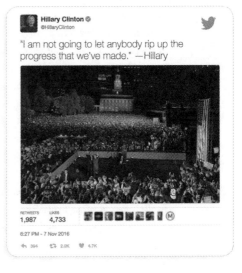

Andra Day sings a song called "Rise Up." The lyrics always remind me of Ruth and Naomi, of what I hope I can do day after day after day. It's what I hope we all can do, setback after setback after setback—rise up no matter how tired and beaten down we may be. Working for justice, trying to live life with forgiveness and love and peace—it can knock us down. God calls us to rise up a thousand times.

------ ★ ★ ★ ------

God of love, thank you for creating me to be resilient and strong. Whenever life knocks me down to the ground, give me the courage to rise up. Guide me to support others in their times of struggle and offer them my arm to stand back up. Amen.

Rev. Brooke Heerwald Steiner

OUR JOURNEY

Joshua 1:9

I n the first several chapters of the Book of Joshua, we have the story of the ancient Hebrews preparing to and entering the Promised Land.

What is striking about this story is the preparation and the ritual. There are numerous instructions about the journey. From the sending out of spies to assess the strength of adversaries; to how to deal with Rahab the prostitute, who sheltered the Hebrew spies against the enemy; to the roles of the priests and the position of the ark of the covenant in the processional to the Jordan River and beyond.

All of this ritual and preparation gives us the courage to continue the journey no matter what we encounter. We learn to manage our fear and doubt and uncertainty. We learn to trust God. In the midst of our battles, as we confront the raging waters of life, we know that God is with us. We need not be afraid.

God of power and might, we trust you to show us the way. We trust you to part the waters of adversity and lead us into the Promised Land of your eternal kingdom. May it be so, always and forever. Amen.

Rev. Frederick A. Davie

GOD IS IN OUR MIDST

John 14:27

The Oxford Dictionary defines the word *crisis* as "a time of intense difficulty, trouble, or danger; emergency, disaster, catastrophe, calamity." More synonyms include: predicament, plight, mess, trouble, and dire straits.

We know this all too well. My guess is that you, like me, have experienced a crisis or two in your lives—moments or even seasons of great loss, indecision, or challenge, in which we have questioned ourselves, our future, even the existence and faithfulness of God.

They seem to pop up everywhere today, in our personal and professional lives, among family and friends, in our nation and world. "Where is God in the midst of all this?" we ask. "How could a loving God allow such things to happen? How will I ever manage to survive or get through this circumstance and land safely on the other side?"

Our tendency is to think of these as questions of the unfaithful when rather, I think, they are questions of the faithful. They are questions that express our sorrow, anger, and frustration but also our dependence—our pain and vulnerability and also our need for God and the need to make sense of it all.

They are often the kinds of questions that drive us to our knees. Most often a crisis will drive us closer to God; closer to faith or far, far away in the other direction.

> The death of Alton Sterling is a tragedy, and my prayers are with his family, including his five children. From Staten Island to Baltimore, Ferguson to Baton Rouge, too many African American families mourn the loss of a loved one from a police-involved incident. Something is profoundly wrong when so many Americans have reason to believe that our country doesn't consider them as precious as others because of the color of their skin. . . .
>
> Progress is possible if we stand together and never waver in our fight to secure the future that every American deserves.[15]
>
> **Hillary Rodham Clinton**
> July 6, 2016

------ ★ ★ ★ ------

I am reminded of the peace of Christ that is beyond our human understanding. "Do not let your hearts be troubled, and do not let them be afraid." May we find that peace that we so desperately need when we are in the midst of life's storms. Amen.

TRUST IN THE LORD
Matthew 14:22-33

In this story, Jesus told the disciples to "go on ahead to the other side." Crossing over from one place to another—whether the move is geographical, emotional, vocational, or intellectual—is never really a simple proposition. The truth is that when you step out from where you have been, you don't know what you are going to find along the way. You step into a liminal space, an in-between space, a space of unknowing.

Being in between, in the place of uncertainty, is not a comfortable place to be. When a debilitating illness strikes and your whole life is forced to adapt, when the company downsizes or the contract doesn't get renewed, when what has been familiar and comforting in your church changes, when you are responsible for sick or struggling family members who live far away, when you have this nagging suspicion that something isn't working in your life, in these and so many other circumstances, we find ourselves in the middle of challenge, uncertainty, and change.

And that place is deeply uncomfortable. It can feel like you have wandered right into the middle of chaos itself. What is the place Christ is calling you to cross over? How are you feeling about it?

------ ★ ★ ★ ------

Lord Jesus Christ, help me to trust that what you have brought me to, you will bring me through. In the midst of chaos and overwhelm and challenge, be my strength. Amen.

Rev. Ginger E. Gaines-Cirelli

* *

FROM: Rev. Bill Shillady
SENT: September 28, 2016
TO: H

Good morning my sister,
It was great to see Bill, Chelsea, and Marc. I didn't realize it was Charlotte's 2nd birthday. How time flies.
Bishop Tom Bickerton was thrilled to meet you, and I thank you for the compliment that you gave him about me.
I am traveling, but Ginger Gaines-Cirelli has sent me a series of devotionals that will grace your morning and mine for the next few days.
Blessings,
Pastor Bill

* *

EVERY SEASON
Ecclesiastes 3:3-8

This sacred list within Ecclesiastes represents all the seasons and the important matters of our lives. Some are happy times, others sad; some are productive while others seem wasteful; some inspire peace and others bring pain. All of them are necessary for us to learn, grow, and evolve as human beings and children of God.

If we remember that there is a gift in every crisis or challenge—in every transition of life—we will be able to go with the flow of life more easily. May we discover the gift in every season, so that we learn to trust God's loving, grace-filled purpose behind it.

If only life's changes occurred smoothly and easily. But it seems when they come at us, it feels like the force of a perfect storm. If we remember that these are intense opportunities for transformation, then maybe we can ride them out more effectively.

------ ★ ★ ------

Lord, in the midst of the storm of these next twenty months, we pray for your presence within, so that the perfect peace of Christ that surpasses our human understanding may dwell in our hearts and the wisdom of truth may be the anchor that holds us steadfast so that we will emerge even stronger, wiser, and freer than before. Help us be transformed into the children you wish us to be. Amen.

The State Department on Thursday released 362 of the 15,000 Hillary Clinton emails uncovered by the FBI during its investigation into the former secretary of state's personal email server.

Many of the documents—comprising about 1,000 pages—are "near duplicates" of documents Clinton provided to the State Department in 2014 and have already been made public, according to the agency.

A "near duplicate," according to the agency, would include emails identical to previously released chains that were forwarded from Clinton to aides with the note "Please print," for example.[16]

The Hill
December 1, 2016

DO GOOD

WE MATTER

Jeremiah 29:7

As I read the stories about Baltimore after the death of Freddie Gray in police custody, I thought of this passage from Jeremiah.

Jeremiah was writing to the Israelites living in exile in Babylon, in a strange land with a foreign culture. Taken there against their will, they were anxious, frightened, and counting the days until their return to Jerusalem. Sadly, it would not be in the foreseeable future. They needed to prepare for the long haul.

But Jeremiah was saying more—they were to seek the shalom (welfare) of the city and pray to God on its behalf, for in its welfare they would find their own welfare.

When the streets of Baltimore are cleared of their destruction, the National Guard ends its patrols of neighborhood streets, and the news cameras pull away, can communities of faith truly seek the shalom of the city?

Can we agree to fix unjust systems and agree that black lives matter, people living in poverty matter, equal justice and opportunity matter, all lives matter?

------ ⋆ ★ ⋆ ------

God of grace and truth, create in us such a thirst for healing and justice that we will strive willingly to train ourselves and our children in the ways of respect and acceptance. Enlighten the eyes of our hearts, that we may see one another as you see us: beloved children and forgiven sinners. Amen.

Hillary Clinton used her first major policy speech to draw attention to the death of Baltimore's Freddie Gray, saying it was part of an "undeniable" pattern in which black men in America are disproportionately targeted by the criminal justice system.

"What we have seen in Baltimore should—indeed, I think does—tear at our soul," said Clinton....

"From Ferguson, to Staten Island, to Baltimore, the patterns have become unmistakable and undeniable," Clinton added.[1]

The Huffington Post
April 29, 2015

GOOD SAMARITAN
Luke 10:36b

Jesus tells the parable of the good Samaritan in response to a lawyer's question about how to inherit eternal life.

It's a story about four people: one who is completely helpless and three others—a priest, a Levite, and a Samaritan—all from different backgrounds, ethnic groups, and socio-economic statuses. The priest and the Levite passed by on the other side of the road from the helpless man. But when the Samaritan saw the poor man beaten, he was moved with compassion. He went over and wrapped the poor man's wounds in bandages. The Samaritan put the injured man on his

own animal, brought him to an inn, and took care of him. The next day, the Samaritan took out two denarii, gave them to the innkeeper, and said, "Take care of him; and when I come back, I will repay you whatever more you spend."

We know nothing more about the Samaritan, not what he does for a living or how much money he makes. The truth is he could have been a shyster on another day, a crook no more noble than the priest or the Levite. On another day and in other circumstances, the priest and the Levite too might have been just as earnest as the Samaritan, perhaps even more so.

So what makes the Samaritan *good*? I think he is called good because in that moment, on that day, he was able to write a different narrative about who he was in the world and who the beaten man really was.

------ ★ ★ ★ ------

Good Lord, help us to be willing to learn and grow and stay the course until healing comes, peace is our friend, and the world changes for good. May we forever be called good because our heart's desire is to be God's good grace in the world.

Rev. Dr. Cathy S. Gilliard

RENEWED STRENGTH
Galatians 6:9

How often have you given it all you had, done your very best, and thought you were doing the right thing just to have your efforts portrayed as being disingenuous and self-serving? No one says thank you, way to go, great job, or anything.

Everyone appreciates being appreciated and feels good when their efforts are recognized. But all too often many of us allow this to keep us from continuing to hang in the fight. Whatever we feel God has called us to do, we must do it for the glory of God and God alone.

Unfortunately, an element of the human condition perpetuates jealousy, envy, and an unending desire to accentuate the negative and nasty. But this passage of Scripture lets us know that there are those of us who must continue doing good and seeking good. When weariness, fatigue, hopelessness, and helplessness set in, remember the words of the song sung by Rev. James Cleveland:

> I don't feel no ways tired,
> I've come too far from where I started from.
> Nobody told me that the road would be easy,
> I don't believe He brought me this far to leave me.

We cannot and must not give up on good. We cannot grow weary doing good because we do it to please God. We must make sure that what we have done and are doing comes from the heart. So, whether or not we hear thank you, we know that God is pleased. Hang in there and stay focused on pleasing God.

------ ★ ★ ★ ------

Father, let us not become weary in doing good, for at the proper time and if we do not give up, we will reap the harvest. Amen.

Rev. Dr. Marvin A. Moss

BE SET FREE
Genesis 41:14

For the past eight years, I've been teaching college-level courses at Sing Sing Correctional Facility. The prison setting has been the best teaching experience of my life. The men are eager to learn and love discussions. They are highly motivated to turn their lives around.

While I was teaching an Introduction to the Hebrew Bible course, we were discussing the Joseph story in Genesis. This is always a favorite of my students. Joseph is falsely accused of sexual misconduct and thrown into prison.

Joseph's story led to a discussion about being in prison. One of my students said, "Being in prison is awful, but the prison within is even worse." He pointed to his head when he said "prison within." Several of the men nodded their heads in agreement.

We talked about the prison within. Some men stay in their cells all day because of depression or fear. Other men are imprisoned by guilt and shame over their crimes.

I think experiencing the prison within is a universal human experience. Being honest enough to admit and name what is imprisoning us is the first step toward release and freedom.

What is limiting you from experiencing the fullness of life?

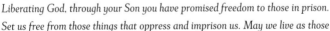

Liberating God, through your Son you have promised freedom to those in prison. Set us free from those things that oppress and imprison us. May we live as those who accept the freedom you have so graciously given us in Jesus Christ. Amen.

Robert Martin Walker

ENDING OPPRESSION

Isaiah 25:7

I n our United Methodist Baptismal Covenant, the second question asked of those baptized or their parents is: "Do you accept the freedom and power God gives you to resist evil, injustice, and oppression in whatever forms they present themselves?"

Note that "oppression" is grouped with "evil" and "injustice," forming a kind of unholy trinity. Oppression is a serious issue, both in the ancient world and in our modern world. It is an abuse of power and authority in a cruel and unjust manner.

Oppression takes many different forms in today's world: human trafficking, terrorism, sexual abuse, abuse of authority, and war. At the root of oppression is injustice and evil.

Hillary Rodham Clinton spoke at the United Methodist Women's Assembly in Louisville, Kentucky. Speaking to 7,400, Clinton advocated for the advancement of women in the United States and abroad. She spent the majority of her speech talking about her upbringing and her lifelong membership in the Methodist Church. She also applauded the women's group for their work to stop human trafficking. "I have seen firsthand how much faith communities can do. I think a lot has been accomplished, not just here at home, but everywhere," she said.[3]

April 26, 2014

Subtle forms of oppression exist as well. Prejudice can be a subtle form of oppression, influencing how we treat those around us. Gender bias can also influence how we behave toward others.

Isaiah 25:7 offers a vision of the end of oppression. This is a vision to be lived into.

What does it mean to live into God's vision of the end of oppression?[2]

------ ★ ★ ★ ------

O God whose son was called Prince of Peace, help us to do our part in ending oppression. Let us accept the freedom you give us to end oppression, injustice, and evil in all of their forms. Open our eyes to the subtle and overt forms of oppression in which we participate. Give us the strength and courage to name the forms of oppression and then to work to eradicate them. Amen.

Robert Martin Walker

GENEROUS KINDNESS
John 13:3-8, 12-15

God does not shy away from grime. Jesus, absconding from any sense of propriety, stoops down and scrubs the dirt away from his disciples' calloused and smelly feet. In performing this act of humility, Jesus reveals to us that, were God to attend a party, you would find the Holy One not seated at the head of the table, but rather bustling between the guests serving drinks, picking up plates, and attending to the spilled wine on the carpet. There is no task too lowly for the Creator of all things to take up and perform with generous kindness.

Our lives must not only mimic the behavior of Jesus, they should seek to be served by it. Opening up our lives to be served by God often requires a tremendous amount of humility from us. We would rather go out and do something great for God rather than sit back and rely on the mercy and unmerited favor of the Most High. Surely there must be a way for us to render ourselves worthy to receive such marvelous love, right? But as soon as we pose this question, we feel the hands of Jesus removing our shoes and socks and dipping our feet into the basin of water, inviting us to reflect on the notion that it is not what we do or accomplish that establishes value in the eyes of God. Rather, God longs to love and serve us because we are God's own children, created in the image of the divine.

------ ⋆ ⭐ ⋆ ------

Most gracious God, help us receive your love without reservation and, in doing so, see our lives transformed as we recognize our value is not found in what we do but in who we are as your children. Amen.

Rev. Kevin K. Wright

"The true measure of any society is how we take care of our children.... No child should ever have to grow up in poverty. Yet every single night, all across America, kids go to sleep hungry or without a place to call home.

We have to do better. Advocating for children and families has been the cause of my life, starting with my first job as a young attorney at the Children's Defense Fund.... I will continue my life's work focused on creating opportunities for children and fairness for families."[4]

The New York Times
September 21, 2016

WHERE YOU STAND
Galatians 6:2

S ending a prayer on your behalf and positive energy toward Nevada!

------- ⋆ ★ ⋆ -------

Lord, throughout our journeys, we are challenged to search our lives, to look deep into our souls, and to root out that which does not work for life. Help us to find the courage we need. Help us to understand that until we look deep inside and embrace who we really are, we cannot come to you in sincerity and integrity.

We admit that sometimes our lives are a bit empty and we are not able to approach you as we should. Be by our side, gracious God.

Constantly encourage us to find the strength to continue. Fill us with determination to grow toward maturity of mind and spirit. Fill us with a passion for mission and to become the people you want us to be.

We remember John Wesley's teaching:
Do all the good you can—offer loving service to others;
By all the means you can—in worship, work, play, and prayer;
In all the ways you can—by building something or doing nothing, teaching or learning, talking or listening;
In all the places you can—in family or church, community or workplace, your homeland or someone else's;
At all the times you can—for an hour or a day at a time;
To all the people you can—Christians, Jews, Muslims, or those who claim no faith at all, one at a time or gathered together;
As long as ever you can—wherever you are in life, for the rest of your life.

Fill us with this understanding of your grace and mercy. Help us remember that these are the things that give us life and life eternal. Amen.

Vice President Joe Biden campaigned on behalf of Hillary Clinton today.... During his speech, Biden spoke about the importance of electing a president and Senator who are pro-union and labor. He said that Donald Trump is anti-union adding, "If [Democrats] don't win the Senate and Hillary doesn't win the presidency, you'll be out of business."[5]

Hillary Clinton Speeches
October 29, 2016

DO MORE
James 2:14-26

I have recently been in an e-mail conversation with Burns Strider, your longtime friend and my new friend in faith. He asked me about your comments at the Al Smith dinner about Catholics and Methodists being similar in the relationship between faith and good works. The letter of James and the above passage came to mind.

In our Wesleyan Heritage we see God's grace and human activity working together in the relationship of faith and good works. Faith is the only response essential for salvation, but the General Rules of the Methodist Church remind us that salvation evidences itself in good works. I have read that St. Ignatius, in his exercise of doing more for God, would encourage people around him by asking them: "What have I done for God? What am I doing for God? and What more can I do for Him?"

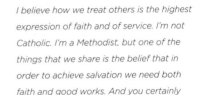

I believe how we treat others is the highest expression of faith and of service. I'm not Catholic. I'm a Methodist, but one of the things that we share is the belief that in order to achieve salvation we need both faith and good works. And you certainly don't need to be Catholic to be inspired by the humility and heart of the Holy Father, Pope Francis. Or to embrace his message.[6]

Hillary Rodham Clinton
Al Smith Dinner, October 20, 2016

"Do all the good you can, by all the means you can, in all the ways you can, in all the places you can, at all the times you can, to all the people you can, as long as ever you can." It is our Methodist magis.

------- ★ ★ ★ -------

Take, Lord, and receive all my liberty,
My memory, my understanding
And my entire will,
All I have and call my own.

You have given all to me.
To you, Lord, I return it.

Everything is yours; do with it what you will.
Give me only your love and your grace,
That is enough for me. Amen

St. Ignatius Loyola

OFF OUR KNEES
Zechariah 9:9-12

A dark cloud has settled over our country and the world. The past few months have been awful with terrorism and racism—the worst enemies of the human race.

I believe in prayer and its unique power. Prayer helps me communicate with God and get inside God's heart and thinking process.

I can't know how God feels about our "thoughts and prayers" or our "moments of silence." But I am positive God would be far more pleased if we would open our eyes, lift up our heads, get up off our knees, and go and do something rather than simply pray. How seemingly foolish it is to continue to tremble over the tragic news and then ask God for comfort when we aren't doing anything to transform the conditions under which these killings and terrorist plots continue to happen.

I don't think God has anything to do with violence, murder, or terrorism. That is our sinful human choice. I would rather believe in an all-loving God who isn't in control than an all-controlling God who would cause such heartache, death, and pain to innocent people.

We can be the people God wants us to be. That is, if we come to the end of our prayers, get up off our knees, and go and do courageous things through love to transform the world, our nation, and our own hearts.

God of love, move us from our prayers and into action to make your kingdom of love come true. Amen.

THE UNEXPECTED
Luke 10:25-37

I t might be the most familiar of Jesus's parables. People who've never read or heard the parable use the words *good Samaritan*. There are the good Samaritans laws, which protect volunteers from liability. Hospitals are named Good Samaritan.

We all know what this parable means, right? It means helping people who need help. Be like the good Samaritan who took time out from his trip to help a man who had been beaten, to see that he got care. We know this. We agree with it.

Actually there is something new here. That first-century audience who heard this parable would have found the combination of the words *good* and *Samaritan* odd and disturbing. There were no "good" Samaritans. Samaritans were bad people who lived in the wrong neighborhood.

He's the wrong person. The "right" people all walk on by without stopping. The wrong person stops, the wrong person helps. Maybe the parable of the good Samaritan isn't only "Be a good neighbor." Maybe it's also "When you and I didn't deserve or expect help, help came. Unexpected. Undeserved. From an unexpected person, a condemned man; from an unexpected place, a Cross." The New Testament calls Jesus's sacrifice "a scandal," sort of like being saved by, of all people, a Samaritan.

Because you have been graciously and surprisingly helped by an unexpected person, be gracious to others unexpectedly.

------ ＊ ★ ＊ ------

Thank you, Lord, that when I've been beaten and down, you haven't walked on by on the other side. You've come to me, come for me, lifted me up, and carried me home to be healed. Amen.

A DIFFERENT WORLD

Isaiah 43:18-19

E lizabeth Barrett Browning wrote:

> Earth's crammed with heaven,
> And every common bush afire with God;
> But only he who sees takes off his shoes;
> The rest sit round it and pluck blackberries.[7]

The risk for followers of Christ in every age is that we miss the new things God wants to do in our world because we are too preoccupied with trivial things around us. Speaking to people in exile, people who found themselves in a radically different world than the one in which they grew up, Isaiah heard the Lord saying:

> Don't remember the prior things;
>> don't ponder ancient history.
> Look! I'm doing a new thing;
>> now it sprouts up; don't you recognize it?

------ * ★ * ------

Creative Spirit of God who is always at work to do a new thing in our world, give us eyes to see and strength to follow the new tasks to which God is calling us. Amen.

Rev. James A. Harnish

Bill [Clinton] addressed some protesters outside of the venue that were holding signs about coal country. He said, "I saw those signs outside. I just want to say, [Mrs. Clinton] was the first and is now the only candidate to say we've got to do something about coal country. We've got to do something about these rural pockets and these inner cities that have been totally left out of this economic recovery. We've got to invest in these areas. You can't leave anybody behind here. And that's what this election is about. If we do this we're going to rise together."[8]

Hillary Clinton Speeches
October 4, 2016

SHALOM ON EARTH
2 Chronicles 6:32-33; Matthew 25:34-36

The evening news carries such vivid images of the refugee crisis. Innocent people fleeing war and hatred are attempting to find new homes and lives. Reports estimate that more than 16,000 migrants have streamed into Austria since the weekend and more than 17,500 people were received in Munich, Germany, alone. According to the United Nations Refugee Agency estimates, more than 366,000 refugees and migrants have crossed the Mediterranean Sea to Europe this year and at least 2,800 have died or disappeared during their journeys.

The Old Testament passage, though related to the dedication of the temple during Solomon's time, reminds us that those who come from afar are to be welcomed as witnesses to the God whom we love. Jesus's teaching from Matthew in the parable of the sheep and the goats reminds us even more of what our actions need to be.

"The Rev. Jack Amick, head of International Disaster Response for UMCOR, the United Methodist Committee on Relief, offers a prayer of action and solidarity for those fleeing conflict and migrating to Europe and other parts of the world."[9]

------ ★ ★ ★ ------

Prayer for a New Vision

God of Shalom,
Grant us hearts that cry like yours
At the sight of dead boys on beaches,
Packed train cars,
And long lines of families on the move.

We confess that we have seen these images for centuries.
Grant us, this time, the wisdom to act in a way that turns history upside down.
And brings your shalom on earth as it is in heaven.
Grant us arms that welcome the stranger;
Grant us hands that feed the hungry;
Grant us feet that walk with those whose feet search
For a new home, a new job, a new life. Amen.

SALT AND LIGHT

Luke 14:34-35

"If you're going to do something, do it." My friend told me those words as I was waffling over whether to sign up for the Marine Corps Marathon in Washington, DC. I had been a casual runner (aka slow jogger) up to that point, but there was something about the allure of running a marathon that had captured my imagination. As the sign-up date for the race approached, I contemplated the intense training schedule, special diet, and time commitment that awaited me.

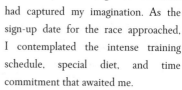

I've tried to say for some time now that our country needs more love and kindness. I know it's not the kind of thing presidential candidates usually say. But we have to find ways to repair these wounds and close these divides. The great genius and salvation of the United States is our capacity to do and to be better.[10]

Hillary Rodham Clinton
July 8, 2016

In today's Gospel text, Jesus has an extreme aversion to the idea that his followers would do anything halfway. For Jesus, if you're going to do something, you need to go ahead and do it.

Salt must be salty. We must be doers of the Word and not just hearers of it. If you have embarked upon a task to live out the gospel in your life, whether it is through private sector work or public service, then put your whole heart into it. Commit to running the race even on the days when your legs feel sore and you wish that you could be off doing something else more enjoyable.

Rev. Kevin K. Wright

Father, help us to be doers in this world, and not just waiters for the perfect time to act. Show us what you desire for us to conquer and then give us the courage and strength to conquer it. Amen.

THE STANDARD
Matthew 7:12

Jesus knew the human heart and its self-centeredness. Jesus's Golden Rule gives us a standard by which naturally selfish people can gauge their actions: actively treat others the way they themselves like to be treated.

People universally demand respect, love, and appreciation, whether they deserve it or not. Jesus understood this desire and used it to promote relational ethical behavior. Do you want to be shown respect? Then respect others. Do you crave a kind word? Then speak words of kindness to others.

Prayer to Practice the Golden Rule

May I be an enemy to no one and the friend of what abides eternally.

May I never quarrel with those nearest me, and be reconciled quickly if I should.

May I never plot evil against others, and if anyone plot evil against me,

*   may I escape unharmed and without the need to hurt anyone else.*

May I love, seek and attain only what is good.

May I desire happiness for all and harbor envy for none.

May I never find joy in the misfortune of one who has wronged me.

May I never wait for the rebuke of others, but always rebuke myself until I make

*   reparation.*

May I gain no victory that harms me or my opponent.

May I reconcile friends who are mad at each other.

May I, insofar as I can, give all necessary help to my friends and to all who are

*   in need.*

May I never fail a friend in trouble.

May I be able to soften the pain of the grief stricken and give them comforting

*   words.*

May I respect myself.

May I always maintain control of my emotions.

May I habituate myself to be gentle, and never angry with others because of

*   circumstances.*

May I never discuss the wicked or what they have done, but know good people

*   and follow in their footsteps. Amen.*

Eusebius of Caesarea, fourth-century bishop

DARE TO BE

Proverbs 29:7

During the early eighteen hundreds, a flood of immigrants from Europe came to the lower eastside of New York City and worked in unsafe conditions in sweatshops for unfair wages. Many lived in conditions of squalor, gang activity, addiction, hunger, and abuse—and children were victimized.

It was to these conditions that the compassionate concern for the needs of children and their mothers gave birth to the zeal of the Methodists to organize ways to feed, educate, and uplift people from chains of poverty.

In the 1830s, the Methodist women of New York City noticed that nothing was being done by politicians or social groups to help the children, so they set out to make a difference at the risk of their own personal safety and health.

In the spirit of John Wesley and the evangelic fires of Methodism— using the Bible as their textbook—these women, rather than hosting camp meetings and crusades, began to teach the poorest children to read. Soon, about 500 children were attending classes and enjoying lunch in a safe, clean environment. These "Sunday schools" eventually touched the lives of thousands of boys and girls.

This was the origin of the societies that became the United Methodist City Society. Today, I celebrate this wonderful diversity and our ministry with immigrants, especially those undocumented who use our Far Rockaway Mission for food and support.

------- ★ ★ ★ -------

Awaken my heart, Lord, to those you care about, including the poor and helpless, the hungry and homeless, the troubled and hopeless in our world. Amen.

LIVE BY THE HEART

Ephesians 4:11-16

I like the phrase "to equip the saints" (v. 12 ESV). Paul usually refers to saints as the faithful in Rome who were enduring great persecution. But here in Ephesians he broadens the term to all who are followers of Jesus— potential saints building up the body of Christ.

Saints are not perfect. Saints are people who have discovered how to live by the heart and take the road to the goal of perfection—the road paved for us by Jesus Christ.

Henri Nouwen writes:

> As God's beloved children we have to believe that our little lives, when lived as God's chosen and blessed children, are broken to be given to others. We too have to become bread for the world. When we live our brokenness under the blessing, our lives will continue to bear fruit from generation to generation. That is the story of the saints—they died, but they continue to be alive in the hearts of those who live after them—and it can be our story too.[11]

We all have saints who live in our hearts. I think of your mother, whose life was filled with difficulties but who let the light shine through it anyway. May we do the same.

------- ★ ★ ★ -------

Gracious God, help us, saints-in-the-making, to be strong and faithful, diligent in our care for one another, and wise in our witness to your power and love. Keep us true to the light of Christ within our hearts, to be both compassionate and courageous in the ways we witness to a better world. Amen.

FOR GENERATIONS TO COME
Psalm 78:1-8

Sometimes, we see history as a great negative, guided only by the tragic and overwhelming mistakes of human hubris. But the future comes. Can we make it a future of hope? We can do so, the psalmist reminds us, as we remember the works of God in the past.

Perhaps we can remember the past but work as an "angel of progress" by advocating for peace and justice. And since God sent his son Jesus to show us how to love one another, we can move forward with a different principle and law.

The social holiness tradition of Methodism has long demonstrated the ways Christians can "love thy neighbor" (Mark 12:31 KJV) in caring for the least, the last, and the lost. I also believe our tradition calls us to advocate for better social, political, and religious policy.

May the spirit empower you, Hillary, a child of these Methodist roots, to "do all the good you can" to effect change so that our world can be a better place for all people.

And remember to tell Charlotte the stories of faith so that as the psalmist says: "the next generation may know them" (Psalm 78:6 ESV).

------ ★ ★ ★ ------

Lord of Abraham, Moses, David, and John Wesley, guide my heart with your skillful hand through the history of today and tomorrow, a Christian life ever in the making. Help me to do all the good I can each and every moment. Amen.

Chelsea Clinton has given birth to a daughter, according to a post on her Twitter and Facebook accounts. The baby was born Friday, a Clinton spokesman said.

"Marc and I are full of love, awe, and gratitude as we celebrate the birth of our daughter, Charlotte Clinton Mezvinsky," Clinton's message read.

Former President Bill Clinton and former Secretary of State Hillary Clinton said they feel "blessed, grateful, and so happy to be the grandparents of a beautiful girl."[12]

CNN
September 27, 2014

MERCY AND FAIRNESS
Amos 5:6-15

Amos came from Tekoa, in Judah, to Israel to work as a prophet. One might consider Amos a migrant worker moving to a more prosperous nation to find work. He was a shepherd and dresser of trees, and even then, such migrant workers were disparaged.

Then God called Amos to leave his work to become God's spokesperson. Amos spoke as an outsider with strong warnings of God's imminent judgment upon the king, the politically powerful, the wealthy and well connected, and the religious establishment.

Amos (v. 6) exhorts his hearers, "Seek the LORD and live." He insists that God may still be open to a deep and heartfelt repentance followed by dramatic new ways of living. Seeking God means seeking "good and not evil, that you may live" (v. 14). Seeking God means doing good for others, especially the poor and vulnerable in the community and society at large.

> If we claim we are for family, then we have to pull together and resolve the outstanding issues around our broken immigration system. The American people support comprehensive immigration reform not just because it's the right thing to do—and it is—but because they know it strengthens families, strengthens our economy, and strengthens our country.[13]
>
> **Hillary Rodham Clinton**
> May 5, 2015

Amos's words have continued to speak powerfully across the centuries wherever the poor are trampled, the distribution of wealth is out of whack, and justice is perverted.

In a world like ours threatened by economic insecurity, global warming, disparities in justice in our legal system, and where twenty percent of the world's population uses eighty percent of the world's resources, the words of Amos continue to bear witness.

------ ★ ------

God of all who are cast down, you call us to seek good and to meet oppression with justice. Help us to love those who have been marginalized. Fill us with grace and courage as we work for the good of those in need, so that mercy and fairness may prevail and your kingdom come in Jesus Christ. Amen.

FOUNDATIONAL TRAITS
Micah 6:1-8

I remember a story about theological students at Harvard who were preparing for the ministry. They were taking their final exam on Immanuel Kant's moral imperative. Kant was a German moral philosopher who argued that fundamental concepts structure human experience, and that reason is the source of morality. The students had two hours to write their philosophies, with a ten-minute break in the middle. They wrote furiously for fifty-five minutes. Then the professor rang a bell for the break. They all went out into the hallway, where there was a person costumed like a homeless person, sitting humped up on the floor, disheveled, looking like a mess. The theological students were busy in conversation with each other, getting a drink of water, taking a bathroom break. Then back into the classroom for the second hour of writing their philosophies of what it meant to be a moral human being.

A few days later, the theological students received their test results: they had all failed. The students thought that their test was what they wrote. The professor meanwhile was standing out in the hallway during the ten-minute break and grading them on who approached the man on the floor and spoke a kind word. Nobody did. Justice, kindness, and mercy are foundational to God's character. God expects people to show love to their fellow humans and to be loyal in their love toward God, just as God has been loyal to them. The ingredient that God requires from his disciples is fundamental human mercy and kindness—to family, friends, work associates, classmates, and strangers in the hallway.

God our deliverer, you walk with the meek and the poor, the compassionate and those who mourn, and you call us to walk humbly with you. When we are foolish, be our wisdom; when we are weak, be our strength; that, as we learn to do justice and to love mercy, your rule may come as blessing. Amen.

A REQUIREMENT
Micah 6:8

Requirements are absolute necessities. You have to do them. You might as well get used to them because requirements are part of everyday life.

Do you remember when you got your driver's license for the first time? Or when you taught Chelsea to drive so she could get her first license?

I learned to drive on the family car—a stick shift. And when I got my license it was a great day. Freedom. Movement. A sign of growing up.

There are rules for getting a license. You take a driver's education course—classroom and behind the wheel. You take the state written and road test. No arguments. No discussion. These are the requirements.

I am required to pay my federal taxes by April 15 to avoid a penalty. I am required to purchase an airline ticket twenty-one days in advance if I want to get that cheaper rate.

Life is full of requirements. The question is this, "What does God require of us?"

Micah 6:8 could have been the inspiration for one of our favorite John Wesley expressions: "Do all the good you can; By all the means you can; In all the ways you can; In all the places you can; At all the times you can; To all the people you can; As long as ever you can."

That is the requirement!

------ ⋆ ★ ⋆ ------

You have shown us, O God, what is good. You have shown us what you require: to do justly, to love mercy, to walk humbly with your God. Let the river of your justice flow through us as we live as you have shown us. Help us to do justly, to love mercy, and to walk humbly with you. Amen.

During her speech, Hillary Clinton, who described herself today as a "Methodist both by birth and by choice," thanked the church for being a place where the Clintons "could worship, study, contemplate, be of service, get some good pastoral advice and step outside all the commotion of life in the White House in Washington."

"That was very, very precious to us," she said. "Here we were not the first family. We were just our family. And we relished and cherished that time."[14]

ABC News
September 13, 2015

HUMBLY WALK
Micah 6:8

"Walk humbly with your God." Focus on the word *walk*. Walking is the opposite of running. Walking is a gentle, deliberate pace.

Focus on the word *humbly*. Not full of yourself. Not preoccupied with yourself.

Jesus said that the greatest person in the kingdom of God is a person who is humble like a little child. He said that the greatest virtue of all the virtues is humility.

Henri Nouwen says, "Often we are made to believe that self-deprecation is a virtue, called humility. But humility is in reality the opposite of self-deprecation. It is the grateful recognition that we are precious in God's eyes and that all we are is pure gift."[15]

Humility is sacrificing your own needs to listen to the needs of others and the desires of God. Humility is the art of actually listening to what God is telling us through Scripture and the Spirit. That message is always that you are loved.

Walking humbly with God is placing our hand in God's as we walk together. Like a parent holding the hand of a child, *God* walks with us and our trust needs to be in that relationship.

To walk humbly with *your* God is not that God is your possession but that God is personal to each of us. Your God who made you. Your God who walks with you every step of every day. Your God who walks with you in the valleys of the shadows of death.

Hillary, may these words be with you. May these words be in your heart and mind as you walk with God every day.

------- ★ ★ ★ -------

What does the Lord require? To do justice, love kindness, and walk humbly with your God. May it be so, O Lord. Amen.

GOODNESS
Psalm 23:6

The word *goodness* wrapped around and captured me as I meditated this morning. The soothing words of Psalm 23:6 came quickly to mind.

Soon, though, the comforting words revealed a new perspective, a new dimension in the form of a question. Does goodness "follow" me as I leave places? Is goodness the natural, expected blessing of my presence in the life of others?

Psalm 23 is clearly geared to a description of God's action and presence in our lives. But, on second glance, this psalm also has an underlying ethical component particularly addressed to folk like me called to be shepherds. It can be read as exhortation on how to live and how to lead, in imitation of the Good Shepherd, revealing fresh insight. It has blessed me with unexpected peace and freshness.

Goodness—does it follow me? Does my presence leave in its wake an aroma of goodness? Goodness, just like mercy, is more than good acts; it's an environment, a realm, a clearing, a hospitality. Goodness is the possibility of further goodness, ever-flowing, self-replicating, life-giving, and transforming.

------ ⋆ ★ ⋆ ------

Merciful, loving, gracious God, source of goodness, giver of every perfect gift, I ask that your goodness be activated, released, and prioritized this day so that my presence creates a realm of hospitality for goodness in this world that needs it desperately. And as I pray, I commit myself to this journey in the name of all that is holy and in the steps of Jesus, the Christ. Amen.

Jorge Lockward

⋆ ⋆

From: Rev. Bill Shillady
Sent: June 24, 2015
To: H

I hear great reports about your statement at Christ the King United Church of Christ in Florissant, Missouri.

It is the right path to address the racial inequality in our country.

Blessings. May goodness follow you and be with you. You are in my prayers.

Rev. Bill

⋆ ⋆

TRANSFORMING LIVES
John 20:18

M ary's encounter with the resurrected Christ opened her eyes to a completely new reality. Her encounter with Jesus in the garden on Easter morning recalibrated her perception of how things were supposed to run.

Just hours earlier she had sat weeping before an empty tomb, and now she is preaching the good news about Jesus's resurrection to the disciples.

Her message is simple and yet startlingly powerful:

"I have seen the Lord."

Where have you seen the Lord lately? Is it on the rope line as you're looking into the face of a young man wondering when his country will accept him for who he is? Is it at a town hall meeting where a veteran shares about her journey to overcome post-traumatic stress disorder? Do you see the Lord in the college student who is terrified about being ripped away from the only country he has ever known?

It is Mary's experience with Christ that wrestles her heart away from the grip of fear and pushes her into the pulpit of proclaiming God's good news for all. So too, then is it our experience with Christ that propels us forward in advocating for and championing the things that matter greatly to God—things like caring for the poor, tending to the sick, and advocating for the incarcerated.

----- ★ ★ ★ -----

Father, may our experience of seeing you transform our reality and cause us to see a hopeful future made possible through God's power and love. Amen.

Rev. Kevin K. Wright

LAMP OF HOPE
Titus 3:3-8

This morning, I was able to watch your speech in Miami. I want to commend you once again for allowing your faith to shine through with the "good" that needs to be held high in this political environment that has become so toxic. After listening to your thoughts, I could not help but find an appropriate Scripture for you today.

The little-read pastoral letter of Titus came to mind. Paul's words to Titus might have inspired the Wesleyan quote that you and I both love. "Do all the good you can. By all the means you can. In all the ways you can. In all the places you can. At all the times you can. To all the people you can. As long as ever you can."

Paul recognized that doing good will be excellent and profitable for everyone. John Wesley, in his notes on the New Testament, wrote about verse 8: "This is a faithful saying, and these things I will that thou affirm constantly, that they which have believed in God might be careful to maintain good works. These things are good and profitable unto men.

"Be careful to excel in good works—Though the apostle does not lay these for the foundation, yet he brings them in at their proper place, and then mentions them, not slightly, but as affairs of great importance."[16] Blessings, my sister. Keep up the good!

------- ★ ★ ★ -------

Lord, today, may I find a way to practice your love and kindness to someone who needs to be blessed. Help my good works to be a lamp of hope to others. Amen.

In Miami, Florida, Clinton delivered a victory speech with supporters at a Super Tuesday rally. During her speech, she congratulated Sanders for his strong showing, then she thanked all her supporters and volunteers who helped make her victories possible. She focused on the future and the road to nomination before taking a shot at Republican front-runner Donald Trump saying, "We know we've got work to do. It's not to make America great again—America never stopped being great. We have to make America whole."[17]
Hillary Clinton Speeches
March 1, 2016

THE WORD
John 1:1-5, 10-14, 17-18

I n the beginning was the Word." Not the angel, nor the manger, but the Word—just that. If John's Gospel were the only one, this is all we would know of Jesus's birth: that before his name was Jesus, his name was the Word, and he was with God from the very beginning of creation.

He was God's self, God's soul, God's life force in the world, invisible and indispensable. He was God's message to the world, and the message was life. The message was light.

This passage helps us to see that God decided to speak in a new way, less mysterious, less invisible. God decided to speak body language. The eternal Word of God took human form, becoming one of us.

"In the beginning was the Word," is hard for us, because we think of a word as a unit of human speech, and we live in a world that is flooded with words.

This Word made flesh is different. It is a way of life. This Word does not deliver medical lectures to sick people; this Word heals them. This Word does not hand out neatly printed recipes to hungry people; this Word feeds them. This Word does not leave inspirational tracts lying on the bedside tables of those who are dying; this Word raises them from the dead.

This incarnate Word does what he says and says what he does. In him, word and reality become one thing.

------ ★ ★ ★ ------

Almighty God, you have poured upon us the new light of your incarnate Word. Grant that this light, enkindled in our hearts, may shine forth in our lives; through Jesus Christ our Lord, who lives and reigns with you, in the unity of the Holy Spirit, one God, now and for ever. Amen.[18]

Rev. Beth Elders

ABUNDANT LIFE

John 10:10b

In the 1970s a greeting found its way into popular culture: "Have a nice day!" Not only would people say this to one another, they would conclude letters and messages with it. At some point, a smiley face got connected with this phrase.

The sentiments behind this phrase are good ones. To say "Have a nice day!" is to wish someone well. However, isn't hoping for just a nice day aiming too low? We don't want nice days; we want great days, wonderful days, amazing days, and remarkable days! Why settle for nice when you can have something more?

In Christian terms, our desire for something more is called "abundant life."

Abundant life is life in its fullness. Abundance is so much more than niceness or pleasantness—it is life in its richness, depth, and wholeness.

Jesus is the one who shows us the way to abundant life: self-giving love. If we want to receive abundant life, we must look for ways to make possible abundance for others. This means putting our love into action with those who are poor, in prison, or suffering.

How do I make abundance possible for others?

------ ★ ★ ★ ------

Good Shepherd, you have come to bring us abundant life. Help us to understand that our own abundance is interconnected with making abundance possible for others. Give us the strength and courage to put our love into action. Amen.

Robert Martin Walker

JUSTICE AND MERCY
Amos 5:6-7, 21-24

One day Amos—not a priest, just a guy—strolled into the thriving town of Bethel from Tekoa, far to the south. God had interrupted his life; God had erupted into his life. He became a prophet.

Amos, like all prophets, is not too popular for speaking the truth. Evidently God is not much impressed by mere talk, hollow rituals, melodious hymns, or eloquent prayers. What God wants to hear is the constant flow of justice and righteousness.

Justice, in Amos, is about life. Let justice roll down like waters, like an ever-flowing stream. Justice is like water; it is a life-giving force. Judgment is not justice—it is what happens when there is no justice. Justice is about healing; justice is about transformation.

We must redefine the word *justice* in our nation. It is *not* when the good are rewarded, and the bad are punished, but when the most needy in society are cared for.

Let justice flow down like an ever-flowing stream! Let justice and righteousness be constant, like the air we breathe.

A reporter asked Mother Teresa, "Mother, why are you so holy?" Her answer was wonderful: "You sound as if holiness is abnormal. To be holy is normal. To be anything else is abnormal."[20]

------ ★ ------

Lord, help us to see those who are in need. Help us to have hearts that are serving others. Grant mercy to those who are in need. Amen.

COMFORT AND COMPASSION
Matthew 25:31-46

Today I get to serve those who attend our Far Rockaway Mission each day for a hot meal, and I think of this scene drawn by Matthew—sheep on the right, goats on the left.

Often we gloss over the harshness of Jesus's words to the "goats" revealing that there is a price tag on God's blessings. In return for God's gifts—love and forgiveness, salvation, redemption, adoption, an eternal life of blessing—there is something required of us: that we love one another.

Nothing angered Jesus more than when good people treated each other badly; nothing got Jesus's goat so much as when people of faith failed to show love for one another, refused to offer help, comfort, compassion to fellow human beings.

Do our security concerns make us hold back the flow of love, hoarding it against some imagined day of scarcity instead of freely, eagerly passing the plate to everyone?

Through the gift of Jesus the Christ, God has offered to us a cornucopia of blessings—ever-loving, ever-giving, ever-present, ever-powerful.

> *If we stand with each other now, we can build a future where no one is left out or left behind, and everyone can share in the promise of America—which is big enough for everyone, not to be reserved for a few.*[21]
>
> **Hillary Rodham Clinton**
> July 8, 2016

------ ★ ★ ------

Lord, help us to be the kind of disciples who act with compassion and caring without thinking about it. Help it to be a natural act in our responses to your love and blessings in our lives. Remind us that every person whom we help is actually the face of Jesus to us at that moment. Amen.

IT'S SIMPLE
Micah 6:6-8

As a woman, I sometimes take John Wesley's "do all the good you can . . ." a bit too literally; it's not enough for me to simply try my best, but to do everything I can to fix unjust systems, be a voice for the voiceless, be a beacon of God's love (to name but a few).

It's exhausting. And it can easily become frustrating. I find myself pleading to God, "What do you want me to do?!" And then I return to this verse from Micah. The first two verses begin with an impassioned plea: "What should I do?" The world that Micah was speaking into was one where corruption reigned and poverty and hopelessness were commonplace. What does a person of faith do in the midst of this mess?

The prophet Micah doesn't give a detailed list of exactly what we are to do to be a person of faith in the world. It's simple, he says—it's not how large your offerings are to God, nor is it how awesome your works are. It's how you live your life. Humbly walking with God, loving God and others authentically, and working for justice. That's it.

------- ★ ★ ★ -------

Dear God, on those days when it just gets to be too much, when detailed plans and exhaustive schedules get the best of me, help me focus on you and your call in my life. Help remind me of what it's all about. Calm my mind and guide my words and actions, that I may humbly follow you, love others, and work for justice. Amen.

Rev. Beth Elders

"As I have had the honor of representing our country, I have learned that women everywhere have the same aspirations for good jobs, healthy families, strong communities," Clinton said.

"They share the drive to be entrepreneurs and builders, agents of change, drivers of progress and makers of peace. All they need is a fair shot."[22]

WFPL News Louisville
April 26, 2014

FRUIT OF THE SPIRIT

John 15:1-5

As I consider these Scripture verses, I am struck by three things: (1) my life is intended to bear fruit, (2) the source of my "fruitfulness" is my connection to Jesus Christ, and (3) that which does not bear fruit needs to be pruned.

It is in Christ's teaching and example that we discern the type of fruit we are to bear. We are called to show the impact that Christ has made in our lives, so that those we know can experience transformation. Too often, we deceive ourselves by saying that our faith is a purely private and spiritual matter.

Connection to Christ is the conduit by which we reach our lives' goal of bearing fruit. It is in Christ that we find strength and life. Jesus says we are to abide in him: our lives take up residence in him (and he in us).

Dead branches are detrimental to the life of the vine; living branches that do not bear fruit literally sap the life away from branches that will bear fruit. The story is told of a man who had a huge boulder in the middle of his front yard. The rock was ugly but way too big to move. One day he found a solution: he'd make it into a work of art. With hammer and chisel, he went to work and in the end had a beautiful sculpture of an elephant. A friend asked him, "How did you carve this wonderful likeness of an elephant?" He responded, "I just chipped away, little by little, the parts that didn't look like an elephant."

------ ★ ------

Spirit of life, may my choices and actions produce your good fruit: love, joy, peace, patience, kindness, generosity, faithfulness, gentleness, and self-control. Amen.

Rev. Matthew T. Curry

RICH AND POOR
Luke 16:19-31

Jesus never held back any punches about our duties and responsibilities as Christians toward helping others. In one incident, he tells a story about a rich man and a poor man. The rich man wears expensive tailored outfits and feasts daily on gourmet meals. The poor man, positioned at the rich man's gate, is hungry, destitute, and covered with sores that wild dogs come by and lick.

Both men die. The rich man is tortured by belated regrets and a conscience that burns with an unrelieved sense of guilt, while the poor man is carried by angels to heavenly places, comfort, and bliss. It is not wealth alone that condemns the rich man to eternal misery; it is his neglect of the needy who are at his door. We are reminded that consideration of and care for those in need, especially those "at our gate," are essential components of the Christian life. This is undeniable.

Jesus seemed to have had a special proclivity toward the poor. I think that is because we are all poor in our own way, if only in small measure. Poor and needy. Whether physically poor and hungry, spiritually poor and in need of someone to love us or someone to love, so withdrawn that we are afraid to give others a chance, or so full of ourselves that we fail to notice those desperate for the crumbs we toss away, poverty is poverty, and we all have our needs.

------- ⋆ ✦ ⋆ -------

Lord, may we be blessed enough to recognize our wealth, but more important, to recognize that the good fight of faith always includes those who desperately need our help in whatever ways we can offer it. Amen.

Rev. Dr. Cathy S. Gilliard

CHESED
James 3:13-18 ESV

There is a wonderful word in Hebrew that is used throughout the Hebrew Scriptures to describe the ways of God. It is *chesed*, which means "kindness and mercy." *Chesed* is the loyal love that God shows to humankind and to the people of Israel no matter how rebellious, rancorous, and hated they (we) become. It is the core of who God is, the love that lasts "from everlasting to everlasting," gracious and merciful and abounding in steadfast concern for us. It's also the love that God wants us to have for each other.

This is the God, Jesus says, that we should model our love after. Love when love is not returned. Love that expands the scope of who is our neighbor to mean every person we come into contact with—and many we don't. This is the love that takes its lead from the one who got this all started, as Jesus says, "Be merciful, even as your Father is merciful." We love others because God loves us—generously, extravagantly, in unexpected ways.

------- ⋆ ⭐ ⋆ -------

Lord, we have all sorts of opportunities to be kind and merciful to other people. Help us to have the eyes and the heart to see them. Amen.

FROM: Rev. Bill Shillady
SENT: September 10, 2015
TO: H

May this bless you!
I hope your voice recovers soon. I hear you will be at Foundry this Sunday for their anniversary. I hope it will be a great homecoming.
Rev. Bill

⋆ ⭐ ⋆

FROM: H
SENT: September 10, 2015
TO: Rev. Bill Shillady

You are such an early riser!
Chelsea and I are speaking together at the Foundry Church's anniversary service in DC on Sunday and I'm reviewing all your daily messages for material. Thanks for everything, H

LIVE BY FAITH

NEW FUTURE
Revelation 21:1

For the new to come, the old must pass away. This is the truth embedded in the above verse from Revelation. The new heaven and new earth are possible because the former heaven and earth are now gone.

As we move through the stages of life we can see this truth in action. When we move into adolescence, we must leave behind acting like a child. As we move into adult life, we leave behind the challenges of adolescence. Paul pointed to this truth in 1 Corinthians 13:11, "When I was a child, I used to speak like a child, reason like a child, think like a child. But now that I have become a man, I've put an end to childish things."

When it comes to growing and developing in our Christian journey, there are things that need to pass away so that newness can come. One thing that we need to let go of is our grudges over past wrongs done to us.

The new heaven and new earth are possible because the past has made way for the future. What things in your life need to pass away to make room for new things?

------- ⋆ ★ ⋆ -------

Eternal God, you are the one who makes all things new. We ask for your help in shedding those past things that are preventing your newness from coming into our lives. Amen.

Robert Martin Walker

Hillary Clinton joined Gov. Cuomo in Queens Wednesday to promote his new tuition-free plan for New York's public colleges.

"You move to New York you can get an affordable college education," said Clinton. . . . "I hope it will be the first of many states [that offer free tuition]," she said.[1]

New York Post
April 12, 2017

TEACH US TO PRAY
Matthew 6:9

Listening God, teach us how to pray. We admit that we are sometimes uncertain in our praying. What is a prayer? Are tears prayers? Can laughter be a prayer? Can prayers be expressed in groans, shouts, screams, or sobs?

We are afraid to put certain thoughts and feelings in our prayers because we believe they might be unacceptable to you. So we clean up our prayers and use nice words and overly formal language. We are afraid of offending you with our real thoughts. Or we fear that if you knew our deepest and darkest thoughts, you wouldn't want anything to do with us.

Yet the prayers of your children in the Scriptures are honest and sometimes raw. Abraham pleaded for the life of his son, Isaac. Moses prayed in anger and frustration for the rebellious Israelites. The psalmist brought the full range of human emotions into his poetic prayers. And your son prayed to escape the agonies of the cross and death.

I pray very specifically for people whom I know by name, people who either have gone through or are experiencing difficult times, illness, divorce, death, disappointment, all of the life experiences that confront most of us.[2]

Hillary Rodham Clinton
March 6, 2016

Teach us to be totally honest in our praying. Reassure us that there is nothing we can say that you haven't heard before and that you're not easily offended. Give us permission to bring all that we are—our true selves—before you.

------- ★ ★ ★ -------

Father, you already know our thoughts and feelings before we put them into words. You know us better than we know ourselves, yet you still love us. Help me pray with the confidence of those who are loved unconditionally. Remind me that prayer encompasses all of life. Amen.

Robert Martin Walker

PRAYERS AND PETITIONS
Philippians 4:6

There is a constant reassurance in Scripture that God is with us in all circumstances. I'm reminded of this presence by this reflection from Henri Nouwen and his encouragement that freedom comes in trusting that.

> When we are spiritually free, we do not have to worry about what to say or do in unexpected, difficult circumstances. When we are not concerned about what others think of us or what we will get for what we do, the right words and actions will emerge from the center of our beings because the Spirit of God, who makes us children of God and sets us free, will speak and act through us.
>
> Jesus says, "When they hand you over, do not worry about how you are to speak or what you are to say; for what you are to say will be given to you at that time; for it is not you who speak, but the Spirit of your Father speaking through you" (Matthew 10:19-20 NRSV).
>
> Let's keep trusting the Spirit of God living within us, so that we can live freely in a world that keeps handing us over to judges and evaluators.[3]

------ ★ ------

O God, fill me with the assurance of your constant presence in my life, through the Holy Spirit living in and speaking through me. Free me from all anxieties and give me the gift of calm inner peace. Amen.

LIFE IS A MARATHON

Hebrews 12:1-2

I n this text we are encouraged to be ready for a marathon. In a marathon, distance is the key factor, and not necessarily speed. Endurance is a must in order to handle the challenges that might come along the way. As life occurs from day to day, we are training for a marathon. Disappointments and setbacks, betrayals and bombshells all serve to get us in shape to continue to run the race. It is not easy but it is possible to stay in the race.

As the text suggests, we have to keep our eyes on Jesus, the one on whom our faith depends from start to finish. When you feel as though you are out of breath, look to Jesus. When the pain seems unbearable, look to Jesus. When the trail is unclear, look to Jesus. When chatter from the sideline seeks to slow you down, look to Jesus. When you feel as though you have nothing left to give, look to Jesus!

So, at the beginning of each day as you hear the command, "On your mark. Get set. Go!" realize that it is just a part of the marathon of life. God will strengthen you, encourage you, and empower you to make it to the end because the victory is sure in Christ Jesus.

Rev. Dr. Marvin A. Moss

---- ★ ★ ★ ----

Lord, help us run with endurance the race that God has set before us. Focus our eyes on Jesus of whom our faith depends from start to finish. Amen.

BLESSED FRIENDSHIP

James 2:23

Friendships are wonderful gifts to our lives. God wants to be our friend as well.

I like the passage I have chosen for today about God calling Abraham *friend*. I'm inspired to share this with you, my friend, Hillary, because I saw a Facebook post involving you and an old high school friend. One of my Facebook friends happens to be one of your friends. What do we say, six degrees of separation?

Well, it just reminded me that I need friends in my life. I don't just mean friends on Facebook, but friends who make me laugh or smile; friends who love me enough to put up with my faux pas, stumblings, and growing edges; friends who respect my strengths and gifts; friends who share what their faith means in their lives and in their work for a better world.

Giving us friends is one of the ways God takes care of us. We need all the things friendship entails—encouragement, companionship, love, honesty, loyalty, understanding, and so much more.

Have a blessed day, my friend, Hillary.

------ ⋆ ★ ⋆ ------

Thank you, God, for the friends you have given me who continue to point me to be a better person and encourage me to live each day one at a time. And best of all, I like that I can consider you as my friend. Amen.

During Biden's 30-minute speech, he called Clinton a close friend who he has known for over 40 years.

"She gets it guys," Biden said to cheers. "I want people to know the Hillary I know."[4]

Times Leader
October 21, 2016

HELP OUR UNBELIEF

John 20:24-29 NIV

On the first Easter, when the other disciples told Thomas they had seen the risen Christ, Thomas refused to believe it. When Jesus later appeared to Thomas, it was an event in one of Thomas's blind spots. Until that moment, Thomas had been relying on his prior experience to tell him what was real.

Experience is colored by what we bring to it—our culture, training, upbringing, and more.

One mother always used an instant mix whenever she made mashed potatoes, and her son grew up thinking that's what everybody did. Then he got married, and the first time his wife fixed mashed potatoes, she peeled and cut up real potatoes. He said, "Why go to all that work? Just use instant." But when they sat down to eat, he found the real mashed potatoes unbelievably delicious and finally understood that there had been a gap in his culinary experience. Such are the limitations of experience.

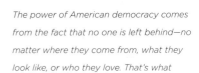

The power of American democracy comes from the fact that no one is left behind—no matter where they come from, what they look like, or who they love. That's what I mean when I say that we're stronger together.[5]

Hillary Rodham Clinton
August 28, 2016

Jesus does not come merely offering instant potatoes; he offers Thomas a new experience.

But Jesus calls for more than experience-based discipleship. He says, "Blessed are those who have not seen and yet have believed" (John 20:29 NIV), and in so saying, he calls for a faith-based model in which all people will have the same opportunity the apostles did—to embrace him as the risen Lord.

Today we walk by faith, trusting in our heart with new insight and spiritual vision for life in Christ's name.

------ ★ ★ ------

God of all creation, we lay before you our Easter hopes and resurrection dreams for a world of wholeness, an end to poverty and violence, the healing of divisions and the mending of brokenness. Send us your grace and your Spirit, that we might make peace, repair broken lives, preach your liberating news, and dream resurrection dreams. Amen.

ONE ANOTHER
John 9:13-25

Jesus routinely broke the rules. He touched the worst of unclean (bleeding women, lepers, and tax collectors) and mingled with sinners. The Samaritan woman at the well was given the role of first evangelist. The despised (Peter, the betrayer) got the commission of feeding the sheep.

Such actions do not draw crowds or enhance popularity. That gospel is not popular and never will be, as it calls us to lay down our lives for our enemies, to put vengeance aside, to relinquish power, not gain it.

I do believe that, with our fellow Christians in community and with God's amazing grace, we will find our strength to live out such a complex call as this—to lay down our lives for others and genuinely love our enemies. We need one another for strength, for guidance, for correction, for collective power to stand for good and against evil and injustice in whatever forms we find them. We must be connected to one another in basic unity to have what it takes to keep going.

------ ★ ★ ★ ------

Amazing grace! How sweet the sound
That saved a wretch like me!
I once was lost, but now am found;
Was blind, but now I see.
Amen.

* *

FROM: Rev. Bill Shillady
SENT: August 7, 2015
TO: H

Blessings this day. I am hoping to see the show "Amazing Grace" to see how the writer and producer have taken the story of John Newton and made it into a Broadway production.
Rev. Bill

* *

PRECIOUS GRACE
John 9:13-25

As a Church of England priest, John Wesley saw that the institutional church had lost its way. It had become a business, burdened with bureaucratic layers and indecipherable requirements. Priests were preaching to empty cathedrals and churches. The poor and marginalized were not welcome. The church had become a place of rules and hierarchy of membership.

Wesley created his methods so that people might really live as Jesus commanded. He preached outside the church walls, ministered to the sick and the poor, established hospitals, schools, and institutions to help care for people. He was a rule-breaker.

As believers, we have to find a way to start over—a way that has grace at its core, not at the periphery. A way that acknowledges that many things are not so guaranteed as truth, a way that we can interpret the "Living Word" differently, a way to genuinely listen to one another, and a way together to find the mind of Christ for such a time as this.

We can't replicate the methods Wesley developed and used. That was a different time, a different world. But we can replicate the foundational theology of grace that informed his teachings. Therein is our hope.

If we choose not to replicate the gift of God in the amazing grace offered to us through Jesus, we no longer can be called true followers of Jesus. We need to speak truth to ourselves and to others, truth that sets us free to love and give, truth that offers generous life and genuine holiness and not just surface rule following.

------ ★ ------

Through many dangers, toils and snares,
I have already come;
'Tis grace hath brought me safe thus far,
And grace will lead me home.
Amen.

OUT OF THE DEPTHS
Psalm 130

In seminary, I took Clinical Pastoral Education, where I worked as a chaplain in training. I was assigned to the children's ward at Duke University Hospital. This involved ministering to families on the floor and being the chaplain in the pediatric emergency room. I met families on what often seemed to be the worst days of their lives.

I would sit with anxious parents while they waited. From time to time, a well-meaning friend would try a little too hard to make everything all right, saying "God meant this for a reason," or "God just needed another angel," or "God doesn't give you more than you can handle."

One of the things I love about the Psalms is that they do not try to make it all better or to sugarcoat the reality of life. The psalmist gives us honesty—grief and pain and doubt. Sometimes even calling to God "Out of the depths" (v. 1).

------ ⋆ ★ ⋆ ------

Compassionate God, on those days when "Out of the depths I cry to you, LORD," *may you bless us with friends like the psalmists, who are able to sit with us and to cry out alongside of us. Amen.*

Clinton started her remarks the way she often does in a house of worship, with a psalm: "This is the day that the Lord has made. Let us rejoice and be glad in it," she said, quoting Psalm 118:24.

Clinton told the congregation about her meeting with several young mothers whose children are suffering from lead poisoning. "I was just heartsick," she said after their conversation.

The former secretary of state started speaking out on the Flint water crisis several weeks ago, releasing statements and calling it a "civil rights issue" on the campaign trail.[6]

NBC News
February 7, 2016

OUR FATHER
Matthew 6:9-13

The Lord's Prayer begins by approaching God as "Father." Jesus probably originally taught this prayer in Aramaic.

The word Jesus used for "Father" would have translated to *Abba*. A group of biblical researchers examined a vast body of prayer literature from ancient Jewish tradition around the first century. They concluded that nowhere else does this personal address ever occur. Only in the words of Jesus is there the boldness to call God "Father."

Today especially, we need to be in solidarity with the people of Nepal as we think of "Our Father" beginning to meet their needs.

Though the prayers of the Buddhist tradition are different from ours, we pray the results in Nepal will be the same—that

help with arrive, that people will be found alive, that those who are injured will be healed. And that those who lost their loved ones, their homes, their livelihoods, and now their sense of hope, will feel God's presence.

-------- ★ ★ ★ --------

Lord, be with the people of Nepal following the devastation. Give them needed help, supplies, and some sense of hope. Amen.

LEARNING TO PRAY
Luke 11:1-13

"Teach us to pray" was one of the few things the disciples ever asked of Jesus. This passage from Luke is a shorter version of the more familiar prayer from Matthew.

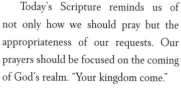

I pray for the will of God to be known so that we can know it and, to the best of our limited ability, try to follow it and fulfill it.[7]

Hillary Rodham Clinton
March 6, 2016

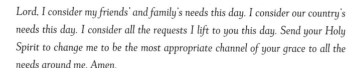

Today's Scripture reminds us of not only how we should pray but the appropriateness of our requests. Our prayers should be focused on the coming of God's realm. "Your kingdom come."

After Jesus's statement of "Give us this day our daily bread," Jesus mentions the parable of the friend at midnight. An unexpected visitor has arrived close to midnight, and the unprepared host knows that hospitality is a sacred act. The host persistently knocks on a friend's door seeking help.

The point of the parable is if a reluctant friend will help, think how much more God will respond to our requests made in prayer. Today, gleaning the task and practice of prayer from the passage, the formula can be found for appropriate praying.

So often we pray for things to change, circumstances to be different, miracles to happen. But until we pray "God, change me!" we may always be caught in a rut of unanswered prayers. Ask, search, knock—receive, find, open.

———— ★ ⭐ ★ ————

Lord, I consider my friends' and family's needs this day. I consider our country's needs this day. I consider all the requests I lift to you this day. Send your Holy Spirit to change me to be the most appropriate channel of your grace to all the needs around me. Amen.

MUSTARD-SEED FAITH

Mark 4:30-32

I n gardening, each season brings new challenges and new blessings. We plant seeds, hoping that the weather warms, the soil nourishes, and the right amount of rain falls so that there can be an abundance of flowers and vegetables. But we need faith that all the elements necessary will come together to make it happen.

As Jesus uses this image in Mark, the seeds of the kingdom are in each of us. God plants us, as mustard seeds. We may not know what type of plant God has sown in us. But when all things come together and our faith grows as a child of Christ, we become a plant so large that the world can receive a blessing from us. I believe each person has the seed for great potential, and if cared for, will become a transformer of our world.

It only takes a mustard seed–sized faith to help us build God's kingdom through the many branches of our lives. Like a fast spreading, strong, and persistent mustard seed, our small seeds of love and hope can grow and become a powerful force for change.

------ ★ ★ ★ ------

I pray that each of us does all we can to help others to grow and mature so we can anticipate and dream of a harvest of transformed lives, nurtured by the love of God in Christ Jesus. May our lives be like the mustard tree, where individuals can "nest" and grow in God's love. Amen.

A HURDLE TO OVERCOME

Mark 11:20-24 NIV

W hatever you ask for in prayer, believe that you have received it, and it will be yours" (Mark 11:24 NIV). Few statements in Scripture have raised as many questions or left faithful prayer warriors as frustrated or disillusioned as this one. The promise that prayer will always result in "what we ask for" is surely not an ironclad guarantee that God will never say no.

People have prayed with sincerity and commitment, over long periods of time, for special requests. Some report great divine interventions, but when there are no great miracles, people often ask, "What went wrong?" or "Were the prayers not uttered correctly?" How desperately we try to find ways of explaining away the mystery of the divine.

My humble belief is that we limit ourselves to what we think God's answers to our prayers should be. My prayers may not change my circumstances, or the situation for which I am praying, but my prayers should change me to look at those circumstances and situations differently. Prayer can and will change me. And God's answers may be totally different than what I expect.

Lord, help me to open my eyes to see your love and presence more clearly. May my prayers to you help me to find comfort and peace. And as I pray, may I be changed to look at the circumstances of my life in new ways, so that your answers to my prayers may be more visible to me than the answers I may expect. Amen.

RISING WATER
Mark 11:20-24

Prayer can and will change us. But God's answers may be totally different than what we expect. I've always loved this story:

A man was trapped in his house during a flood. He began praying to God to rescue him. He had a vision in his head of God's hand reaching down from heaven and lifting him to safety. The water started to rise in his house. His neighbor urged him to leave and offered him a ride to safety. The man yelled back, "I am waiting for God to save me." The neighbor drove off in his pick-up truck.

The man continued to pray and hold onto his vision. As the water began rising in his house, he had to climb up to the roof. A boat came by with some people heading for safe ground. They yelled at the man to grab a rope they were ready to throw and take him to safety. He told them that he was waiting for God to save him. They shook their heads and moved on.

The man continued to pray, believing with all his heart that he would be saved by God. The floodwaters continued to rise. A helicopter flew by, and a voice came over a loudspeaker. The voice offered to lower a ladder and take him off the roof. The man waved the helicopter away, shouting back that he was waiting for God to save him. The helicopter left. The flooding water came over the roof, caught him up, and swept him away. He drowned.

When he reached heaven and asked, "God, why did you not save me? I believed in you with all my heart. Why did you let me drown?" God replied, "I sent you a pick-up truck, a boat, and a helicopter, and you refused all of them. What else could I possibly do for you?"

------- ⋆ ⭐ ⋆ -------

God, thank you for answering our prayers. May we recognize the right answers! Amen.

CONSTANT PRAYER
2 Thessalonians 1:11-12

In Thessalonians, Paul hammered home to this congregation its new identity, not as Roman citizens, not as Thessalonians, but as people entirely defined by their relationships with God and Jesus. Paul, being like a concerned father, used such words as *encouraging, comforting,* and *urging* as he sought to lead them into lives worthy of God.

Here, Paul reminds them that he has always prayed for them—and the prayers have worked. A good lesson for us is to be in constant prayer for others, especially for the conflicted places of our nation and world.

------ ⋆ ⭐ ⋆ ------

Gracious Lord, in your mercy you are always present with us. Help us remember to pray to you for the people and concerns that matter most to us and for the places that need peace in our world. Amen.

FROM: Rev. Bill Shillady
SENT: June 15, 2015
TO: H

I hope you are doing well and that you feel good about Saturday and your journey. You are in my prayers.
Rev. Bill

⋆ ⭐ ⋆

FROM: H
SENT: June 15, 2015
TO: Rev. Bill Shillady

Rev. Bill–
Belated thank you for continuing the daily messages, even when you were fully occupied.

Yesterday, in Iowa, a woman who had just attended their conference said their Bishop urged every church to address early childhood needs— thru programs to provide child care, help close the "word gap," do more to support parents under stress, etc. Is that a national priority [within the church]?

All the best from rainy New Hampshire—H

HORIZONS OF PRAYER
Luke 11:1-4

A woman, her body inflamed by the spread of cancer, lay in a hospital bed. On my hospital visits, day after day we prayed for healing. Each day I could see her silent disappointment that she was not making progress. One day she said to me, "Today, let's not pray that I'll be healed. God knows that I hate this illness. God knows I want to be healed. Let's pray, whether I'm healed or not, that I feel closer to God because, even if I'm not healed—especially if I'm not healed—that's what I really want: God."

Prayer didn't change her circumstances, but it certainly changed her. She reminded me that, when all is said and done, we want not simply peace, justice, health, wholeness, and bread. We want God in our lives through Jesus Christ.

We pray that God's will be done. Our prayer should focus on how we can change to allow God in the Holy Spirit into our lives, to ask for the appropriate change in perspective, to seek alternatives that we may not have thought of before, and to knock on the many doors available to us especially as we open our horizons of prayer.

------- ★ ★ ★ -------

Lord, teach us to pray! Amen.

FROM: Rev. Bill Shillady
SENT: June 15, 2015
TO: H

Hello again,
There isn't necessarily a national movement that has been adopted by the General Conference, but one of the four primary foci of the church is "ministry with the poor."

The UMC has always been supportive of public education, and now at a time when public education has become a political battleground, the church is called to remember, first and foremost, the well-being of all God's children. Education is a right of all children and is affirmed by Scripture which calls us to "train children in the right way" (Proverbs 22:6 NRSV). Furthermore, the Social Principles affirm that education "can best be fulfilled through public policies that ensure access for all persons to free public elementary and secondary schools and to post-secondary schools of their choice."
Rev. Bill

A REDEFINING LIFE

Genesis 32:22-32

In today's passage, Jacob is about to meet his brother, Esau, again. He has stolen Esau's identity, his wealth, and his position—his blessing and birthright—and is worried that his brother will seek revenge and will not forgive him. For his whole life, Jacob has been on the run.

Just as Jacob wrestles with his life situation, we too grapple with life's difficulties with no easy answers. Our struggle may include a period of wrestling with God—without a winner. After a dark night, in the act of wrestling, without a winner, without the answers—we emerge, as does Jacob, a new, better person.

The story of Jacob and Esau haunts me, but it also reminds me that the crucial transformations and reconciliations in our identity and faith happen when we allow ourselves to be vulnerable, when we admit our past sinfulness, and when we wrestle with the right path that we know God wants us to take— the path of love and forgiveness.

God is not the adversary in the dark night of the soul, but the advocate who wants us to redefine ourselves, in a way that leaves us blessed, possibly even wounded, and leads us to reconciliation with our brother, our sister, our enemy, and our friends.

------ ⋆ ★ ⋆ ------

God beyond all seeing and knowing, we meet you in the night of change and crisis and wrestle with you in the darkness of doubt. Give us the will and spirit to redefine ourselves as your children who seek the path of reconciliation and love. Bless us and help us to live faithfully and to love as we are loved by you. Amen.

Clinton, the former secretary of state and first lady, left the campaign trail in New Hampshire two days before the pivotal primary election to highlight the Flint water crisis yet again, framing the issue as one of failure. . . .
"Do not grow weary doing good. The road is long and I know there will be a lot of bumps along the way. But this is the most important work we're ever called to do" [said Clinton].[8]

Detroit Free Press
February 7, 2016

TRANSFORMATIVE POWER

1 Timothy 2:1-6

Some years ago, in conversation with a spiritual guide, I was busy whining about how boring I was finding prayer and how it seemed to be a waste of time. He looked at me and asked whether I did not know that the effects of prayer would be in my life and not in the prayer itself. This was life changing for me, realizing that prayer is about changing me and not about changing God's mind.

I had been taught that if our prayers of petition and intercession—asking God for things on behalf of ourselves or others—are not answered it is because we are not asking right; or we are not asking for things in accord with God's purposes; or that we do not have even the faith of a mustard seed; or that they would be answered in God's time, and so on. Answers we've been told to explain why we do not get what we want when we pray.

I am a praying person, and if I hadn't been during the time I was in the White House, I would have become one because it's very hard to imagine living under that kind of pressure without being able to fall back on prayer and on my faith.[9]

Hillary Rodham Clinton
March 6, 2016

Things do not happen in the world because I pray. But things do happen in the world when I pray. I am changed by prayer because I opened myself up to God's Spirit. And then, somehow, I become a small pebble in the pond of God's transformative power.

------ ★ ★ ★ ------

Lord of the universes, thank you for the grace offered through our mediator in Christ Jesus. We pray that our lives may reflect the love and grace of your son in all that we do. Amen.

A RACE TO WIN
Psalm 61:1-8

Mothers take pride in hearing their children's first words. They marvel at their children's ability to string words together to create phrases and then sentences. By the third grade, children will know approximately a million words! While words are important tools for communication, there are times when words are not enough. We may be moved to use inappropriate words, or we may not be able to speak at all. Tears can somehow convey to God the deepest concerns.

God hears our prayers. Find time to listen and allow God to lead you. The psalmist reminds us that the steadfast love of the Lord endures forever. You have something that is greater than the challenges you experience. You may not have all the answers, but God is able to make all things well. God promises to protect you and keep you. God brought you this far, and God will see you through. Do not give up on God because God will never give up on you. You are in the race to win!

Rev. Dr. Denise Smartt Sears

———— ★ ⭐ ★ ————

God, we will continue to celebrate your goodness. Continue to bless us on this journey of life. Amen.

THE REAL THING
2 Corinthians 11:16-30

A group of military veterans has published the names of more than five hundred people who falsely claim to have been prisoners of war during the Vietnam conflict. For whatever reasons—recognition, respect, or perhaps financial gain—these phony POWs speak of places they've never been and experiences they've never had.

But an association of former POWs says to them, "We're on your trail, and we'll unmask you at the first opportunity." The veterans group's goal is to stop those who would steal another's valor and to have a searchable repository of all earned medals of valor—a place where the public can read stories about the true heroes.

When a group of phony apostles threatened to undermine the gospel of Christ in Corinth, Paul denounced them as deceitful workers and ministers of Satan. To establish the authenticity and authority of his own apostleship, he "boasted" not of his successes but of his sufferings, including physical danger, mental anguish, and spiritual exhaustion.

Paul was a hero for Christ, and he made sure to "out" all those who were false. Our faithfulness to Christ and his kingdom may cause us to bear the marks of a true veteran in his service. In the kingdom of God, it's not ribbons and stars but redemption and scars that set you apart as the real thing.

Dear Lord Jesus, thank you for the work you have entrusted me to do. I ask only to be worthy of that trust. Help me to be faithful to the great treasure of the gospel you have placed in my care. Please, Lord, be with me when I am fearful and make me faithful. Be with me when I am faithful and make me fruitful. Be with me when I am fruitful and make me humble—for it is only by your grace that I wish to serve you; only by your strength that I am able to serve; only by your faithfulness that I am still serving you today. Amen.

ANSWERED PRAYERS
Luke 18:1-8

I n this parable about prayer, Jesus is suggesting that God is listening—that we must always keep the faith and never lose heart. Sometimes prayer will be all that we have, and we need to learn how to pray without losing heart.

I pray on a pretty regular basis during the day because I need that strength and I need that support.[11]

Hillary Rodham Clinton
March 6, 2016

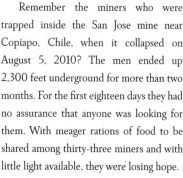

Remember the miners who were trapped inside the San Jose mine near Copiapo, Chile, when it collapsed on August 5, 2010? The men ended up 2,300 feet underground for more than two months. For the first eighteen days they had no assurance that anyone was looking for them. With meager rations of food to be shared among thirty-three miners and with little light available, they were losing hope.

Mario Gomez, the oldest, had made it through his dangerous life as a miner and was to retire in a couple of weeks. At home, his wife prayed—morning, noon, and night. With darkness all around him and no evidence of any reason to hope, he found hope in his prayers and the knowledge that his wife was praying for him. He became the leader for all the miners in prayer. In those prayers, hope became welded to the steel core of their beings, of their community.[10]

------ ★ ★ ★ ------

My sister, with every ounce of strength, continue to be persistent, determined, and prayerful. Do not lose heart; God is with you. Amen.

BE NOT AFRAID

1 John 4:18

Last October during the children's message, our director spoke to our tots about their experiences of Halloween and what sorts of costumes they were planning to wear. As you might imagine, the conversation took on a life of its own, and several brave souls acknowledged that they are not afraid of anything—including ghosts and goblins.

The conversation got me thinking about how often our adult lives are fraught with fear: fear of the unknown; fear of not getting a great job, of losing it, or not having enough money; fear of never getting married or being unable to sustain the relationship; fear that we will let others down, that we will not be liked or accepted, respected or admired. We fear what *might* happen in life. Fear seems to have a way of overshadowing us even when we are committed to living otherwise.

It seems to me that the only emotion greater than fear is love.

If you are wrestling with something that is motivated by fear, let me encourage you to take a deep breath, step back a bit, pray about your circumstances, and be open to the love of God that is present to you. It may not be easy to recognize, but I assure you it's there. Receive it.

------ ★ ★ ★ ------

Lord, I am not always as brave as I like to think I am. Sometimes, I am afraid. Help me to find the courage to live in the strength of your love. Amen.

Rev. Dr. Cathy S. Gilliard

"For me, this is a personal commitment. I will stand with you every step of the way. I will not for one minute forget about you. I will do everything I can to help you get back up, get your strength and resilience flowing through this community again."[12]

Detroit Free Press
February 7, 2016

GLORIOUS SEASON
Psalm 19

All I need to do is look out my office window to see the beautiful fall colors of Riverside Park and the New Jersey Palisades. I am in awe of nature's wonder in the fall, as the trees turn into a collage of radiant maroon, red, orange, and yellow.

My creative left brain loves the scene. My logical right brain knows the reason. Trees are green in the summer because chlorophyll, a green pigment in the leaves, absorbs red and blue light from the sun. The light reflected from the leaves appears green to our eyes. Chlorophyll is an unstable substance, and bright sunlight causes it to decompose rapidly. Therefore, plants must continuously synthesize and regenerate it. The shortening days and cool nights of autumn, however, interfere with this process. As chlorophyll breaks down, the green color of the leaves begin to fade. This beautiful artistic palate of nature seems to serve no practical purpose—at least none that scientists can discern. And why are there photoreceptors in our eyes that enable us to see it?

I believe that God's goodness and love is the point of God's creation. And thank God it is a beautiful tapestry for us to enjoy and of which to be good stewards. Another Psalm states that God is "good to all, and God's tender mercies are over all God's work."

God colored the world for our childlike delight. God's like that, you know.

------- ⋆ ★ ⋆ -------

What a gift you have given us, Creator God. Help us to be good stewards of all you have given to us so that this world might continue to be beautiful and good. Amen.

⋆ ⋆

FROM: Rev. Bill Shillady
SENT: November 4, 2015
TO: H

Have a blessed and colorful day, my friend. I am praying for you, Bill, Chelsea, Marc, and Charlotte. Enjoy this season!
Bill

⋆ ⋆

ILLUMINATED PATH
James 1:16-25

There is a story told about a pastor who stood before his congregation one Sunday and said, "I want to apologize. I have no sermon today. I hope you will forgive me, but this past week was so full of emergencies I had no time to develop a sermon." Then he sat down. The organist froze, as did the liturgist, choir director, and congregation. No one moved. After about sixty long, painful seconds, the pastor moved back to the pulpit, and said, "This is what God must feel like when we tell God we are just too busy to seek God and do God's will."

There is a great debate among scholars as to whether God needs us—but of this we are sure: God wants us to be covenant partners in working out our salvation, in developing a living, breathing, "first name" relationship with God.

The Epistle of James is a pithy little sermon that unabashedly advocates for doing good works. The character of this community is not about "me." It starts with God, whom James calls "the Father of lights." God, whose first creative act was to make light—light that then gives life, never changes. God is always the giver of life and light.

James's message is true. Doers of the word work in God's spirit, giving light and life for others. He is encouraging all followers to put love, light, and life into action; to let Christ's Spirit focus and shape our doing with each other in the church and in the larger community as well.

------ ★ ★ ★ ------

Lord, when I am feeling lost, send rivers of light to illumine my path. And as I journey in faith toward my future, may I constantly reflect that light to others so I may always be finding the balance between my faith and the good works you want me to do. Amen.

REFINING FIRE

Daniel 3:19-30

In the story of Shadrach, Meshach, and Abednego, we have a wonderful image for keeping the faith when life is hard.

These three Jewish boys, living under the rule of the Babylonian King Nebuchadnezzar, refused to worship a golden idol that was ninety feet tall and ten feet across, one which was most likely a likeness of the king. Nebuchadnezzar responded as a raging lunatic executioner, bound them, and had them thrown into the furnace. When the king looked into the fire he saw the three boys and a fourth, who had the appearance of a god, unbound and walking around in the fire. Humbled and defeated, Nebuchadnezzar decreed that all were to worship the God of the Jews.

In the hard times, Shadrach, Meshach, and Abednego experienced the presence of God with them and they remained faithful.

It is very clear throughout Scripture that we can keep faith in hard times because God is with us all the time, perhaps especially when we feel we are walking through the fire of having our faith tested.

Remember, my dear sister, Christ is with you on your journey.

———— ★ ★ ★ ————

Come Holy Spirit, guide us through all our hard times until, in faith, we can look back and see how much stronger and how great a witness our times of refining fire have been for our lives. Amen.

FAITH AND WISDOM

James 1:2-6

The Book of James states that life is hard and the world will test us, but this testing is a joy because endurance produces maturity of faithful living. James encourages his hearers to pray, asking God for understanding, and it will be given.

In difficult times, we are not to be double-minded—seeking God's help while hedging our bets by operating on the world's standards of grasping for easy outs or simple solutions. Rather, James wants us to be faithful people seeking God's will and living it fully by caring for the needs of the world.

Difficulties in life may be captured in that famous phrase, "When the going gets tough, the tough get going." In hard times, with the confidence of God's presence with us, we may press on to the call of God.

C. S. Lewis once said that the most frequently spoken word in heaven will be, "Oh!" As in, "Oh, now I understand." Or, "Oh, now I see the reason for all those difficulties."

May you and I do the same!

------- ★ ★ ★ -------

Lord, guide us through all our difficult times in this life until, in faith, we can say, "Oh, now I see!" Amen.

"Our greatest leaders are often the most humble because they recognize both the awesome responsibilities of power and the frailty of human action," Mrs. Clinton told an audience that was almost entirely black. The nation, she added, needed "a president who will pray with you and for you."[14]

The New York Times
September 9, 2016

STAND TALL
Luke 6:46-49

Over the last few days, I have been thinking of this passage from the Sermon on the Mount. What foundations do those who wish to lead our country stand upon?

A man of wisdom often offered me this simple piece of advice: "Bill, stand tall." My dad meant that I should be courageous in my decisions, not compromising principles, not violating my faith values, and not shrinking from responsibility.

I have tried to follow his advice for most of my life, and when I have stood tall, life has been very good. When I have failed to stand tall—when I compromised my values, when I ignored my faith—life has been difficult or even unpleasant.

I used this idea for a children's sermon, and when I asked the kids to stand tall, all of them rose and stretched to their tippy-toes. And when I told them about my father's words and about Jesus being our foundation, one little boy shouted, "Jesus wants us to do what is right." No need for any additional words, so we prayed.

My sister, continue to stand tall for God!

------ ★ ★ ★ ------

God of all people and of many names, thank you for sending your son into the world to show us the way, the truth, and the life. He taught us to stand tall on the foundation of your love, mercy, and grace. As your beloved and redeemed child in Christ, help me to live a life worthy of that "tall" calling; in Jesus's precious name I pray. Amen.

SWEET FRAGRANCE
2 Corinthians 2:14-15

Every time I get close to a rosebush or a bouquet of flowers, I'm unable to resist the temptation to pull a flower toward my nose to savor the fragrance. The aroma lifts up my heart and triggers good feelings within me.

Writing to the Christians in Corinth centuries ago, the apostle Paul says that because we belong to Christ, God uses us to spread the aroma indicative of life and not the stench of death. Through Christ we can live a victorious life, exchanging our selfishness for his love and kindness and proclaiming the goodness of life-giving salvation. When we do this, we are indeed a sweet fragrance to God.

Despite all the problems the Corinthian church was facing, Paul continually reassured them of both his own affection and God's affection for them. Paul's message is clear that we are part of a victory parade, the sweet smell of successful living. Yes, we will experience problems that need to be corrected, but God leads us to be his presence in the world.

------ ★ ⭐ ★ ------

Lord, let your splendor fill my life, so that I may draw people to you. Help me walk in the way that spreads the fragrance of your love to others. Amen.

FROM: Rev. Bill Shillady
SENT: September 29, 2015
TO: H

Hillary,
I hope you are doing well. I just realized I missed Charlotte's birthday. I hope you had a nice birthday celebration for her first year. Please give her a birthday hug from me.
Bill

MORE LIKE HIM
Matthew 8:5-13

A Prayer for all:
God of love and compassion, we speak to you as those who are too narrow in our loving.

We love those in our families (well, mostly); we love our neighbors and friends.

But that's about as far as we go in our loving.

We find it difficult to extend our love to those outside our inner circle. We view strangers with fear rather than acceptance. We look at those of different nationalities, religions, and social classes with indifference or even fear.

We have even more trouble loving those who don't return our love. Too often we respond in kind to those who don't like us or even those who hate us. When it comes to love, we are reactors, not initiators.

Yet your love is generous, even extravagant. You love everyone with an unconditional, grace-filled, totally accepting kind of love. You overlook all the faults and imperfections we so clearly see in others but can't see in ourselves. You forgive everyone's sins and failures.

Can we learn to love more like you, Lord? Can we learn to reach outside of our narrow circles of love to a world in desperate need of love? Can we find the strength within ourselves to love the unlovely, the difficult people, and our enemies?

You have shown us the path to such a love in Jesus Christ, who embodied your love. He sought out those on the margins of his society—the tax collectors, prostitutes, and poor—and proclaimed a message of good news to them. He shared table fellowship with those whom society rejected.

Break down the barriers that we have erected between ourselves and others. Break through the hardness of heart that views others with indifference. Break into our consciousness so that we can truly see others as persons created by you and, therefore, worthy of our love and respect.

We pray this in your loving name. Amen.

Robert Martin Walker

ROOTED IN CHRIST
Colossians 2:6-7

I can picture it now. A long driveway with oak trees planted on either side. It seemed to be the only part of the landscape that was not devastated from Hurricane Katrina. Our group from Park Avenue had gone to Biloxi, Mississippi, with UMCOR to help rebuild. There were hardly any houses, trees, or landscapes that were not destroyed—except the long line of oaks, still standing strong, leading to a house that had vanished with the winds.

The pastor of the church told me their story. "When live oak trees are planted together in a row," she said, "their roots not only intertwine but fuse together. This interdependent root system allows the live oaks to share water and nutrients and to form a stronger hold in the ground." She told us that when Katrina swept through, the live oaks sustained little damage because they were held strongly together in the earth.

What a great image. What if we as the Christian community, rooted in Christ, were so intertwined that we could resist the buffeting winds of difficulty and trouble? What if we poured out the strength, wisdom, and love that God has given us in faith and with thankfulness shared it with those experiencing hardship? God did not design us to stand on our own but created us to be a family, firmly bound together by our roots in Christ Jesus, our Lord.

------ ★ ★ ★ ------

Gracious God, while other trees fell all around, the oak tree held its ground. Remind us of the rootedness that we have in Christ Jesus, just as the oak has its roots stretched deep in the earth. May our faith in Christ and our love for our brothers and sisters help us to withstand the forces trying to knock us down. Amen.

DARE TO HOPE

A PURPOSE
Psalm 138:7-8

I cannot imagine a greater living hell than going through life without a purpose. For me, futility is the ultimate enemy. If my pains are not connected to any greater wisdom; if my struggles have no meaning beyond their current reality; if my tears are not tailored to teach me anything about a greater good, then I would rather not take my next step. Anguish is never easy, but it is bearable as long as we are assured that we do not suffer in vain.

Faith in God's direction or providential purpose for our lives is one thing, but the promise that nothing can block, thwart, or derail that purpose ushers us into a whole new arena of faithful expectation.

I know it is easy to get discouraged. But here's the blessed assurance: God not only has a purpose for us, but God's purpose will be fulfilled and will happen for our good.

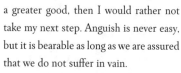

We've got to keep working together and that means creating common ground and common purpose wherever we can. There will always be naysayers; there will always be haters. But we can't let them drive our agenda. What we're trying to do is much bigger than them and much more hopeful than they even understand.[2]

Hillary Rodham Clinton
September 7, 2016

My hope is built on nothing less
Than Jesus' blood and righteousness.
I dare not trust the sweetest frame,
But wholly trust in Jesus' Name.

On Christ the solid Rock I stand,
All other ground is sinking sand;
All other ground is sinking sand.[1]

------ ⋆ ★ ⋆ ------

May you continue on your journey to the purpose our God has for you, and may you find your strength and anchor in your faith in Jesus Christ. Amen.

ALL IS WELL
Hebrews 11:1

German theologian Jürgen Moltmann wrote his popular book, *Theology of Hope*, in 1964. It was translated into English in 1967 and immediately became a theology bestseller.

Moltmann argued that there are two ways the future is related to us. The Latin word *futurum* is one way. This word refers to the future developing out of the past and present. We draw conclusions about the future based on past and present experiences.

This extrapolative thinking captured by the concept of *futurum* is important when we're projecting what could happen in the future. We see clouds building on the horizon and expect rain. Optimism is based on extrapolative predictions.

Moltmann insisted that hope, unlike optimism, is independent of our circumstances. Hope isn't based on the correct extrapolation of the present into the future. Christian hope is *adventus*, a Latin word referring to a future coming from the outside of past and present. This is the future that comes from God.

Hope doesn't develop; it breaks into our lives as a gift from God. That's why hope can spring up even in the darkest and direst of circumstances.

------- ★ -------

Eternal Friend who calls us to live in hope, help us not to give in to despair when the future seems dark and difficult. Give us the reassurance that, in the words of Julian of Norwich, "all shall be well." Amen.

Robert Martin Walker

"What do we do in the small world of our own lives?" [Chelsea Clinton] asks. "How do we ensure that we are being the best parents, friends, citizens that we can be in our own day-to-day interactions? And then how do [we] start from that place to then engage in the wider world? You simply have to start . . . regardless of whether you're feeling hopeful or angry."[3]

Refinery29
January 18, 2017

VALLEY OF VISION

Isaiah 22:1

I recently came across a book of prayers, *The Valley of Vision*, a compilation written by Arthur Bennett. One prayer, called the Valley of Vision, speaks of the distance between a sinful person and holy God. The person says to God, "Thou hast brought me to the valley of vision . . . ; hemmed in by mountains of sin I behold Thy glory." Aware of his or her wrongs, the person still has hope. "Stars can be seen from the deepest wells, and the deeper the wells the brighter Thy stars shine."[4]

I'm reminded of Jonah, who finds God's glory in the ocean's depths. He rebelled against God by not going to Nineveh where God had called him to preach. He attempted to flee to Tarshish, far away. Thrown overboard, Jonah ended up in a fish's stomach, overcome by his humanness, self-centeredness, and rebellion against God. There, Jonah cried out to God and God heard his prayer and his repentance.

Although life is filled with difficulties and our self-centeredness creates distance between God and us, we can look up from the lowest points in our lives and see God's holiness, goodness, love, and grace. When we turn from our sin and selfish ways and confess to God, it will be forgiven. God answers prayers from the valley.

------ ★ ★ ★ ------

Lord, in the darkest of times, the brighter your stars shine. Let me find your light in my darkness. Amen.

FROM: Rev. Bill Shillady
SENT: September 30, 2015
TO: H

Good morning, my sister Hillary. I hope you are doing well and enjoy today's devotion!
Rev. Bill

★ ★ ★

FROM: H
SENT: September 30, 2015
TO: Rev. Bill Shillady

I've never seen that phrase "the valley of vision" or the prayer before. Another mind-opening gift from your daily message. As always, thank you.

BE PERSISTENT

Luke 11:5-13

Tradition interprets this parable—"Suppose one of you has a friend"—to believe we are the ones who approach the door. But what if Jesus was saying something entirely different?

What if God were knocking at our door? How often does God knock, but we are too ashamed to answer or don't want to respond? We don't want God to know our deep, dark, awful mess behind that door. We say to ourselves, "God doesn't want to know that," or "God wouldn't like me if God knew." But God knows what kind of mess lies behind the door and continues to wait shamelessly and persistently for us to open.

This parable reminds us that God is always there. This isn't a love that will go away. Our God is persistent and acts in our lives at all times, despite the doors or barriers that we build between us and God. This parable highlights the importance of a relationship with God. The man knocking at the door isn't just a stranger, or even a neighbor, but he is directly named as a friend. God is our friend who cares enough to stand at the door and continue to knock even when we are ashamed or full of ourselves or too busy watching television to get up out of the chair and open the door. What a love God has for us!

------ ★ ★ ★ ------

God of grace and God of glory, come into our lives. You may need to keep knocking. We forget about your love and grace, yet you are persistent in reminding us. Keep knocking until we come to find once again that you are always present and always ready to receive us. Amen.

FINDING TRUTH

John 5:39-47

Many of the religious thinkers of Jesus's day were troubled by Jesus, by his thoughts about God, by his approach to truth. The same was the case in the early church when the Gospel of John was written. Some of these people were not ready to let go of cherished ideas and theological doctrines that may have held for a long time. The more they hardened their understandings, the more calcified they became. In the end, they could neither see nor accept that their own Scriptures pointed to one who would love God, love truth, and love all people like Jesus did.

When we seek validation from Scriptures, we are more preoccupied with our glory than the glory of God. We want the Scriptures to validate our position. We want to win the debate. Convinced that we are right, this self-gratifying approval trumps the honest inquiry and a passion for the truth.

There is another way to gain the truth from Scriptures. Stand in the path that opens the Scriptures, and be prepared to go wherever the Scriptures lead. As we know from our United Methodist quadrilateral, Scripture is primary in our search for truth but must be validated by tradition, reason, and experience. As we use our minds, the history of the church for 2,000 years, and our personal and collective experiences, we can then find the truth not to validate what we already believe but to be challenged to what God has in store for us. We will not be disappointed.

------ ★ ★ ★ ------

God, light a fire in my heart and mind for your truth. Make me a lover of your truth. Amen.

"I think there are lots of ways to make a difference, to work in all sectors of our society, the for-profits, the not-for-profits, looking for ways that you can help people live their own lives better, tell their own stories better."[5]

Business Insider
April 7, 2017

RENEWED ENERGY
Ecclesiastes 3:1

I've never understood why we begin the New Year on January 1. The middle of winter is a terrible time to be thinking about new beginnings. In contrast, springtime is the natural season for turning over a new leaf, hatching new schemes, celebrating the renewal of life, and rejoicing in the life that makes all things new.

Winter is a season of dormancy and hibernation. Spring and summer reveal light and warmth and new growth. It's a time for planting seeds and making plans: a time when all the world seems young and blessed with great potential for the days to come.

As we celebrate the changing of each season, let's take a moment to delight in the sunshine or the rain, cherishing the new dawn, which follows every dark night of the soul.

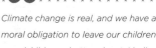

Climate change is real, and we have a moral obligation to leave our children and grandchildren a better planet. I believe we can fight climate change and create millions of good-paying jobs at the same time.[6]

Hillary Rodham Clinton
October 20, 2016

------ ★ ★ ★ ------

Loving Creator, we thank you for springtime and its message of hope to a world tiring of winter's starkness. Springtime is our yearly reminder that to a world that was dark and cold you sent your Son to break through sin's icy blanket and, arms outstretched on a cross, he brought us hope. In the sense of that springtime warmth and hope, I pray for Hillary and Bill, Marc and Chelsea and Charlotte, all their family, friends, and Hillary's team, that with renewed hope and energy, they too may blossom in the need for springtime hope in our nation. Amen.

HOW THE LIGHT COMES
John 1:1-9

The word *Advent* comes from the Latin verb *advenire*, which means "to come toward, to draw near, to approach." During Advent, we remember and celebrate God's drawing near to us in Jesus Christ—in the past, the present, and the age to come.

I love how the Gospel writer John tells the story of God's coming. His version of the Christmas story is absent of anything we can put into a manger scene—no baby Jesus, no Mary, no Joseph, no shepherds, angels, or far-traveling, gift-bearing Magi wafting in on the fragrances of frankincense and myrrh. John pares away the Christmas story in five verses to its essence: The Word. The Light. The Life. Dwelling among us. In the flesh. Glory and grace and truth.

In his telling, John the Evangelist then invokes John the Baptist, who is utterly at home in John the Evangelist's telling of the story that enchants with its poetic simplicity and beauty. The Baptist knows about the basics, knows about getting to the heart of things, knows what it means to divest ourselves of anything that hinders us from preparing a way for the Word and proclaiming its presence in our midst.

Lord, may we tell the story and testify to the light that the Word may take flesh in us this day and in all the days to come. Amen.

LIGHT HAS COME
Psalm 27:1

I love lighting candles. When I was a child, lighting candles represented birthdays and the fun of rising to my full height, inhaling deeply, and putting out every small flame with a swift and long breath.

When I was old enough, I became an acolyte at church. I remember how important it was to carry in the light of God every Sunday. My Sunday school teacher would say to me, "Little Billy, you are going to be a minister and bring God's light to the people in church."

Now I light candles to mark special occasions with friends or light an Advent wreath. But candles to me still represent the presence of God.

The beautiful thing about light is that it shines not only to expose potential pitfalls and dangers but also to reveal what is lovely. Without light, we have no ability to behold beauty. Jesus came to rescue us from the darkness of sin and despair. For those who are walking in darkness now, there is hope—light has come.

The light of Jesus is more powerful than the darkness of our circumstances or even the darkness of evil in our world. The light shines in the darkness, and the darkness has not overcome it because it cannot overcome it. Christ is our light. By him we see. By him we live.

And as the Spirit enlightens us, may we become light to others.

------- ⋆ ★ ⋆ -------

Lord Jesus, we give you thanks for illuminating our lives with your grace and light. We give you thanks as we mark this time with the light of Advent candles and Christmas bulbs, which will constantly remind us that you are the Light of the world, the One who is our salvation. Amen.

⋆ ⋆

FROM: Rev. Bill Shillady
SENT: December 5, 2016
TO: H

Good Morning,
Back from vacation as I begin the 5 a.m. ritual of spiritual disciplines of prayer, meditation, a devotion shared with you, and walking Lilly in Riverside Park.
Blessings of light this day.
Rev. Bill

⋆ ⋆

HEAR OUR CRIES
Psalm 106:47

Once again, violence and death penetrate our daily lives. Words fail amid another unspeakable tragedy at a Christmas party in San Bernardino, California.

The world mourns those struck down by another horrific act of violence. Silence can be seen as assent or indifference, so we pray, believing that God can bring new life from our inarticulate, often impotent cries.

------ ★ ★ ★ ------

God of justice, God of love, be with your people in San Bernardino. This recent shooting feels overwhelming. Surround those directly involved with your loving presence. Comfort the families of the dead and injured, sustain those waiting for word of those they love. Protect, strengthen, and uphold the police and emergency personnel.

Help all of us to remember that your love is bigger and stronger than despair and destruction. Guide and strengthen us to reach out to those affected in ways that will bring healing. Give them and us a sense of your peace and hope. Make us into people of light and love. We are a people of hope. Guide us, Lord Jesus. Amen.

"It is a very political, difficult issue in America," [Clinton] said. "But I believe we are smart enough, we are compassionate enough to figure out how to balance the legitimate Second Amendment rights with preventive measures and control measures so that whatever motivated this murderer, who eventually took his own life—we will not see more deaths, needless, senseless deaths."[7]

The Washington Times
August 26, 2015

WE ARE THE CHANGE
James 5:7

The Letter of James is offered to the church scattered throughout the Roman Empire. The fledgling Christians are uncertain about their future. James provides a way forward, encouraging the church to live differently so that it will be ready when the Lord returns.

Real wisdom, God's wisdom, begins with a holy life and is characterized by getting along with others. It is gentle and reasonable, overflowing with mercy and blessings, not hot one day and cold the next—not two-faced! You can develop a healthy, robust community that lives right with God and enjoys the results from the hard work of getting along with each other and treating each other with dignity and honor.

My prayer is that the light of Christ will ignite within you so passersby will see that light and will want to know Christ, too.

We are Easter people living in Advent time, living into our faith as those who are called, and sent to be actively engaged with God. We are building new relationships in new places, making disciples for the transformation of the world. Friends, go into all the world and be the change agents it so desperately needs: faith, hope, peace, and love in action, changing lives one block at a time!

------ ★ ★ ★ ------

Lord, help us to be the change that this world needs. Amen.

Rev. Dr. Denise Smartt Sears

THE DIVINE LIGHT
John 1:4-5

The days grow shorter and the nights are longer. Darkness is all around us. It is hard when we know there is still so much death, pain, and tragedy around us. The attacks in Paris and San Bernardino have overwhelmed our world once again. There are 59,568 homeless people in New York City alone, including 14,361 families with 23,858 children, sleeping each night in the municipal shelter system.[8] Darkness is all around.

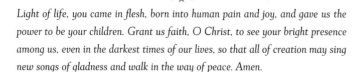

I believe we have a moral obligation to protect our children no matter what ZIP code they live in—to reduce violence, especially gun violence. To stand up against systemic racism and to promote justice and equality. I believe we owe that to our children, and we owe it to the parents who love their children more than anything, especially those whose love persists after they were so tragically taken from them.[9]

Hillary Rodham Clinton
May 23, 2016

As people of faith, we find that the true journey is toward the source of the light shining in the darkness. Christ Jesus came into the world as our Light. I find this image comforting. It reminds us that no matter our difficulties, no matter the confusion we may be experiencing, no matter how dark our lives may be, the light of Christ still burns. We may cover it, hide it, or run from it, but the true source of light is God in Christ Jesus. This divine light cannot be snuffed out.

So as we move toward the Light, may we find our hearts truly warmed and blessed, and may we experience attitudes of hope, love, joy, and peace flowing more readily through our lives.

★ ★ ★

Light of life, you came in flesh, born into human pain and joy, and gave us the power to be your children. Grant us faith, O Christ, to see your bright presence among us, even in the darkest times of our lives, so that all of creation may sing new songs of gladness and walk in the way of peace. Amen.

Rev. Matthew T. Curry

GOD IS FAITHFUL

Psalm 80:1-7

L ast night, I went to the homeless shelter we host in the winter months at our church. A boy there with his mom greeted me with hugs and joy.

I met him at a difficult time, when he was only a baby, when his parents were divorcing, and when his mom became a single parent. Baptizing an entire family at once is a rare occasion for me, so I remember how special it was to baptize him, his sister, and his mom, all at the same time.

Over the years, I wondered if they would make it as a family, to be healed and made whole again after many spiritual, physical, and financial ups and downs. Well, almost a decade later, here they were, full of joy and gratitude and serving at the shelter. God has been faithful.

In the midwinter night with the moon shining bright, in the shelter serving food, listening to questions, and praying to God, this boy reminded me that it is God who saves, God who restores, and I was unexpectedly surprised by the turning of my heart towards the One for whom we yearn, wait, and anticipate and who comes to us as God's gift of salvation.

------ ⋆ ★ ⋆ ------

God of grace, we give you thanks as we remember your saving and restoring ways in our lives, in the past, even now, and still coming. We pray without fear and with humble adoration that you surprise us again and again. Amen.

Rev. Wongee Joh

FROM: Rev. Bill Shillady
SENT: December 20, 2016
TO: H

Good Tuesday Morning,
I hope you are warm and feeling God's presence as we approach this holy season.

Once again, our world is torn by forces of hatred and evil causing the suffering of innocent people in Berlin.

May the peace of Christ come to our world and bring healing of the people.

Prayers during this season for all of you: Bill, Chelsea and Marc, Charlotte and Aidan.

Rev. Bill

THE HARVEST WILL COME
Hebrews 11:1-3; Mark 4:26-29

We can hope in God because, even when we cannot see the evidence, God is present and at work in our world. Faith is the assurance of things hoped for, the conviction of things not seen.

The Letter of the Hebrews was written to people who had many questions because they had not seen Jesus or his ministry. Sure, Jesus had promised that he would one day return and that in the meantime his spirit would be with them. But, they, like most of us, were like the little child who replied to its mother's words, "Go to sleep now, God is with you," with, "Yes, but I would rather have a God I can see."

We like to see evidence for the things we believe in, the things we put our trust in, and the things we build our lives on. Yet Jesus teaches us that one of the mysteries of God's power is that it is not always evident in our lives. Like the parable of the sower of seeds in Mark 4, we are to live in faith, trusting that the harvest will come. When one scatters seed on the ground, Jesus tells us, the person does so with the conviction that the seed will sprout and grow, even though the person does not know how those things happen.

Lord, give me hope amid the cloudiness of my life. Even when I cannot see clearly, create within me that hope which cannot and will not disappoint, no matter how deep my longing for clarity. Amen.

LIVING WATER
Mark 1:9-13

We are big J. R. R. Tolkien fans. I tend to watch the *Lord of the Rings* trilogy when world events seem dictated more by darkness than by light. That's when we need to be reminded that there is good and hope in the midst of darkness.

There is a scene in *The Fellowship of the Ring* that reminds me of baptism—Galadriel, the elf queen, draws water from her fountain into a silver pitcher and pours it into a basin, encouraging Frodo and Sam to look into it. She says something like, "The water will show you what has been, what is, and some of what might be."

Every time I baptize a child, I am reminded that the Spirit of God breaks through and comes upon that child. Yes, there can be uncertainty in that vision, but there is affirmation as God affirms that child and looks with hope to the future. Baptism is where God breaks into our reality. The Spirit tears apart the distance between God and us and descends, and we hear, "You are my beloved child, with you I am well pleased."

We share by our faith this common symbol, this initiation, this rite, this power of God over the deep and often raging chaos of life. How thankful we are to know water!

------- ★ ★ -------

God of grace and truth, we remember the peaceful warriors through whom you have worked to increase dignity and liberty for all. We turn to you in hope, for the task is not yet complete. Inspire us mightily, that we may continue the work of freedom in the cause of peace; for the sake of Jesus our Lord. Amen.

HIS LIGHT
Matthew 5:14-16

There are different kinds of light described in the Bible. In this Matthew passage, light is associated with God shining forth in humans. There is a warning not to hide this light of God but to let it shine.

There is also light that we see by. Lanterns and flashlights are examples of this kind of light. They light paths that we travel and allow us to see the way forward in the darkness. Jesus says, "I am the light of the world. Whoever follows me will not walk in darkness, but will have the light of life" (John 8:12). Jesus illumines the path for us to travel as we follow his way, truth, and life.

Light must have a source, and God is the source of light. In its different forms, light can provide guidance, illumination, energy, and life. God's presence is inner light that can shine forth in how we live our lives. Thank God for light!

Eternal Light, we thank you for the gift of light and for the ways it shows us who we are and what you want us to become. May we be bearers of your lights of truth, goodness, compassion, and love. We pray this in the name of the Light of the World. Amen.

Robert Martin Walker

FROM: Rev. Bill Shillady
SENT: January 16, 2016
TO: H

Hillary,
Blessings from your preacher friend. I am praying for your light to shine tomorrow night!
Bill

OUR NIGHTLIGHT
Matthew 5:14-16

Many years ago, I had a parishioner who never took down her Christmas tree or unplugged its lights. They stayed on, twinkling in her picture window, day and night, all year long, year after year. I thought it was odd.

Then I visited with her and heard her story. She loved Christmas—the time of year that made her happy and filled with joy. In the middle of summer during her husband's terminal illness, he had asked for the Christmas decorations to be put on the tree. Now she left them out as a reminder of him and his love for her. She said she felt closer to Jesus because of the lights blinking out to the world. I understood.

She also hoped that, since Christmas was when people treated each other kindlier, they might see her Christmas tree and have Christmas spirit all year round. I began to see that she was prudent, realistic, even brave, because some of us go through life thinking we already have all the light we require. But we don't—we need all the light we can get.

We need reminding that the Christmas story of angels telling the shepherds to "fear not" should happen all year long. We need to see the Christmas lights and remember that God so loved the world that he sent Jesus, born in a manger in Bethlehem.

I think of Jesus as the bright and constant light in the world's window, a nightlight that God leaves on in the places that are darkest for us, shining so we won't be afraid. As we learn to trust Jesus, something strong and bright begins to shine in us too, a light as old and as new as creation.

------- ★ ★ ★ -------

By your light, O Christ, remind us of your love. Kindle anew your light within us. Keep us constant in shining a bright light for all in the world. Amen.

THE POTTER
Jeremiah 18:1-11

I once tried to make a clay pot, and it was a disaster. The clay spun so rapidly on the wheel that each wrong move I made created a weird imperfection. First, I made one side higher than the other, so I molded the clay into a ball and started again. I made the edges too thick, then too thin. I finally made a rounded object, but my thumb slipped and created a lip I didn't want. I gave up and made an ashtray.

Jeremiah watched a potter at work and saw the analogy to God's work with humans. Sometimes pots get marred on the wheel; and sometimes humans, created to do good, go astray and do bad things.

With clay, you can roll it back into a ball and start again, but with humans, we are more challenging—we have minds of our own. We had free will breathed into our nostrils after God created us from the clay in Genesis 2, so we are always being molded and changed.

This reminds me of the way God works in my life. It is so much better when I let God take my life and shape it. Every time I try to do it myself, I seem to create an ashtray. I must remind myself constantly to let God shape me into what God wants me to be.

------ ★ ⭐ ★ ------

Dear Lord, every time I try to take control of my life, I wind up as an unshapen blob or an odd ashtray. Help me to let you to make me into what you want me to be. Amen.

ANGELS ON HIGH

Luke 2:8-14

I like to sit in churches and enjoy the light through stained glass windows. I find myself humming Christmas carols—often "Angels from the Realms of Glory." And as I hum in these sacred spaces, I can almost hear the angels sing: "Glory to God in the highest, and on earth, peace" (Luke 2:14 ESV).

In 2006, on my European sabbatical, we saw carved stone and gold-leafed angels in the great cathedrals and beautiful paintings of angels in museums and churches. In Vienna, I climbed to the top of Karl's Kirsch, and there, hundreds of feet above the sight of worshipers or visitors, there were cherubs and angels carved into the woodwork and painted on the ceiling.

One angel especially intrigued me. It was a serene and beautiful face, carved long ago by the church sculptors—far above where anyone would visit. And as I looked beyond her in the dim light, I realized that she was not alone. She was but one of a heavenly host of carved angelic faces on the ceiling.

What a wonderful inspiration—angels above us, ever praying for us, ever interceding with God for us—permanent and very beautiful, carved or painted, helping us to take the right direction in our lives.

------ ⋆ ★ ⋆ ------

Angels from the realms of glory,
Wing your flight o'er all the earth; . . .
Worship Christ, the newborn King.
Amen.

FROM: H
SENT: December 29, 2015
TO: Rev. Bill Shillady

I particularly love this lesson and the image of the angel. My mother loved angels and collected cherubs all her life. Whenever I see one, I think of her and am grateful for all the "guardian angels" I've had, starting with her.
    Here's to all our angels here on earth and in the realms of glory!

TURN ON THE LIGHT
Matthew 5:16

As a pastor, I've seen folk move from wandering in the dark toward the light that is Christ. I know that most of the time church is rather conventional, rather predictable. But I've seen church be dramatic when someone's eyes are opened—the first time they see.

> We have learned over the years that America's problems won't be solved by building walls and dividing our country between "us" and "them." We know our diversity is a strength, not a weakness.[10]
>
> **Hillary Rodham Clinton**
> April 13, 2016

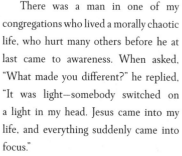

There was a man in one of my congregations who lived a morally chaotic life, who hurt many others before he at last came to awareness. When asked, "What made you different?" he replied, "It was light—somebody switched on a light in my head. Jesus came into my life, and everything suddenly came into focus."

Jesus once criticized us for having a bad habit of hiding our lights "under a basket" (Matthew 5:15 CEB). But sometimes, through the power of Christ, we shine.

May I remind you that you are light with all the good you do. Continue to shine for God in this darkened world.

$$\star \; \bigstar \; \star$$

We are here today because, in some way or another, the light of Christ has shone in our lives. Let us remember that we are to shine in the world as the light of Christ. Amen.

FRUIT OF THE LIGHT

Psalm 89

Although we can survive for a while in less-than-ideal conditions, we can't thrive. We have spiritual needs that can't be met by any substitute.

Scripture reminds us that we are children of light. We are to live in the full light of God's presence to thrive. Otherwise, no matter what we do, we will produce nothing but fruitless deeds. Paul's words to the church of Ephesus remind us: "For you were once darkness, but now you are light in the Lord. Live as children of light (for the fruit of the light consists in all goodness, righteousness and truth)" (Ephesians 5:8-9 NIV).

If we are to bear the fruit of God's love, we are to

Hillary Clinton ✔
@HillaryClinton

Scripture tells us: Let us not grow weary in doing good, for in due season, we shall reap, if we do not lose heart.

RETWEETS 69,339 LIKES 212,849

10:55 AM - 9 Nov 2016

11K   68K   213K

be living in the light of Jesus. He came as the Light of the world, and the darkness cannot overwhelm it. Let us allow the fruit of his light, which is good, faithful, and true, to blossom in our lives.

------ ★ ★ ★ ------

Dear Lord, thank you for redeeming me and giving me new life. Help me to live as a child of the Light. Amen.

CHRIST'S LIGHT
Matthew 5:16

The room is dark. Someone lights a candle, just a small candle. But light suddenly floods the room. It doesn't take much light to lighten a dark room.

Last summer, I decided to take a late night walk without the aid of a flashlight. *It's not all that dark,* I said to myself. But it was dark, very dark. I had forgotten just how dark it can be in our area, away from streetlights and city lights. And when it's that dark, you can't see a thing. Even the smallest light would have been enough.

Today's Scripture reminds us that we are here as Christ's light in the world. It is a stirring image of Christian discipleship. We are not only to allow Christ to enlighten us, to show us the way, to shine in our lives, but we are also to let our light shine for others. You are light, even as Christ is our light and life.

And one reason you are a Christian is because someone was luminescent, iridescent to you; that is, you saw Christ's light shining through someone else. You came toward that light. It is a wonderful thing when the world can look through someone's life toward Christ.

------- ★ ★ ★ -------

Lord Jesus, help me to be your light in the world. May I shine forth in all my ways with the glory of your grace. Amen.

★ ★

FROM: Rev. Bill Shillady
SENT: March 5, 2015
TO: H

A little late today. Actually slept in a bit.
Guess I need to stop being a sloth!
Blessings.

★ ★ ★

FROM: H
SENT: March 5, 2015
TO: Rev. Bill Shillady

Or, start being a little slothful from time to time. Did John Wesley ever sleep in? Probably not as we understand it today, but without electricity he most likely slept longer anyway most days. How's that for a Methodist rationale for more sleep?

★ ★

BOLD REMINDER
John 11:17-44

Lazarus being called from the grave and coming out is a bold reminder of God's power to transform our lives. When we are overburdened, pressed down, pulled down, pulled apart, can we live again? Can we get over the anger we feel toward God for seeming to be absent?

This story from John boldly reminds us that Jesus was in control of an uncontrollable situation. Those gathered beside the grave saw no hope, but Jesus shattered the barrier between Lazarus and a new day. We are challenged to set our goals on what God can do through us—the difference between what we are and what we might be. We're like Lazarus, being called to a new day even when the situation seems hopeless. We can trust in Jesus, maybe not on our time schedules, but on his.

We can claim from this story the power of Jesus to call us out from where we are buried: in our fears, our pain, our grief, our worries, and life's pressures.

------ ✦ ✦ ✦ ------

O gracious God, so often we find ourselves buried by the pressures of life. Remind us of the freedom that comes from the hope and the power that Christ can free us to be your children. Let us know that no matter how dark the day or hopeless the situation, you will be with us and, in your time, you will deliver us. Amen.

Hillary Clinton made history this year by becoming the first female nominee of a major party, but she has been breaking ground for women during her entire career. From her groundbreaking commencement speech at Wellesley to declaring for the world that "Women's rights are human rights," Hillary has been an inspiring voice, fighting for the rights of women around the world.[11]

Hillary Clinton Speeches
October 31, 2016

PERSISTENCE
Luke 18:1-8

Do not lose heart. When we persist, when we do not lose heart, it's possible to go the distance.

This parable reminds us of the power of persistence in prayer. A widow asks for justice from the judge. He ignores her. She asks again and receives the same response. She continually persists in asking—until he finally decides to grant her justice, just so she'll stop bothering him.

This would be a great story whatever the context, but in Jesus's time widows were utterly powerless. There were no respectable jobs for widows, so they relied on the charity of others to survive. This widow knew there was no chance of compassion from the unjust judge. She had no power, no way to assert her case.

The first time she asked for mercy, she likely went home feeling defeated, crushed by despair. Possibly she lay there weeping, losing hope of any justice. But something very interesting happened—she realized she couldn't let it go.

Somewhere, deep in her soul, she discovered a steel core welded to justice and hope. And no one was going to take it from her. Day after day, week after week, she went to the judge and demanded her due. Relentlessly, unfailingly going the distance, and eventually, she wore him down. Persistence!

I pray you find deep within you the spiritual fortitude that has helped you before. The finish line is in sight.

----- ⋆ ★ ⋆ -----

Holy One, we lift our eyes to you in hope and awe. Grant that we may reject all apathy of spirit, impatience, and anxiety, so that we may lift our voice again and again to seek your justice. May our nation move to civility, hope, and true community once again. Amen.

PILLAR OF FIRE
John 7:37-39; John 8:12

At the end of the seven-day festival of Sukkot, commemorating the Exodus, Jesus, in the Temple, dramatically calls people to him, saying, "I am the light of the world" (John 8:12).

In the Old Testament, the image of light refers to God's presence, God's salvation, and God's revelation. We remember from the first story of creation that God created light to penetrate the darkness. In this setting of Sukkot, celebrating the Israelites' deliverance, Jesus is claiming to be the divine presence that saves God's people from their bondage.

The Israelites followed the presence of the Lord in the pillar of fire as they escaped Egypt and journeyed to the Promised Land. Now Jesus says that those who follow him will never walk in darkness but will have the light of life. Here is a promise of salvation much greater than the deliverance Israel experienced, for it is liberation not just from a human enemy but from the forces of rebellion against God that lie behind every form of evil in the world.

In our world now, with all the killings in Beirut, Egypt, Paris, and Nigeria and with so many conflicts, racial tensions, and fears, we seem overwhelmed by darkness. We need the Light of the world, King Jesus, to remind us of the goodness of humanity.

------ * ★ * ------

Lord, help us to be lights in the darkness of today's world. Help us to show you through our daily tasks of living for you. Amen.

LET YOUR LIGHT SHINE
Matthew 5:14-16

Many of us learned a song in Sunday school with the chorus: "This little light of mine, I'm going to let it shine; This little light of mine, I'm going to let it shine, let it shine, let it shine, let it shine."

Our Christianity is to be visible, noticed, not hidden. People are to know you are a Christian by what you say and do, by who you are.

There is no such thing as a secret Christian. At home, at work, at school, your discipleship is to be seen. How does it shine? By good works!

You let your light shine by using your light to bless others—with acts of kindness and generosity. The light, which God has placed in the center of our souls, is not for us, but to bring light, hope, and love to others.

So my sister, let your light shine! You have the essence of that light within. You are light for this darkened world.

—————— ★ ★ ★ ——————

Lord, may the Light of the world, Jesus, shine through me in all that I say and do. He is the essence of my spark and flame. Help me to not hide it. Amen.

FROM: Rev. Bill Shillady
SENT: January 31, 2016
TO: H

Dear Hillary,
You, Bill, Chelsea, Marc, and Charlotte are in my prayers. I hope you are feeling them! Keep up the courage and strength. After this week and the articles about your faith and Methodist upbringing, this old sermon came to mind. I share a part of it with you.
Rev. Bill

DEAD TO LIFE
Isaiah 9:1-7

When all hope appeared to be sunk, Isaiah lifted his head and shifted the tone in his prophecy—to a time when the flood would subside. Waters will dry up, the anticipated Messiah will come, and the darkness will flee. The radiant presence of the Savior will not only shine bright but also bring the dead to life.

The flood of humanity's sin is not final. It is as if we dwell at the bottom of the sea, but we, through the illumination of the Spirit, look up from the deep dark to the shafts of light beginning to break the surface. The distant shimmering, the Great Light, would come to Israel as a child—the incarnated Son of God who would change the world. Like Israel, all who feel the flood of despair put their hope in the Light coming through the dark, and so they wait on the Lord—our present help in the midst of the evil and distress affecting our world.

------ ★ ★ ★ ------

God our Savior, help us to follow the light and live the truth in this season. In you, we have been born again as sons and daughters of light. Help us to radiate the love of Christ to the world. We ask this through our Lord Jesus Christ, your Son, who lives and reigns with you and the Holy Spirit, one God, forever and ever. Amen.

Following news that the FBI had charged three Kansas men for plotting to use a weapon of mass destruction against an apartment complex in Garden City, Kansas, that is home to many Somali immigrants, Hillary Clinton issued the following statement: "I applaud law enforcement for detecting and disrupting a highly disturbing terror plot in Kansas, in which men were allegedly planning an elaborate attack directed at Muslim Americans. . . . This plot is an affront to all Americans. We all must stand firm in fighting terror and rejecting hateful and divisive rhetoric—and we must do it together."[12]

Hillary Clinton Speeches
October 15, 2016

BEARERS OF HOPE

Romans 12:12

Have you ever felt like you are being booed off the stage? Nothing you say or do is right, and no one seems to care.

On days when I have felt a deep sense of loneliness and despair, it seems that God has always provided a way once again for me to find hope and encouragement. When I could not find my way, God has always sent someone to encourage and support me in my time of need.

We parents...work hard to give our kids a sense of confidence to send them out into the world believing in their own value, and it really is important that we don't let anybody take that away from them.[13]

Hillary Rodham Clinton
November 3, 2016

Are you in need of someone to encourage you today? Keep your eyes open! There is an angel of God who can and will bring you words of encouragement, mercy, and grace.

And when was the last time you jumped over the rail and embraced someone who was being booed? Who is the person who needs you the most today? How can you be an angel of God who brings mercy and grace? It's often true that when we give, we get back immeasurably more than we ever anticipated.

Today, open your eyes and ears to the people around you. There is someone who will surprise you today with a blessing you need most. Receive it. And there is someone who needs words of hope and encouragement on the journey. Give it. In the process, you might just discover the face of Christ in yourself and in those special people around you.

O God, use me today to be a blessing of hope and encouragement for someone in need. Amen.

Bishop Thomas J. Bickerton

DAZZLE THE WORLD
Revelation 1:12-16

I don't like the Book of Revelation. It's filled with such symbolism and apocalyptic images that it's hard to swallow. Plus, everyone misreads this book and decides that the world will end soon. But today, I focused on these words of the image of the reigning Christ. Take a minute, go back, and slowly read—maybe out loud—these verses from Revelation.

Amazing, eh? Eyes like a flame, feet like shining bronze, a voice like the sound of many waters, and holding a handful of stars.

Sometimes I wonder, with a Lord and Savior like this, how my own way of being a Christian seems to come out so safe, colorless, and conventional. Might we hear in this dazzling, shining vision of the Christ an invitation to shine just a bit ourselves?

Imagine today that you hold stars in your hand. Imagine just now your own eyes burning like a flame. Consider the possibility of allowing God to set you on fire, even if just a little. Dare to dazzle. God has put a light within you and upon you. Dare to shine, for you are a child of God. You are made in the image of God and are quite wondrous. Yes, let your light, joy, and knowledge dazzle the world.

Thank you, Holy One, for words and images that fire the mind and stir the heart. May your light shine from within us this day. Let your love for the world live in us so that we may live in you. Amen.

WHAT NEWS . . .

Romans 8:39

L ong ago in a faraway village there was a man who had only one son. The son was the pride of his life. One day a nearby farmer gave this young man a horse. The neighbors all said to the man, "What good news!" The man replied, "Good news, bad news, who knows?"

Not long after that the boy fell off the horse and broke his leg. The neighbors went to the man and said, "What bad news!" And the man said, "Bad news, good news, who knows?"

A few months later the neighboring warlords began fighting with one another. A band came through the village and drafted every young man there, taking them off to probable death. But the boy was not drafted because of his broken leg. "Good news, bad news, who knows?"

Nothing in life is wasted—the challenges, the joys, the tragedies, the defeats, the victories, the relationships, the experiences both good and bad. We are the sum total of all that is, and God uses it all to increase our wisdom, sensitivities, compassion, understanding, patience, and—yes—love.

------ ★ ★ ★ ------

Lord, no matter what might come my way, may I always say, "Good news, bad news, who knows?" Amen.

Bishop Jane Allen Middleton

DON'T GIVE UP!
2 Corinthians 4:4-12

This Scripture came to mind for you today. I know the last few days have been difficult, and you have been in my intense prayers. I remembered an old sermon story that I used in the past that is a great image for this Scripture.

The great boxer Joe Louis was fighting Tony Galento when Galento knocked him down with a surprise left hook. Louis bounced back from the mat before the referee could even start his ten count. Louis's trainer was furious, saying to Joe, "I keep teaching you to take a count when you're knocked down. Now why didn't you stay down for nine like I've always taught you?" Louis angrily responded, "What . . . and let him get all that rest?"

Like Joe Louis, we bounce back. We will not give our opponents and those who seek to hurt us the pleasure of even one more second on the mat. Our lives represent the Resurrection each and every day. Paul tells us in this Scripture to allow the death of Jesus to be a part of our souls, so that the Life of the resurrected Jesus can be the outward appearance of our faith.

God is with you. Onward and upward. Don't give the opponent any time to rest.

------ ★ ★ ★ ------

Dear God, give me the light of Christ each and every moment so that my spirit can be resilient and cope with being crushed and perplexed but never without hope. Help me to face this day even in the shadow of yesterday's challenges. Help me today to bounce back. Amen.

★ ★

FROM: H
SENT: July 7, 2016
TO: Rev. Bill Shillady

Thanks, Bill, it has been a stressful few days, so words of encouragement and reminders of the True Light from Scripture are most welcome. Onward!

★ ★

OVERCOME FEAR

FORGIVENESS
Matthew 18:21-22

I was moved by the responses of the families to the murders that happened last Wednesday at Mother Emanuel AME Church in Charleston.

When fear, religious doubt, and the desire for revenge would have been expected, forgiveness, a foundational aspect of our faith, has been found. It is a fundamental part of Jesus's teachings and a doctrine that is ingrained in us. But its practice is the most difficult thing we are called to do and is sometimes rarely found.

Hate cannot win. And forgiveness is the first step in the journey toward that victory.

Jesus tells us to forgive seventy-seven times. Can we? Can we all find the depth of our faith available to forgive as many in the Emanuel AME Church family have done?

What can one say about events like these? What can people and leaders of faith say about events like these? It's hard, isn't it, even to know where to start. But let's start here—let's take a moment to pray for all the families and the loved ones suffering today.[1]

Hillary Rodham Clinton
July 8, 2016

------ ★ ★ ★ ------

Lord, we read in your Word that we are to forgive others, yet it's difficult to do so in times like these. Please let those around us who show such grace and forgiveness be an example of how I too should forgive when it seems impossible to do so.

A HOPEFUL FUTURE
Exodus 3:1-12

Hillary, I hope and believe you have heard among all the voices calling for you to enter the presidential race a divine call to move this nation out of the current political crisis and into a new era.

I am one of many people whose prayers will be answered by your leadership for our nation—to move us from this state of deep negativity and stalemate to a place of hopeful compromise and optimism.

I think you are the one to confront sexism, racism, ageism, pessimism, discrimination against the LGBTQI community, the immigration crisis, the polarization of our nation, religious absolutism, and the many other "isms" that confront us. And you are the one to lead us to a more peaceful world.

------ ⋆ ★ ⋆ ------

Lord, as you promised to be with Moses as he confronted the evil powers of his day and as he led his people, so be with your servant this day and every day. Amen.

[Clinton] called on attendees to participate in organizations that would foster progress on human rights and for the United States to call out abuses of gay people abroad, like the reported homophobic killings in Chechnya. She said due to the Trump administration's posture on gay rights, people needed to "never stop fighting" and focus on winning upcoming elections, from the midterms on.[2]

CNN Politics
April 21, 2017

LIFE'S STORMS
Matthew 7:24-27

The weather forecasters were predicting a big snowstorm, so I was at the grocery store picking up some last-minute necessities. The lines were long but everyone was courteous. I enjoyed looking at what appeared in people's shopping carts. One man had four quarts of goat milk, a bag of grapefruit, and six liters of mineral water. Another shopper's basket was filled with hydrangeas that looked like fluffy snowballs. "If we are going to be cooped up in the house, we should try to enjoy it," I overheard him explain.

I won't let anyone take us backward, deny our economy the benefits of harnessing a clean energy future, or force our children to endure the catastrophe that would result from unchecked climate change.[3]

Hillary Rodham Clinton
November 29, 2015

There is a spiritual lesson in this: Do you go through life prepared for its storms? I'm not asking if you are paranoid or anxious—quite the opposite. If you were stopped and asked what you had in your basket today, would it be the things that are helpful: the bread of life, the milk and honey of God's blessings? Or are you carrying around things that are unnecessary or even harmful—envy, resentment, addiction, distractedness?

May this season be a time for reflection and re-evaluation of our lives. May we be wise enough to build on a solid foundation, and may we pass through the storms with God's presence and peace.

------- ★ ★ ★ -------

Grant us your wisdom, dear God, that we might replace anxiety with wisdom and worry with grace. Be present in the lives of those who are most vulnerable to life's storms, and help us to be responsive beyond our own places of safety and security. In the name of Christ, who calmed the storm. Amen.

Rev. Matthew T. Curry

ONE IN CHRIST
Ephesians 2:13-22

This passage is a wonderful statement of the great ministry of reconciliation that Christ offers to the world. The writer declares that Christ broke down the wall so that Jews and Gentiles could see they are really one people, equal citizens of God's realm.

Paul says to the church at Ephesus: first, in Jesus Christ, Gentile strangers to the covenant have been brought near and saved; second, our reconciliation to God is accompanied by reconciliation to one another so that there is now one humanity in place of two.

We are called as people of faith when confronted by brokenness to be the healing power to the world and to each other to bring wholeness to

humanity. Let us break down the walls that divide us, and let us work towards reconciliation with people of all faiths, traditions, and cultures—including our own.

------ ∗ ★ ∗ ------

Lord Jesus, even before we dared to reach out to you, you reached out to us. You came searching for us even when we were the lost sheep. Help us to be welcoming so that the world might be transformed into your family, a dwelling place of peace and love. Amen.

I NEED HELP!
Proverbs 17:17

It seems to me that three of the most difficult words to utter are "I need help." Perhaps it is because there's a deep-rooted need inside of us to try to make it on our own. Or the realization of a vulnerability that we would rather be in denial about. Or fear that once our need is confessed no one—at least not the ones we hoped—will respond in a favorable manner.

Of course, there is the issue of pride—not the kind that allows us to feel good about ourselves or an accomplishment but the kind that suggests that we would rather die than let someone know how bad things are. And sometimes, we do die—a thousand little deaths.

Regardless of the reasons, every once in a blue moon, most of us have to face the reality that we need help of one sort or another. I know I do. Asking may be risky, but I have discovered that letting others in on what's going on can also be liberating. It holds the potential for all kinds of positive outcomes that we might never have imagined.

Most people I know would rather help than be helped. We are moved with compassion to assist others in need—even strangers. There is a shared vulnerability about life that helps us realize that, at any given moment, our luck, chance, grace, or whatever can change, and we too can find ourselves in similar situations as those we've helped.

Being in community means realizing that helping is a two-way street. We give and we receive. We help and we are helped. So, how about the next time you really, *really* need help, why not take the risk, let someone in, and see what happens? It might save you from greater despair and give you the strength to carry on.

------ ★ ★ ------

Lord of life, I am humbled by all those who have helped me along the way. Bless them this day. Help me to recognize when others need my help and give me the insight, patience, and compassion to do what I can. Amen.

Rev. Dr. Cathy S. Gilliard

HE IS WITH YOU
Matthew 14:22-33

Our lives are fraught with change and challenge. We constantly have to navigate the in-between places, the crossing-over places. And chaos (with its henchman, fear) threatens to overtake us all the time. This is part of the drama of being human. The good news is that we know the One who is stronger than chaos and who has the power to make the seas lie down and to tread upon the deep.

This is none other than our God made manifest most fully to us in Jesus the Christ. And Jesus is also the one who sees and knows all that you are facing in your life. Jesus knows where you need to cross over. Jesus knows your struggles and how hard you are trying. Jesus knows your giftedness and strength and what you have sacrificed. Jesus sees your pain and knows your confusion. Jesus yearns to be close to you in your loneliness and grieves as you grieve.

Amid the changes and challenges of life, Jesus draws near, sees you, and speaks to you, saying, "Don't be afraid—I AM. I am here. I am with you. I believe in you."

------- ★ ★ ★ -------

O God, you are the alpha and the omega, the beginning and the end, the first and the last. You are the creator of all that is, yet you care about me and about my life and my challenges. You believe in me. Help me believe in you. Amen.

HOUSE OF MERCY

John 5:1-9

The legend of Bethesda, which in Hebrew means "house of mercy," was that many people waited for the stirring of the water by an angel, which would then cure the first person to enter the pool.

For me, when Jesus asks the man sitting by the pool, "Do you want to be made well?" I think he's asking us the same question: "Do you want to be free of whatever is holding you back?"

I think of this story whenever I'm in Central Park, since the Bethesda Fountain there is commemorative of this story. The fountain was designed by Emma Stebbins, the first woman to receive a public commission for a major work of art in New York City. The statue depicts a female winged angel touching down upon the top of the fountain, where water spouts and cascades into an upper basin and into the surrounding pool. Beneath her are four cherubs representing Temperance, Purity, Health, and Peace. The statue refers to John 5—our Scripture passage today.

------- ★ ★ ★ -------

Lord of healing mercies, we want to be made well. Let us hold nothing back from your healing grace. We resoundingly say yes to being in your house of mercy. Amen.

FROM: Rev. Bill Shillady
SENT: April 20, 2015
TO: H

Blessings! You are in my prayers today on this rainy, wet day, in New York City.

★ ★ ★

FROM: H
SENT: April 20, 2015
TO: Rev. Bill Shillady

Love the idea of Central Park and the fountain there being a source of inspiration and healing like the original Bethesda. Onward to New Hampshire!

TIMING IS EVERYTHING
Mark 13:32-37

Ask a good comedian, stock market sage, or real estate investor, and each will tell you timing is everything. This Scripture is about being prepared—expecting the unexpected.

It's a story about a wealthy landowner going on a trip. The servants who were left behind were given charge of the estate, and when the master returned—which was unexpected and unknown—he would check on their stewardship. It is a story about being prepared, getting ready, and staying awake for the unexpected.

Each of us has a heart that longs for things to be better. We want peace even though much of the world clamors for war. We want justice even though many tell us to take advantage of every opportunity to get more, often at the expense of others.

God's time is everything. It compels us to have a heart for truth, mercy, and justice and to find ways and time to work for those things because they are the things God cares most about. God invites us to have an abundant life that is more spiritual and less material. He invites us to put our faith and trust in his mercy and divine intervention.

------ ⋆ ★ ⋆ ------

Lord Jesus, break into the routine of my life. Help me experience your grace in special ways. Help me prepare my heart to welcome your love. Amen.

"Fighting to give women and girls a fighting chance isn't a nice thing to do," Clinton said. "This is a core imperative for every human being and every society. If we do not complete a campaign for women's rights and opportunities, the world we want to live in, the country we all love and cherish will not be what it should be."[4]

The Daily Beast
April 5, 2013

REFUEL YOUR SPIRIT
Isaiah 40:27-31

The whole idea of waiting goes against our nature and culture. When our natural inclination is to step on the gas, maybe we need to hit the brakes. Waiting is often difficult because we equate it with inactivity. But waiting, which can also be translated in this passage as hoping, means to wait with expectation.

"It's important to sit with your thoughts every now and then . . . and that did help me reconnect with what this whole campaign is about." Clinton went on to say she feels lucky that she can afford to take days off when she's sick, whereas "millions of Americans can't."[5]

Hillary Rodham Clinton
September 15, 2016

During these periods of waiting, in the middle of hectic lives, God is often refueling and refining us for what is in store. Waiting does not have to be simply a physical waiting. It can be the pause between emotions, between significant events, even between relationships.

It is good to remember that we all need to be refueled after energetic times. Why can't this be the case with our spiritual lives as well? What may seem like inactivity from our perspective is often purposeful preparation from God's perspective. Be encouraged that those who wait end up even stronger after the Lord renews them.

------ ★ ------

Everlasting God, help us to wait upon your presence in our lives. The hope in our waiting is that you will give us strength to rise above the fray and work to help the powerless. Make us agents of healing and wholeness. Give us strength and power so that your good news may be made known to the ends of your creation. Amen.

STANDING FOR EACH OTHER
Luke 13:10-17

This Scripture text contains a fascinating, multi-layered narrative that offers exciting possibilities for preachers like myself to discuss.

Jesus notices a hurting woman while he's preaching, stops everything, and tends to her needs. That's astounding in Jesus's culture and time. One might explore how we notice or don't notice certain people in our own communities, or how women—two-thirds of the world's enslaved and impoverished population—are often overlooked and untended.

Or you may note that when the synagogue leader gets outraged at Jesus for healing a woman on the Sabbath, he doesn't go and talk to Jesus about it. Instead, he triangulates communication and complains to the crowd. Props to Jesus who isn't afraid to call out the hypocrisy.

Or the preacher could talk about what it means to be in need of healing, physical or any other kind of healing, and the powerful and profound way in which Jesus invited the woman to stand up straight.

When I read this text, I wonder if she was afraid of being seen, of hoping, of making people mad, of seeing the world from a different perspective, of being healed . . . of change? I wonder if she was bent over in body but crippled even more profoundly by fear.

As counterintuitive as it seems, sometimes the painful situations in which we find ourselves feel more comfortable than the fear of the unknown. Fear itself can bend us over, crippling us so that we cannot live with freedom and hope in a world that so desperately needs people who will gather the courage to face our fears and help each other stand up straight.

It seems to me that this is a common individual human experience, but even if we prefer not to get personal, we can see it playing out in living color in our national political discourse. Fear drives division between us. Fear invites bad decisions. Fear limits possibilities. Fear leads . . . to death.

I wonder what would happen if we set fear aside and if we stood up straight. And what if we opened our hearts and our arms to possibilities, to hope, to each other?

------- ★ ★ ★ -------

Lord, heal our fears so that we can stand up to praise you. Standing straight and firm, we can go forth with hope to transform the world. Amen.

Rev. Dr. Amy K. Butler

ARE WE THERE YET?

Habakkuk 1:2-4; 2:2-4

I t is hard to wait for things to get better when, in our heart of hearts, we aren't sure that things *can* be different or that *we can* be different. We look around at the world and see that it is full of senseless violence, injustice, prejudice, systems that fail, public discourse that is anything but civil, and a culture that makes idols of material wealth and fleeting fame. And the words of the prophet Habakkuk sound painfully current.

The book of Habakkuk is only three chapters long. The prophet takes on God with challenge after challenge and question after question. He wants an answer for his complaints and, in the first lines of chapter two, Habakkuk stands watch, waiting for a response from God. The response comes: "If it delays, wait for it; for it is surely coming."

"Wait for it. . . " Really? Haven't we waited long enough? Yet this is the word we receive—a word of promise for the future. The promise of God that raises up the lowly and oppressed, that sets the captives free, that brings healing, mercy, justice, reconciliation.

------ ★ ★ ★ ------

Loving God, help me to wait upon you, to rise up with wings like an eagle. You have promised that I will run and not be weary, that I will run and not faint. Help me to wait, to trust, to offer my life for the sake of your vision of shalom. Amen.

Rev. Ginger E. Gaines-Cirelli

HURTFUL ACTS
Isaiah 35:5

This quote from Simone Weil recently captured my attention: "A hurtful act is the transference to others of the degradation which we bear in ourselves."[6]

It got me thinking about all the hurting people in the world: all those who callously inflict pain, the pain they themselves must be experiencing, the pain I have caused (knowingly and not), and the pain I have received.

Isaiah paints a startling picture about the radical nature of God's work among humanity. Strange and marvelous things

happen when the Lord appears. Things are changed for the better, and there is reason for joy and gladness.

Today, I visualize all the hurting people I know and imagine myself standing beside them. I imagine God coming to stand in solidarity with us until there is no separation.

------- ★ ★ ★ -------

Healer of our every ill, light of each tomorrow, give us peace beyond our fears and hope beyond our sorrows. Amen.

Rev. Dr. Cathy S. Gilliard

THE RHYTHM OF LIFE
Ecclesiastes 3:1-8

There's a lot of talk these days about balance in our lives. We strive for the right balance between our work lives and the rest of our lives.

Frankly, to me the whole concept sounds exhausting, like balancing on one foot or balancing a tray of full glasses while walking on a rocky path—I can do it, to be sure, but not for long.

Balance is not a biblical virtue. The way of life that is commended in the Bible is more about rhythm than it is about balance. When we respond to the rhythms of life, it is more like taking part in a dance—first one foot and then the other.

I pray that you can find the rhythms of your life. May your dance with life provide time for your spiritual reflection with God, time for your family, and time for your own renewal—time to restore and revive your spirit. May your days be filled with joy and seriousness, with laughter and tears.

------ ★ ★ ★ ------

God, help me to know how to move my feet, first one and then the other, in the rhythmic dance of your creation. And if I lose my balance, help me to get back up, dust myself off, and start all over again. Amen.

During Chelsea's speech at the DNC, she talked about Hillary Clinton as a grandmother to 2-year-old Charlotte and 5-week-old Aidan.

Charlotte, Chelsea said, "loves Elmo, she loves blueberries and above all she loves face-timing with grandma." She explained that Grandma Hillary "can be about to walk on stage for a debate or a speech" but will make time for a reading of "Chugga-Chugga Choo-Choo" via video chat.[7]

Heavy
August 2, 2016

FIGHT THE GOOD FIGHT

Esther 8:3-17 NIV

I n this story are the often quoted words of Mordecai to Esther, "Who knows but that you have come to your royal position for such a time as this?" In essence, Mordecai was saying to Esther, "Do not hide behind position and privilege. Step out, for you are in a unique place of power to become the advocate of a just cause against evil and a defender of your people."

What if all humans, and all of creation, were kindred to us? What if we took up a just cause against all plots that would result in the destruction of people's ways of life—their livelihoods, their environment, their security, their future, and their very dignity?

What if, like Esther, we could not bear to see the calamity that is coming on our people?

------ ⋆ ★ ⋆ ------

O God, remind us of our true identity and mission, and make of us advocates and defenders of life for all people, near and far. Amen.

FROM: Rev. Bill Shillady
SENT: August 27, 2016
TO: H

Dear Hillary,
It has been a rough couple of weeks for you. Stand tall with the truth, and it will set you free.

With all that you have been enduring, the story of Esther came to mind. In the face of evil, she stood tall and told the truth to her king. And Haman got his comeuppance.
Blessings,
Rev. Bill

FEAR NO EVIL

Jeremiah 31:15, Psalms 23 NKJV

This Scripture comes to mind as our nation once again deals with a shooting, this one at Emanuel AME Church in Charleston. The memories come flooding back. One minute you feel safe and secure; the next, all the horror of previous shootings, all the tragedies of Oklahoma City, 9/11, Newtown, Boston, Virginia Tech, Columbine, and others all come surging back.

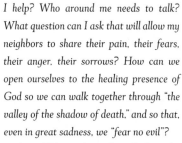

In the spirit of the Charleston Nine, let's bridge our divides, fight for change and remember that love never fails.[8]

Hillary Rodham Clinton
June 17, 2016

I immediately ask myself, *How can I help? Who around me needs to talk? What question can I ask that will allow my neighbors to share their pain, their fears, their anger, their sorrows? How can we open ourselves to the healing presence of God so we can walk together through "the valley of the shadow of death," and so that, even in great sadness, we "fear no evil"?*

"I will fear no evil, for You are with me." The psalmist doesn't deny the reality of evil. But the psalmist has adopted a resolute stance in the face of this real threat—no fear. Not because the police, the Justice Department, and the FBI are already on the scene. Not because the shooter can never hurt anyone again. But because "You, God, Yahweh, the Essence of Love, are with me."

------ ★ ★ ★ ------

O God, when tears fall, when horror grips us, and when words fail us because of the enormity of the loss for which we would pray, we claim your promise that your Spirit intercedes on our behalf with sighs too deep for words. Help all people of faith who value the sacredness of human life and the dignity of all cultures to denounce such hatred that leads to innocent lives being lost. Move us to the deeper dialogue of forgiveness and reconciliation and a new future of hope with all lives being valued. Amen.

UNLIMITED MERCY
Matthew 18:23-35

This is a fascinating and violent parable. Using exaggeration and hyperbole, Jesus helps his listeners see that justice prevails. The answer to how much we should forgive is impractical, if not absurd. Those who hear are to forgive many times and no matter the debt. One must be willing, if asked, to forgive even the unforgivable, unpayable debt because such is the mercy of God.

One may be a bit overwhelmed by the violence and punishment in the parable. But we know so well that our world is filled with violence, with too many terrible acts of retribution, revenge, and recompense.

Our brothers and sisters who died at the Emanuel AME Church are but another example of the evil of racism, hatred, the gun culture, and our lack of movement on changing our society. But the words of forgiveness by those in that church community are a witness to God's amazing grace. As God has been merciful to the believer to an infinite degree, so too must believers be merciful to one another and not to any lesser degree.

------ ★ ------

Lord, thank you for your unlimited mercy and forgiveness. Help us to do for others as you have done for us. Weeping may endure for the night, but we trust in your grace and hope, O God, that joy will come in the morning. Amen.

I FORGIVE YOU
Luke 11:4

The words from Luke 11:4 are spoken every time we pray the Lord's Prayer. Since that prayer is repeated so often, we may not realize the radical nature of what we are praying—tying our forgiveness of others with God's forgiveness of us.

Even though we eagerly receive God's forgiveness, we may not find it easy to forgive persons who have done horrible things to us or to those we love. I stand in awe of the members of Emanuel AME Church who said to the murderer of their pastor, family members, and friends, "I forgive you."

They were being true to the transformative nature of forgiveness. Only those whose lives have been made new by being forgiven can forgive a person who has committed such a heinous act of racial hatred.

To forgive others not only allows them the possibility of a new start, it allows us to let go of destructive emotions that can harm us. Without forgiveness, there is no possibility for inner healing or the healing of a broken relationship. This is true not only of our relationship with others but also our relationship with God.

------ ★ ★ ★ ------

Eternal Friend, out of unconditional love you have unconditionally forgiven us. Give us the strength and courage to forgive those who don't deserve our forgiveness but who need the same healing and freedom we have found in your forgiveness of us. Amen.

Robert Martin Walker

In court, one by one, grieving parents and siblings looked at the young man who had taken so much from them and said, "I forgive you." And the entire Charleston community—black and white, Christian, Muslim and Jewish, and so many others—came together to stand up to hate and bigotry, providing love to one another instead.[9]

CNN
June 17, 2016

RETURN TO CENTER
Luke 4:1-13

We understand power. We especially understand and resent abuse of power by those who should wield it for the benefit of others. Scholars point out that in the Gospels, Jesus wields no power at all except toward spirits and demons. This story is Jesus's refusal to abuse the power he already had.

We are on journeys of faith, and there will be tests, temptations, and struggles. Yes, there will be many opportunities for each of us to forget the divine commandment—to love God with all your heart, mind, soul, and strength and to love others as much as you love yourself. The tester wants you to believe that if you only love yourself, you will be great. But Christ's gospel offers a new way of living, a new perspective on life!

Henri Nouwen reminds us:

> Our true challenge is to return to the center, to the heart, and to find there the gentle voice which speaks to us and affirms us in a way no human voice ever could. The basis of all conviction is the experience of God's unlimited and unlimiting acceptance of us as beloved children, an acceptance so full, so total and all-embracing, that it sets us free from our compulsion to be seen, praised, and admired and free for Christ who leads us on the road to service.[10]

----- ★ ★ ★ -----

Lord, free us up to be your children fully in this world. Forgive us when we fail on our journeys. Help us to love with all our being all those who test us, confront us, and whom we find most difficult to love. Help us to look to the Scripture and our heart for your grace and acceptance and allow that to flow from us to the world. Amen.

PRONE TO WONDER
Luke 15:8-10

At Disney World, the parking areas include more than 50,000 slots, and every day, a good number of guests cannot remember where they parked. Visitors arrive at the theme park revved up, and they aren't paying attention or are driving a rental car whose color and make they haven't embraced.

Disney employs a small army called the Parking Cast whose job it is to help reunite families with their cars. The Parking Cast uses an array of tools, including perseverance, technology, and clues elicited from the guests. Through one means or another, Disney usually manages to reconnect vehicles with guests, who may feel that, no matter where their car really was found, they had parked in the Dopey lot.

Jesus tells us that God goes about the business of seeking us purposefully. That is great news, whether we are parked in Dopey or wandering through the day wondering where we are. God looks for us because it is God's great joy to find us. And when we are found, heaven rejoices.

------ ★ ★ ★ ------

You have found me, O God, and rejoiced. Seek me when I am feeling lost, and help me to guide others to the bread of heaven and the living water so that they may be found. In the name of the one who came to find us all, Jesus the Christ. Amen.

FROM: Rev. Bill Shillady
SENT: May 16, 2015
TO: H

Dear Hillary,
You are in my prayers.
Bill

★ ★ ★

FROM: H
SENT: May 16, 2015
TO: Rev. Bill Shillady

I haven't heard or read many lessons on the lost coin parable and think the Disney link really works. All is well with us, thankfully, and I'm forging ahead. Onward! -H

WHERE WE ARE

1 Samuel 3:1-10

I was talking with a board member of the United Methodist City Society about how she manages people under her supervision. She told me, "I believe that I always articulate my expectations and ground rules, and follow up with meaningful feedback. In return, I expect, at least, an honest effort and a commitment to improve. When my efforts to lead and guide are met with resistance or worse, I become disappointed, frustrated, and angry. I personalize the encounter: *How could she let me down? Wasn't he listening? How many chances do I have to give them?*

Then she wondered whether she has let God down too—because God's expectations of her are similar to the ones in her employ, and she knows she isn't always good at meeting God's hope for loving others unconditionally. The story of the call of Samuel popped into my mind.

I do pray for people in authority. I try to think about what they're going through even when I disagree with them. Trying to find some common ground, some common understanding that perhaps can make me more empathetic.[11]

Hillary Rodham Clinton
March 6, 2016

How fortunate we are that God does not hold us to what we think should be God's standards . . . that God meets us where we are and accepts us for who we are . . . that God appreciates our limitations and sent his Son to show us the way.

------ ⭐ ------

Dear Lord, thank you for the infinite chances you give me to renew and deepen my relationship with you. Please help me develop the patience and humility to listen, discern, and respond appropriately to you through my daily encounters with others. Amen.

OUR CHOICES
Luke 23:32-43

When tempted in the wilderness, Jesus had choices to make. He chose to trust God instead of the enemy and to do what was good for us instead of what was good for himself. Jesus made these choices out of love. That love led to the cross with a criminal on both sides. These criminals also had choices to make.

The first criminal echoed the enemy, selfishly tempting Jesus: "Save yourself and us!" This criminal also echoed worldly, mocking voices demanding proof from Jesus: "If you really are the king of the Jews, save yourself." In contrast, the second criminal, in the presence of Jesus, who is innocent, recognized his own guilt. This criminal humbly chose faith in Jesus as he said, "Jesus, remember me when you come into your kingdom." He didn't say "*if* you come into your kingdom." This wasn't some kind of last-ditch effort. This man, guilty and dying, looked at Jesus and saw hope, life, and love. He saw the sign tacked above Jesus's head and knew it was true: Jesus reigns.

Each and every day of our lives, we make choices that signal where we place our faith, choices that point toward who or what we truly serve. Who or what rules your life? As you ponder the question, remember that Jesus always remembers you and longs for you to live in the kingdom.

------ ★ ★ ★ ------

Lord, when faced with difficult choices, remind me of my call to be a disciple of Jesus Christ for the transformation of the world. Your kingdom comes through the choices that I make. Amen.

Rev. Ginger E. Gaines-Cirelli

WHY, LORD?

Psalm 46

L ast night, there was a terrible Amtrak accident. In the last week, some 200 tornados have touched down in the Midwest, killing many. A 7.3 earthquake in Nepal killed more people, and six U.S. Marines have gone missing.

Tragedies are tests of our faith. We cannot help but cry out to God, "Why?"

God understands that question—it is not that God allowed this to happen. We humans are responsible for our actions. So many intricate and interwoven decisions people have made in the past led to such tragedies. Devastation so often is caused by human-made decisions.

Notwithstanding our feelings and questions, there is one response that must be evident within the life of all Christians—empathy. There is no place for indifference in the hearts of Christians. We are to weep with those who weep. We are to respond to their needs as well. This should be grounded not in our own strength, skills, or qualities, but in our overwhelming sense of wonder at the grace of God.

------ ★ ------

Lord, we pray for those devastated by recent atrocities. Lord, help us to find the time to be still and know you more deeply. Continue to lead and guide us as we respond in compassion and action to those around us who need your love. In the name of Christ, we pray. Amen.

SLEEP IN PEACE
Mark 4:26-29

There never seem to be enough hours in the day. Despite time spent sorting through email, returning phone calls, and typing away on our smartphones, we still go to bed each night with what seems like piles of unfinished business. And so we wake up ready to tackle the world, only to feel like we're leaving more and more unfinished. Despite our best attempts, we cannot outrun the pace of life in our modern twenty-first-century world.

Yet, Jesus shares with us a profound truth designed to lighten the burdens we carry. No matter how much we toil and labor and try to exert control over every detail of life, there will always be things completely out of our hands. Just as the farmer must allow nature to take its course in nurturing a plant from seed to stalk, so must we learn to allow God to handle things outside of our control. As Victor Hugo wisely said, "When you have laboriously accomplished your daily task, go to sleep in peace. God is awake."[12]

------ ★ ★ ★ ------

Dear God, help us to remember that your steady hand guides us always. Help us to trust in your love and power when we find ourselves facing uncertainty and discouragement. Teach us what is ours to carry and what is yours to bear. Amen.

Rev. Kevin K. Wright

* *

FROM: Rev. Bill Shillady
SENT: November 12, 2015
TO: H

Hillary,
I don't know how you do it! I have been amazed at your schedule and travel these last few months. I pray you are still able to sleep on the plane as you mentioned once to me. And I will be praying especially for you during the debate on Saturday night.
    I think this devotional is very appropriate for you!
Rev. Bill

* *

WE WAIT
Psalm 27:11-14

I love what Henri Nouwen says about waiting:

> Waiting is essential to the spiritual life. But waiting as a disciple of Jesus is not an empty waiting. It is a waiting with a promise in our hearts that makes already present what we are waiting for. We wait during Advent for the birth of Jesus. We wait after Easter for the coming of the Spirit, and after the ascension of Jesus we wait for his coming again in glory. We are always waiting, but it is a waiting in the conviction that we have already seen God's footsteps.
>
> Waiting for God is an active, alert—yes, joyful—waiting. As we wait we remember him for whom we are waiting, and as we remember him we create a community ready to welcome him when he comes.[13]

------ ★ ★ ★ ------

Bless us, Lord, as we realize the grace of patience and perseverance in our daily living. Remind us at times to stop and take a deep breath, and in that moment of pausing, come to us and give us strength and courage for the next few moments and for the facing of our day. Amen.

SUCH WISDOM
1 Kings 3:16-28; James 3:17

Many people give advice, while others are sources of wisdom. How can you tell one from the other? Advice typically comes in the form of opinion and reflects the viewpoint of the person offering it.

The Book of Kings states that Israel's great King Solomon was twelve years old when God promised him that he would be granted great wisdom. According to Jewish tradition, he turned out to be the wisest man ever to live. As an illustration of the fulfillment of this blessing of wisdom, the Book of Kings reports a well-known case that was brought before King Solomon's court in Jerusalem, in which two women claimed the same child.

Wisdom, the kind of wisdom that Jesus exhibited in his life, has the ring of God's truth about it, an overarching truth that transcends human understanding. Even his enemies marveled at Jesus's selfless, God-centered wisdom.

May you be blessed with advisors like Solomon around you who offer the wisdom that you need. And may you have the continuing presence of the Holy Spirit to give you the eternal wisdom that we all need.

------ ★ ⭐ ★ ------

Jesus, thank you for offering me your eternal perspective and wisdom through Scripture and your Spirit. I don't want to offer people temporary fixes or self-serving opinions. I want your wisdom to shape my perspective and my words today. Amen.

A LIFE WELL-LIVED

Psalm 39:1-13

One reason the Psalms are loved is that they capture the emotions of people facing real situations. It gives us comfort to know that we are not alone in our struggles. In today's psalm, David comments on the brevity of life and has an understandable reaction. If we only knew the number of days of our lives! But life is so fragile, and there are too many tragedies that end lives too quickly.

When I look back on my life, I certainly lament the mistakes and wasted efforts. But David reminds us that, in the face of all our sins, it is God who remains our hope. No matter how much of a mess we have made of our lives, they are never too cluttered for God to redeem.

I think part of the message that I certainly have tried to understand and live with is to look at yourself first, to make sure you are being the kind of person you should be in how you are treating others.[14]

Hillary Rodham Clinton
January 25, 2016

------ ✦ ★ ✦ ------

God, your Son reminds me that you want my life to be fruitful, full of rich abundance that multiplies into the lives of others. Give me grace and peace to know what will make my life abundant and joy-filled. And give me the time in my calendar to live life to the fullest as your disciple who makes a difference at such a time as this. Amen.

ENDURES FOREVER
Psalm 136:1-26

More than ever, we live in a disposable culture. We often simply ignore the impact of all the things that are made to be thrown away—razors, water bottles, lighters, paper plates, plastic eating utensils. Products are used, tossed, and replaced.

This disposable culture is also reflected in more significant ways. Many times, true commitment in relationships is considered optional. Relationships struggle to survive. Recently there has been a string of abandoned babies. Long-term employees are discharged just before retirement for cheaper options. It seems as if nothing lasts.

Hillary Clinton @
@HillaryClinton

The energy we're seeing on this campaign isn't about what we're against but what we're for—an inclusive America where everyone counts.

RETWEETS LIKES
4,911   13,593

12:25 PM - 5 Nov 2016

Our unchanging God, however, has promised that loving mercy endures forever. In Psalm 136, the singer celebrates this wonderful promise by making statements about God's wonder, work, and character. The psalmist then punctuates each statement about God with the phrase, "For God's mercy endureth forever" (KJV). Whether it is the wonder of God's creation, the rescue of God's people, or the tender care for God's own, we can trust God because God's mercy will never fail. In a temporary world, the permanence of God's mercy gives us hope.

------ ★ ★ ★ ------

I give you thanks, steadfast God, that your grace is immeasurable, that your unwavering grace is the anchor that holds me in this fast-paced, disposable world, and that your mercy is inexhaustible. May your peace endure forever in my heart and soul. Amen.

LIFE RESTORED
Ezekiel 37:1-6

It technically wasn't a desert, but the five-year drought had rendered the land like a desert. About the only vegetation in sight were the eucalyptus trees, water-soaking trees that absorbed every possible drop. And there were bones—not human bones but sheep bones. San Juan Island, one of the Channel Islands off the shore of California, was harsh and barren.

The idea of bones ever coming to life is hard to believe. But that's the promise of the prophet: life can be restored.

That's what this passage is about—hope. When the situation seems hopeless, when there is no way forward, when it seems that all forces are working in a negative way, God intervenes and possibilities emerge which only yesterday, only moments ago, were unimaginable. This is the life that God promises.

------ ★ ★ ★ ------

Dear God, when bones are scattered all around, when there is no hope, let your life-giving breath flow to us. Amen.

Bishop Jane Allen Middleton

EXPRESSING OUR LOVE
John 13:14-15

Persons in our communities are in great need of food, shelter, medical care, and education. The greater need, however, is for people to serve others. Service is a natural outgrowth of faith. Spirituality without service becomes narcissistic and shallow.

We're not asked to love each other, not urged or requested. We are commanded to love. Indeed, Jesus made it his greatest commandment.[15]

Hillary Rodham Clinton
September 8, 2016

To serve is to follow the example of Jesus. In a dramatic action that united service and forgiveness, he humbly knelt and washed his disciples' feet (John 13:1-15). This means that he washed Judas's feet even though he was aware of Judas's intention to betray him!

How can we follow Jesus's example? By expressing our faith through actions that help others live fully and abundantly. The important thing is not so much the specific course of action that we take in faith but to incorporate service and forgiveness into the patterns and movements of our daily life.

★ ★ ★

God of humble love, your Son gave us the example of humble service. We admit that we want to serve in ways that win the recognition of others. Help us to quietly, even anonymously, put our faith into actions of love and forgiveness. Help us also to recognize our deep need to serve others. Amen.

Robert Martin Walker

WHY SHOULD I FORGIVE?

Luke 23:34

M ost people have read stories of individuals and communities who have forgiven great atrocities. We have our own stories, too, and my guess is that each of us has forgiven our fair share of faults—some smaller and easier, others that have taken years. And still others that are being worked and prayed out day by day.

I love the image of Jesus sitting on the right hand of God, leaning over and whispering, "Father, forgive them. Forgive her. Forgive *my daughter*, for she does not know (the impact) of what she is doing." Jesus calls us to also forgive one another, however difficult that might be.

A few days ago, I ran across a reflection that I wrote back in April 2001. It reminds me of that time in my life and how far I have come. Might this be our prayer today.

------- ★ ★ ★ -------

Why I Should Forgive

Holding on to past wounds and hurts;
carrying grudges and not resolving issues is costly—very costly.
It costs me present joy, peace, and sometimes my sanity.
It renders me immobile, paralyzed; unable to think and act clearly.
Who or what is worthy of that?

Often the offender has gone on merrily living his or her life
oblivious or unconcerned that the infraction ever occurred,
while I spend hours, days, weeks mourning and grieving my wounded self.

Today, I choose to start fresh;
certain that this day will have its own measure of things to learn,
*   experience, enjoy AND forgive. It's something I choose to do.*
Forgiveness sets me free and gives me back my life.

Forgiveness sets me free and gives me back my life.

Rev. Dr. Cathy S. Gilliard

BE BLESSED

THE BEATITUDES
Matthew 5:1-12

I thought I would do a series of devotions for you about the Sermon on the Mount.

Jesus begins by telling us about the essence of who God is because of whom God blesses.

The Beatitudes are revolutionary assaults on some of our dearest and most widely held values. Here, sketched out for us, is a kingdom quite unlike our earthly standards, where those whom the world ignores, marginalizes, and even curses are those who are blessed. Martin Luther said that the Beatitudes, especially the blessing of those who are poor in spirit, go against the "greatest and most universal religion on earth," namely "faith in success."

Now that does not mean we should go out and fail for the sake of being blessed. The word for "poor" (*ptochoi*) comes from the Greek meaning "to cower, to cringe." We're talking about the abysmally poor, those who are at the ends of their ropes—for whom God's presence and grace is their only hope.

We are to be the agents of that blessing. Do we accept people and love them as they are, as God would do, or do we place limitations on our blessings? Maybe we are blessed as we bless those whom we find difficult!

May God bless us all—troubled souls, questioning minds, insatiable skeptics, fallers from grace, stumblers in the dark, moral bunglers, failures at faith, inept believers.

------- ⋆ ★ ⋆ -------

God of the prophets, God of Christ, we are reminded today that your blessings do not necessarily follow the logic of the world. The world believes that the rich are blessed, but Jesus reminds us that it is the poor who are blessed, the poor in spirit and the materially poor as well. We pray for a more just world in which all have enough and none are left behind. Amen.

POOR IN SPIRIT

Matthew 5:1-12

Some have suggested that the true way to understand the Beatitudes may be when they are inverted or reversed. I would like to suggest that we become dyslexic Christians and read a new meaning to the Beatitudes:

> The way to Heaven is through poverty . . . the way to consolation is through genuine sorrow . . . the way to earthly possessions is through a gentle spirit . . . the way to satisfaction is through a hungering and thirsting for justice . . . the way to mercy is through mercy . . . the way to God is through the open, unobstructed, pure heart . . . the way to a full relationship with God is through the active practice of peace . . . the way to God's Kingdom is through the struggle for right that leads through conflict, pain, and even death itself.[1]

From this perspective, the Beatitudes become something other than a recipe for reward. They are instead more like a road map for life. They tell us not so much how we might arrive at our destination but rather present us with the directions for the journey.

------ * ⭐ * ------

Gracious God, give us the strength and courage to follow this roadmap of faith. We can only reach our destination of the kingdom as we strive to live these principles and, when we fall, to ask in our hearts for forgiveness. Amen.

Mrs. Clinton [spoke] about her views on Christianity and the Bible. Below is her . . . response:
      "The famous discussion on the Sermon on the Mount should be something that you really pay attention to. . . . What does the Sermon on the Mount really mean? What is it calling us to do and to understand? Because it sure does seem to favor the poor and the merciful and those who in worldly terms don't have a lot but who have the spirit that God recognizes as being at the core of love and salvation."[2]

The New York Times
January 25, 2016

THOSE WHO MOURN

Matthew 5:4

W_e don't walk through the valley of the shadow of death in our culture. We like to run through it quickly. I don't think we've taken the time to stop and appreciate the blessings of our mourning.

Mom lived a long and full life. . . . I wept not for what she would miss but for how much I would miss her. I spent the next few days going through her things at home, paging through a book, staring at an old photograph, caressing a piece of beloved jewelry.[3]

Hillary Rodham Clinton

But they are there. Blessings are there with the widow who sits in the chair where her husband used to relax, just so she can remember the sweetness of his presence. They're there when you sort through clothes and suddenly are enveloped with a waft of perfume that reminds you of Christmas with your mom. And in how the ways we've hurt each other seem to fade and the resentment is replaced with understanding. The blessings are there as we defrost the homemade casseroles that the church ladies delivered. And as we eat a meal after the funeral and tell each other stories until our sides ache with laughter as well as pain.

Everyone knows the pain of sorrow. Can we find its blessing? As difficult as mourning can be, especially after a loved one's long or shocking process of death, somehow, I know that I am blessed.

------ ★ ★ ★ ------

O God, our Creator, surround us in our blessedness, in our grief, and in our sorrow; by the power of your Holy Spirit. Amen.

THE MEEK

Matthew 5:5

I n the workplace, the arrogant and powerful seem to win, but in the end, they lose. They don't win in personal relationships. No one wants an arrogant, self-seeking friend. Men and women who are hungry for power are often lonely people. Nor do they win in financial security. They think they possess the world, but the world possesses them. The more money they have, the less financially secure they feel.

In contrast, Jesus said that the meek "will inherit the earth." As we have seen, the earth has become the location of the kingdom of heaven. We tend to think of the kingdom of heaven as *heaven*, a place completely different (golden streets, gates of pearl, a mansion over the hilltop) from anything we know here. But God's promise of the kingdom is "a new heaven and a new earth" (Revelation 21:1). Those who submit their power to God will inherit the perfect kingdom coming to earth. In this kingdom, we receive by God's grace the good things the arrogant fruitlessly strive for in the present earth and more.[4]

------ ★ ★ ★ ------

God of the new heaven and the new earth, help me to use my strength and power for the benefit of others so that your kingdom of love can truly be a reality. Amen.

★ ★

FROM: Rev. Bill Shillady
SENT: August 14, 2015
TO: H

I found this text so helpful that I thought you would enjoy this interpretation of the passage. As I like to say, I couldn't have said it any better . . . maybe that is starting to be meek!

Have a blessed day. You are in my prayers every day, but especially the last few days.

Rev. Bill

★ ★

THIRST FOR RIGHTEOUSNESS
Matthew 5:6

To understand the fourth beatitude, we need to have some idea of what Jesus meant by righteousness. In ancient Judaism, *righteousness* meant "to acquit, vindicate, restore to a right relationship."

I am sure that you have received the blessing of right relationships, which begin as we move from making our actions from a self-centered perspective to what is right for the other person.

Do you hunger and thirst for right relationships—with God, family, friends, enemies, community? Jesus reminds us in this beatitude that we will have God's grace and blessing as we hunger and thirst for right relationships, first and foremost our relationship with God and then with the people around us whom we wish to like and love. Even with those who are most difficult to love.

Jesus says that those who have this hunger will find their appetites filled. It is easy to see the wrongs in our society and the need for right relationships among people of different cultures and backgrounds. If we are hungering and thirsting for righteousness, our utmost desire is to see wrongs righted. Then we will be "satisfied."

May we remain hungry and longing for righteousness!

------ ★ ------

Lord, may your righteous kingdom be the goal of every day of my life, and may it come into fruition in our world now so that peace and justice may be found everywhere. Amen.

THE MERCIFUL
Matthew 5:7

There is an old saying: "You can't really understand another person's experience until you've walked a mile in his or her shoes."

In 2001, Frank Baird created a new concept on this idea. What started out as a small group of men daring to totter around a park in women's high-heeled shoes for a fun and different experience has grown to become a worldwide movement raising millions of dollars for local rape crisis centers, domestic violence shelters, and other sexualized violence education, prevention, and remediation programs.

Walk a Mile in Her Shoes asks men literally to walk one mile in women's high-heeled shoes. It's not easy, but it's fun, and it gets the community talking about gender relations and men's sexualized violence against women.

Walking in another person's shoes! Much easier said than done. Having a sense of another's feeling and suffering to this degree is very difficult because we are normally so self-concerned, so aware of our own feelings, that sensitivity for others to this depth often requires a great effort of the will.

Normally, when we feel sorry for someone, it is an exclusively external act. We don't make the effort to get inside another's mind and heart until we can see and feel things as she does. It is not easy to walk in another person's shoes, but we are blessed and receive God's mercy when we do.

Lord, help me to understand others by putting myself in their shoes. With your mercy, love, and grace blessing me, may I be a conduit of that blessing as I try my best to look at the world from another person's perspective and circumstance. Amen.

PURE IN HEART
Matthew 5:8

Perhaps the easiest way to understand this beatitude is to say the pure in heart are those who give themselves as fully as they can to the great commandment: "You must love the LORD your God with all your heart, with all your soul, with all your mind, and with all your strength" (Mark 12:30 NLT).

This love is to dominate every other love in our lives. The purity of heart that results from this soul-fulfilling love of God translates to clarity of vision for what life is truly meant to be; thus, Jesus says, the pure in heart will see God.

The more we unclutter our lives and the more of our soul that we allow and eventually give over to the fullness of God, the clearer and more presently we can experience God.

Blessed are the pure in heart, those who make their hearts vulnerable, for they shall see God. The covenant of God's love is already written on our hearts—it's just that some of us have more in the way.

------- ★ ★ ★ -------

God our deliverer, Jesus reminds us that you are a God who walks with the meek and the poor, the compassionate and those who mourn, and you call us by a pure heart to walk humbly with you. Help us to shed all the barriers in our hearts that keep us from focusing on loving you with all our being. Amen.

Hillary Clinton is known to hold a deep and private Christian faith, and her devotion to it may surprise many voters. On occasion, in interviews and at events over the years, she has spoken about her long-held membership of the Methodist church (she was a Sunday school leader and long-term prayer group member), and the strength and purpose she draws from God.[5]

Christian Today
May 20, 2016

THE PEACEMAKERS
Matthew 5:9

The seventh beatitude calls every Christian to the task of conflict resolution. Conflicts arise over differences of opinion, and the human tendency is to ignore conflict or to suppress it by using avoidance, force, threat, or intimidation.

In the ideal of God's kingdom here and now, it's a blessing to bring together people in conflict. Only then is it possible to resolve the conflict and restore the relationships.

Of course, I think this passage has even more fruit to bear. To be peacemakers may begin with our own souls. We need to find inner peace in the depth of our being—to take the time to become quiet and still in our souls and find the "peace that surpasses our human understanding" at the center. If we can approach life with an inner peace, it can lead to better relationships in our families, in our work, and eventually, as you have shown as secretary of state, in our world.

We are resilient, determined, hard-working. There is nothing America can't do—if we do it together.[6]

Hillary Rodham Clinton
August 11, 2016

In a time when there's violence and racial tension in our cities, war and conflict in so many places in our world, and alienation as people are pulled further apart, we need to hear afresh Jesus's message to become peacemakers . . . persons who bring people together to transform conflict into peace.

------ ★ ⭐ ★ ------

Our loving God, we bow in this moment to thank you for Jesus and his teachings on how to live into your kingdom. Thank you for his willingness to die on the cross, to go the full measure to demonstrate your unconditional love for all and to bring peace on earth. May we follow in his way. Amen.

THE PERSECUTED
Matthew 5:10-12 ESV

U p to this point, the Beatitudes have focused on humility, meekness, right relationships, mercy, purity of heart, and peacemaking—all positive qualities. But here, Jesus includes the possibility of persecution

"for righteousness' sake." This arises from living the path of the first seven. Persecution—be it physical, verbal, or otherwise— comes from the forces that oppose God's truthful ways.

Jesus brings the Beatitudes to a close with the fact that there is a price to pay when we commit to following him. If you always pursue honesty, integrity, and justice, you will encounter first the cold shoulder, then the caustic remarks, and finally persecution.

Blessed are you for doing good. Keep doing it, my friend, Hillary. God is the one who ultimately evaluates our lives and sees what we did in the secrets of our hearts and the differences we made in this world.

------ ⋆ ★ ⋆ ------

Our loving God, we thank you for Jesus, because we know through his life, his teachings, his death, and resurrection that we have the opportunity for meaningful, kingdom living here and now and then in eternity. May we follow in his way, doing good in this world and knowing that you ultimately are the one who gives the glory. In Christ's name, we pray. Amen.

INTO THE FUTURE
Matthew 6:33-34

People who are prone to dwell in the past, rehashing the failures of earlier days, can be prisoners to their failures and not their successes. Often, people concentrate on the negative and seem to drown in anger or sorrow about what has happened rather than using those experiences as building blocks for the future.

But some recognize the past, learn from it, and dream of the future, reflecting on and rehearsing how it will be. We call them idealists. Jesus calls them disciples.

To lead like Jesus involves learning from the past as God draws us into the future. So those lessons from the past can help us to dream better visions, enhance our goals, implement better strategies for transforming the world. To be a disciple means that there will be trouble each day, but we need not worry because we learn from it and move on to the future kingdom filled with righteousness and good.

I seek God's perspective on the past so I can learn for the present and future. Then I can not only dream of a better world, but can begin to transform it, one relationship at a time.

------ ★ ★ ★ ------

God of the past, the present, and the future, thank you for lessons learned. Give us hope for tomorrow and strength for today. May we leave yesterday in your hands. As we look with confidence toward the future, we seek your wisdom and strength as we serve others and build Christ's kingdom brick by brick. In the name of Jesus, we pray. Amen.

LIVE FROM THE HEART
Matthew 5:3-12

The Beatitudes are what happens when the human heart is touched by God. Here we find a vision of God and ourselves that challenges common perceptions, including our own. What Jesus teaches seems absurd to our rational thinking. There appears to be contradictions.

They say the greatest distance in the world is between one's mind and heart. The Sermon on the Mount presents great teachings by Jesus that on the surface make sense, but when you explore them more deeply, you see the teaching must move from the mind to "heart living"—living in God's grace and love without expecting rational response.

I recently read an article from Dr. Suzanne Steinbaum about what it really means to live from the heart:

> Living from the heart feels much different than living from the head. When you live from your heart, you feel at peace, at ease, and in control of yourself because of a deep inner knowing. You lead with love. You learn how to care for yourself and love yourself. You relax because you know that everything is going to be okay. Living from the heart coaxes your body back into balance. When the heart is in control, your body finds optimum health and starts acting like a well-oiled machine instead of a broken-down car.
>
> We are so used to letting our heads be in charge of our lives that when we start reacting with our hearts instead, it feels like a miracle, like a whole new existence. And it is! . . . Let your heart be the center and watch your whole life transform.[7]

May you have a heart-filled day!

------ * ★ * ------

Lord, help me narrow the gap between my head and my heart so that I may live wisely in faith. May your love guide my decisions, and may your grace sustain me when I am wrong. Amen.

SALT OF THE EARTH
Matthew 5:13

When Jesus tells the disciples they are the salt of the earth, what he may be intending to say is this: "You disciples may seem so small in the big scheme. Yet sprinkle a few of you around in places like your little neighborhood or mine, and no telling what you'll stir up or melt. No telling what you'll flavor."

The lesson expands. "You disciples, without you, the whole earth would lose its zest; without you, it would be boringly dull and insipid." Are we salty characters who dare to follow the teachings of Jesus?

Love your enemies. Turn the other cheek. If asked by the Roman soldier to carry something one mile, go two. People of faith caring about others— that's what's going to flavor this world.

------ ★ ★ ★ ------

Creator of the universe and ruler of my heart, your Son called us to be the salt of the earth. Help me to be salty so that I can flavor the world in the grace and love of Jesus Christ. Help me to bring out the flavors of righteousness and mercy in this world. Amen.

If you had to name one book that made you who you are today, what would it be?

"At the risk of appearing predictable, the Bible was and remains the biggest influence on my thinking. I was raised reading it, memorizing passages from it and being guided by it. I still find it a source of wisdom, comfort and encouragement."[8]

The New York Times
June 11, 2014

TRANSFORM THE WORLD
Matthew 5:14-16

I n today's Scripture passage, Jesus says that God has given every human being a spark of God's light within them to share with the world.

The Mount of the Beatitudes is a wonderful place where tourists are taken to see the gentle slope down to the Sea of Galilee. The mountain is topped by a Roman Catholic Franciscan chapel built in 1937–1938 following plans by Italian architect Antonio Barluzzi.

My faith has sustained me, it has informed me, it has saved me, it has chided me, it has challenged me.[9]

Hillary Rodham Clinton

To a very unlikely group of people Jesus says: "You are the light of the world." You are the ones who will bring light into the darkness of the world. You are the ones through whom God is going to transform the world around us. Remember, Hillary, that this message comes to you and me each morning and reminds us that we must be the light of the world. Let your light shine before others, so that they may see your good works and give glory to God in heaven.

Lord, help me to be a flame of your love to this world. One flame can penetrate the darkness and begin to move the world toward the Light of your kingdom. Amen.

NEW KINGDOM
Matthew 5:38-44, Luke 6:35 NIV

Jesus describes a new lifestyle of a child of the kingdom, not a child of the world. Followers of Jesus are called to an antiestablishment establishment—a network made up of the marginalized, the hungry, the heartbroken, the oppressed, and those who are seeking justice for the world. It is an establishment that depends on God for its survival and salvation.

The Beatitudes are not a bunch of moral laws. We are being offered a new vision of our world and our lives—a new way of relationship that concentrates on love and mercy rather than hate and vengeance, judgment and punishment.

Jesus says to the citizens of his new kingdom, "Your reward

Hillary Clinton ✔
@HillaryClinton

With threats & hate crimes on rise, we shouldn't have to tell @POTUS to do his part. He must step up & speak out.

RETWEETS   LIKES
18,259   48,374

10:04 AM - 27 Feb 2017

4.6K   18K   48K

will be great, and you will be children of the Most High." As children of God, we are given a place in this coming kingdom where our hunger will be filled and our sadness will be replaced by joy. As a citizen of Jesus's kingdom we stand apart, over and against the culture of our world, defying conventional wisdom. Jesus helps us look at the essence of God and discover all sorts of new possibilities for ways to make our world better.

------- ⋆ ★ ⋆ -------

Lord, I promise to do my best to follow Jesus. I will remember that he calls me to a higher level of love and relationships with those who are easy to love and those who are difficult to love. Help me to look at my enemies and those who hurt me with a new sense of loving and to go the second mile in the sharing of grace. Amen.

WHO COULD BE SAVED?
Matthew 5:17-20, Galatians 5:14 ESV

The Pharisees accused Jesus of being a law-breaker—in particular, of being a violator of the Sabbath law. Here, Jesus states clearly that his purpose in coming is not to destroy the law, but to fulfill it. Jesus concludes this revelation in verse 20 with a startling statement: "I tell you, unless your righteousness exceeds that of the scribes and Pharisees, you will never enter the kingdom of heaven."

Ordinary people in his day revered the apparent righteousness of the religious leaders and could not imagine ever matching them in their piety. Jesus shocked them by stating that entrance into God's kingdom was available only to those whose righteousness exceeded that of the scribes and Pharisees. Who, then, could be saved? The problem lay in equating righteousness with external piety. But the word *righteousness* throughout the Bible always denotes right relationships—with God and with people around us.

In Galatians 5:14, we read, "For the whole law is fulfilled in one word: 'You shall love your neighbor as yourself.'" We are to love not only our neighbors but our enemies as well. It is not enough not to murder someone; we must guard against harboring anger that leads to insults and broken relationships. Jesus is clear that a right relationship between you and your brother or sister is so vital that your entrance into the new kingdom is dependent upon it.

———— ★ ★ ★ ————

Creator God, your Son called us to love and serve you with body, mind, and spirit by fulfilling the law. Open our hearts in compassion as we fulfill his teachings. Jesus, our teacher and Messiah, modeled for us the way of love for the whole universe. So we offer our prayers of love on behalf of ourselves, our neighbors, your creation, and all of our fellow creatures. Amen.

LOVE YOUR ENEMY
Matthew 5:38-48

Jesus did not leave us many clues as to how to deal with violence and injustice from others. But in Matthew 5, the teachings make clear that Jesus's third way of creative, loving, non-violent resistance is the only way to love our enemies and to bring the reign of God's love and peace into our world and personal lives.

Jesus never taught passivity in the face of evil or that violence is the appropriate response to evil. We are called to love our enemies and do good to those who misuse us. We are to love our enemies when we show them how they are being unjust, when we give them opportunities to grow and learn from those experiences, and to be open to God's grace to change their violent and unjust and oppressive ways.

These are not calls to be passive and take whatever abuse oppressors want to place on us. These are guidelines from Jesus for nonviolent resistance.

------ ★ ★ ------

Lord, help me to love my enemies. Give me the wisdom to teach them, through my action and attitude, that their injustice will not win. And help me to embrace them as children of yours who need your love and grace through me. Amen.

Hillary Clinton believes that no child should face bullying or harassment, and children who do engage in bullying should receive supports to help them change their behavior.[10]

The Briefing
October 27, 2016

TURN THE OTHER CHEEK

Matthew 5:38-39

The Bible contains the word of God, but we have to dig out the meaning for ourselves. I like to consider the social situation at the time to understand what it meant to listeners then.

Today's directive from Jesus is a way of showing creative, loving, non-violent resistance. The illustration is to turn the other cheek when someone hits you. This makes no sense. How is this loving? How is this just?

But wait. Matthew records Jesus as saying "turn the *left* cheek." Why such a specific direction?

The first century was a time of slavery. Jesus usually talked to the common folk, and many of his listeners were slaves. Slaves were reprimanded by a slap with the back of the right hand to the slave's right cheek. But to strike a peer, someone your equal, you would have used your fist and hit directly, usually the left cheek.

Jesus directs us to turn the other cheek—the left cheek—forcing the hitter to strike you as an equal. By showing yourself as an equal with your abuser, the directive to turn the left cheek meshes with everything else that Jesus tells us to do to enter the realm of God's heaven on earth. We are to show love for our neighbors even when they abuse us.[11]

Protecting all of God's children is our calling.[12]

Hillary Rodham Clinton
February 24, 2017

---

* ★ *

Grant us, Lord God, a vision of your world as your love would have it: where all your children are treated as equals; a world where the weak are protected and none go hungry or poor, where the riches of creation are shared, where different races and cultures live in harmony and mutual respect, where peace is built with justice, and justice is guided by love. Give us the inspiration and courage to build it; through Jesus Christ, our Lord. Amen.

LOSE IT ALL
Matthew 5:40

The crowd listening to Jesus included poor farmers and peasants as well as wealthy landowners who often tried to grab more and more land through lawsuits before the scribes and the Pharisees. This teaching is about the Levitical law, about word of honor, about the role of the coat and cloak, but also about greed, distrust, and manipulation by the wealthy.

Without a cloak, any peasant would be without a covering at night, and it gets cold in the desert. Getting chilled night after night weakens the body, making one susceptible to disease. In such a weakened or ill state, peasants couldn't tend to their crops so their harvests would fail. Then landlords could claim the land back for nonpayment of debt, leaving such peasants without any means of support. Jesus is talking to people who were being sued and taken to court literally for the shirts off their backs.

This is often interpreted as an example of the non-resistance Jesus advocated. Other theologians see this verse as linked to Jesus's renunciation of property and the material. If one has faith in God, one should not be afraid to lose all material possessions. The people who do lose their possessions, even if it leads to great hardships on earth, will be properly rewarded by God.

By the debtors stripping naked for all to see, the brutality of the creditors and the entire system is exposed for what it's really doing and how it's treating people. After the unmasking, there's a chance for renewal and repentance.[13]

------ ★ ★ ★ ------

Lord, there are no things in this life that mean more to me than you do. Give me the strength to let go of anything that sets precedent over you. Amen.

* *

FROM: Rev. Bill Shillady
SENT: August 30, 2015
TO: H

Dear Hillary,
I hear you are on vacation. I hope you are getting some well-deserved rest and spending time with Charlotte. Blessings!
Rev. Bill

* *

TWO MASTERS
Matthew 6:19-21

One of the great teachings from the Sermon on the Mount came to mind today. It is a reminder of what is really important. So, with some fear about my retirement account, I will focus today on the treasures in heaven.

Matthew Henry's commentary on this passage states:

> Christ counsels to make our best things the joys and glories of the other world, those things not seen which are eternal, and to place our happiness in them. There are treasures in heaven. It is our wisdom to give all diligence to make our title to eternal life sure through Jesus Christ, and to look on all things here below, as not worthy to be compared with it, and to be content with nothing short of it. It is happiness above and beyond the changes and chances of time, an inheritance incorruptible. . . . God requires the whole heart, and will not share it with the world. When two masters oppose each other, no man can serve both. He who holds to the world and loves it, must despise God; he who loves God, must give up the friendship of the world.[14]

So, we must focus on our heart faith: loving God with all of it, loving ourselves, and loving our neighbor—all neighbors, not just the ones we like.

Lord, we live in disturbing days, across this nation and across this world. Loving God, meet us in this fear and help us keep our eyes on you. Amen.

BE GRACIOUS TO OTHERS
Matthew 5:21-26

My father used to say, "Never let the sun go down on your anger." I always thought my father was a great philosopher with that statement. The phrase is simple and wise, but it comes from the Bible. Paul writes to the church at Ephesus, "In your anger do not sin: Do not let the sun go down while you are still angry, and do not give the devil a foothold" (Ephesians 4:26-27 NIV).

In today's Scripture, Jesus is not saying that the emotion of anger is sinful. He is saying that anger is dangerous and to be careful. We are to seek to resolve the conflicts that anger us as soon as possible and to do so with love.

If we give in to angry feelings and justify them, the next thing we want to do is to act on them and get even. Jesus's point here is don't seek revenge; God is gracious with you, so you be gracious to others. Treat conflict and injustice as opportunities for God to bring out the best in you, not the worst, so that you grow in your capacity to share the kindness of Christ.

------ ★ ★ ★ ------

Lord, help me to let go of my anger and admit that I can be wrong. Forgive me as I forgive those who have hurt me. Amen.

GO THE SECOND MILE
Matthew 5:41

In Jesus's day, a Roman soldier could conscript a Jew to carry his pack for one mile. This meant the individual had to stop what he was doing and follow the command of the foreign invader—the enemy. But it was an unacceptable practice to make someone carry the pack beyond one mile. It was a punishable offense for the soldier.

Jesus directs his followers to offer to go a second mile. Once again, he is calling us to act and think differently about serving God in the world. Our attitudes are to change so the grace of God can be known. We are to be non-violent revolutionaries who change the world by changing ourselves first.

This second-mile teaching is about being kind to others even when they've made us perform hard tasks. Jesus reveals a way to fight evil without being transformed into the very evil we fight.

As my mother used to say, "Billy, I know he has been mean to you, but why don't you 'kill him with kindness' rather than try to get even?" Living a Christ-centered, non-violent life calls us to go the second mile with grace and love.

------ ★ ★ ★ ------

Lord, help us to develop second-mile eyes and hearts so that we can aid those who need kindness with Christ-centered attention. Help us to find ways to change the world through the kingdom-living teachings of the Sermon on the Mount. Amen.

Hillary Clinton sent a message Monday to close out the year, thanking her supporters and urging them to push "onward."

"Before this year ends, I want to thank you again for your support of our campaign. While we didn't achieve the outcome we sought, I'm proud of the vision and values we fought for and the nearly 66 million people who voted for them," she wrote.[15]

The Hill
December 26, 2016

THROUGH YOUR ACTIONS
Hebrews 11:1-3

The assumption that being a Christian is solely a matter of a personal relationship with God that makes no observable difference in a person's behavior is a uniquely American religious idea. It is deeply rooted in our tradition of individualism but has no basis in Scripture or Christian tradition.

When Jesus called people to be his disciples, he was inviting them into a process of training by which their lives would be reoriented around his vision of the kingdom of God becoming a reality in this world through their actions.

If you read the Sermon on the Mount and the parables, you will see Jesus calls his followers to a radically different way of living—to observable behaviors, not merely to intellectual agreement with a set of beliefs or to an inner spirituality that does not transform external behaviors.

If you read letters from the apostle Paul, as a teacher and theologian, he proclaims the content of the Christian faith, and as a faithful pastor, he questions, challenges, guides, and models for his people the specific behaviors that bear witness to faith in Christ.

Being Christians is about the way the Spirit of God is at work to shape our lives around observable behaviors that demonstrate a growing consistency with the way, words, and will of God revealed in Jesus Christ.

The question for each follower of Christ is, *Would anyone know that I am a Christian by the way I live?*

James A. Harnish

Lord, I want to be a Christian in my heart, in my heart,
Lord, I want to be a Christian in my heart, in my heart,
In my heart, in my heart,
Lord, I want to be a Christian in my heart, in my heart,
Lord, I want to be more loving in my heart, in my heart,
Lord, I want to be more loving in my heart, in my heart,
In my heart, in my heart,
Lord, I want to be more loving in my heart, in my heart,

BE SIGNIFICANT
Matthew 5:13-16

S alt—once one of the world's most sought after commodities. The demand for it led to the creation of major world trade routes. Medically, it's helped to preserve and sustain life. Its tiny grains are utterly essential in their uses. Salt is not significant in itself (nobody eats just salt), yet it is indispensable in what it enables to happen.

So I think you have to keep asking yourself, if you are a person of faith, "What is expected of me? Am I actually acting the way that I should?"[16]

Hillary Rodham Clinton
January 25, 2016

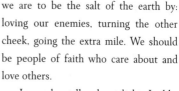

The Sermon on the Mount tells us we are to be the salt of the earth by: loving our enemies, turning the other cheek, going the extra mile. We should be people of faith who care about and love others.

Jesus also talks about light. It, like salt, is mainly of significance in that it enables us to see something else. When Jesus tells his disciples, "you are the light of the world," he is saying, "Without you, the world cannot see what it is." The world has no means of seeing that it is self-centered and violent. The light of Christ reflected in us can show the value of love and grace over the world's values of self-centeredness and manipulation.

God who created salt and light, may we be both salt and light in all that we do to reveal the truth of your love to the world. Help us brighten the day and be salty characters who make a difference.

LEAST OF THESE
Matthew 5:14-16

In the Sermon on the Mount, Jesus distilled the essence of his message to his disciples and to us. The crucial point that Jesus was making is that God has given to every human being a spark of God's light to share with the world.

That day, Jesus gathered his followers on a hillside overlooking the Sea of Galilee. Imagine Jesus in front of this large group of people sitting on the ground. Many were fishermen with their wives and children. They came with the smell of fish, having worn the same clothes for weeks. Some were farmers who worked the soil, walking behind donkeys pulling a plow, and they had dirt under their fingernails. Others were shepherds who spent nights out on the hillsides protecting their sheep and goats. They smelled like their livestock.

There was at least one former tax collector, looked down on because of his profession. There were women who had hard lives—bearing children, working in the fields, cooking meals, or even selling themselves to survive.

It is to this group of very unlikely people that Jesus says, "You are the light of the world." You are the ones, he tells them, who will bring light into the darkness of the world.

Pharisees, on the edge of the group and dressed in elaborate robes, must have scoffed when they heard Jesus call this rag-tag group "the light of the world." But Jesus saw the spark of God in every one of them and fanned that spark into flame. Those ordinary folk became those who glowed with the light of God, and God transformed the world through them.

------- ⋆ ★ ⋆ -------

Jesus, thank you for the reminder today to be "the light of the world." Help us to let your light shine to others. Amen.

YOUR CONNECTION
Matthew 6:9-15

Martin Luther once said, "Just as the business of the tailor is making clothes and the business of the cobbler is making shoes, so the business of the Christian is praying."

The Lord's Prayer is a wonderful formula for the appropriate way to approach God. Luke and Matthew differ slightly on the Lord's Prayer. In Matthew, as Jesus teaches this prayer to his disciples, he tells them to begin with "Our Father."

The opening word, *our*, shows that we have a connection not only to God but to others. This prayer unites all Christians, expressing a profound unity within the fellowship of all believers, regardless of denomination.

Yet few people seem to understand how Jesus really intended his prayer to be used. Instead of being an invitation to a rich, deepening life of prayer, to a new relationship within a family of faith, for many, it's just words.

I invite you to use the Lord's Prayer to approach God with intimate familiarity yet appropriate reverence and awe. This prayer is the invitation Jesus gives us when he teaches us to pray, not to just say prayers, but to enter into a deepening, rich life of authentic and intimate communication with God.

------ ★ ★ ★ ------

Lord, we thank you that we can come before you, knowing that you hear our words, but also our thoughts. We give thanks today for the many blessings you give us. Our cup overflows with your goodness. Amen.

★ ★

FROM: Rev. Bill Shillady
SENT: March 7, 2016
TO: H

Dear Hillary,
Wonderful answer on prayer last night. Have you ever thought about becoming a United Methodist pastor?
So your answer on prayer provides me with some fodder for a mini sermonette today.
Blessings,
Rev. Bill

★ ★

LILIES IN THE FIELD
Matthew 6:25-34

The best cure for worry is to observe a worried man." This traditional Chinese saying is designed to scare us away from worry. But Jesus has the opposite approach. He asks us to look at the lilies of the field and the birds of the air. They don't worry.

Of course, this is easier said than done. We still worry, regret the past, and strive to prepare for the future without really living in the present.

How much time do we spend worrying about things that never happen? In a world where people don't even know the people next door or down the street, is it important what others think about our possessions?

The answer lies first in striving for the kingdom of God—a kingdom not of power, not of might, but a kingdom of mercy, justice, and grace. It is a kingdom of forgiveness and love, where prejudice is unheard of, and pride and conceit do not exist. It is a kingdom where greed is absent.

Today's struggle is enough for today, and living well is what God wants us all to do.

------ ★ ★ ★ ------

Great God, I thank you for today, for this moment. The present is a gift from you that each of us must use to its very best. Help us to seek your kingdom right now, in the present, and to fill our lives with kingdom thoughts so that every tomorrow is better because today has been lived well; in Jesus's name. Amen.

Nearly 40 percent of Americans between the ages of 25 and 60 will experience a year in poverty at some point. The best way to help families lift themselves out of poverty is to make it easier to find good-paying jobs.[17]
The New York Times
September 21, 2016

NOUN AND A VERB
Romans 12:9-21

In today's Scripture we see that genuine love is not just being nice to people. Genuine love has a moral orientation toward the good. To love someone is not simply to cater to specific likes and dislikes of that person. It is rather to act toward them in ways that help them experience more of God's goodness.

I love the image that President Jimmy Carter shares in his book, *Living Faith*. He wrote about the ways his Christian faith guided and sustained him, as well as the ways it challenged and encouraged him to seek a closer relationship with God and his fellow human beings.

President Carter also made a statement that seems to capture the essence of this text. He wrote, "To me faith is not only a noun, but also a verb." He went on to say, "In Christian tradition, the concept of faith has two interrelated meanings, both implying fidelity: confidence in God and action based on firm belief."[18]

You're doing what is the most important thing to do, it's continuing to study and learn what the scripture says and what it means.[19]

Hillary Rodham Clinton
January 14, 2016

The challenge is to hold the two dimensions of faith in proper balance— being and doing. Paul wrote this letter to remind the church and its followers (us) that it is not enough to "be right" but to "do right." And one can turn it around and say it is not enough to do right but to be right.

------ ★ ★ ★ ------

Lord, may your true love abound in my heart and my soul. May that love inspire me to live my faith each moment, day by day, as I seek to care for the least, the last, and the lost. Amen.

MODEL PRAYER
Matthew 6:7-13

Saint Thérèse of Lisieux (1873–1897) was a Roman Catholic French Carmelite nun, widely venerated in modern times. She is popularly known as "The Little Flower of Jesus" or simply "The Little Flower."

Thérèse has been a highly influential model of sanctity for Catholics and for others because of the "simplicity and practicality of her approach to the spiritual life." Her approach to prayer is an example of that simplicity. Thérèse felt an early call to religious life, and overcoming various obstacles, in 1888, at the early age of 15, she became a nun and joined two of her elder sisters in the cloistered Carmelite community of Lisieux, Normandy. After nine years as a Carmelite, she died at the age of 24 of tuberculosis. Her writings and thoughts project us into the presence of God.

> I do not have the courage to force myself to search out beautiful prayers in books. There are so many of them it really gives me a headache! And each prayer is more beautiful than the others. I cannot recite them all and not knowing which to choose, I do like children who do not know how to read, I say very simply to God what I wish to say, without composing beautiful sentences, and He always understands me. For me, prayer is an aspiration of the heart, it is a simple glance directed to heaven, it is a cry of gratitude and love in the midst of trial as well as joy; finally, it is something great, supernatural, which expands my soul and unites me to Jesus.[20]

May you find the aspiration of the heart this day that can expand your soul!

------- ★ ✦ -------

God of Mercy, often we do not know what to pray. Here our spoken prayer, and hear our heart prayers. Amen.

HOW HAPPY ARE YOU?

Matthew 5:11

Most Sundays I set my DVR to record Oprah's "Super Soul Sunday" series. A recent episode was titled "How Happy Are You?" and featured author Robert Holden, who founded the Happiness Project.

The audience members were invited to rate their happiness on a scale of 1 to 7 on the following statements:

1. In most ways my life is close to ideal.
2. The conditions of my life are excellent.
3. I am satisfied with my life.
4. So far, I've gotten the important things I want in life.

A higher score suggested the person was extremely happy, while a lower score—well, the person probably needs help.

I'm not sure how much stock to put into such exercises; however, it did get me thinking about the state of my own happiness these days. For me, the key lies in my faith and overall outlook on life. It also helps to have an attitude of gratitude even for small things. Come to think of it, there are probably no "small things," as every act of goodness received or given in love goes a long way in making life better.

Lord of all joy, help me to find happiness in your way and to recognize how blessed I truly am. Amen.

Rev. Dr. Cathy S. Gilliard

A FRAGILE LIFE
Matthew 7:7-8

F all arrives in just a few days. The ancient Hebrew lunar calendar begins its new year in the fall. Rosh Hashanah, the end of summer, and the reopening of schools signal a time of new beginnings.

We feel the pulse of this more deeply than ever, as we also now remember the anniversary of 9/11. Our remembering 9/11 requires us to renew our faith and start out fresh. We try to take a deeper look at what we are doing with our lives and at what is most precious, as we witness yet again how fragile life is and how swiftly material things can be swept away.

Renewal is important for all of us. The arrival of fall helps us set new goals. May we cross the thresholds of the season, asking God for strength, seeking new beginnings, and being persistent in our quests to find God's doors for our journeys.

------ ⋆ ★ ⋆ ------

Jesus, we know that you said that whatever we ask for, through faith, we shall receive and if we seek, we will surely find, and if we knock, doors will swing open. Lord, we seek you with all our hearts. We need to be wrapped in your loving arms and warm presence. We know we will receive the things we ask for: love, joy, peace, and purpose for our lives. Give us strength to pray even when we feel like surrendering. Amen.

It was 26 August 2003, almost two years since 9/11, and the sickening plume of smoke that hung over Ground Zero in lower Manhattan had long since dissipated. But steam was rising from the steps of city hall, three blocks away, where Hillary Clinton was venting her rage at the Bush administration for having lied to the American people.

"I don't think any of us expected that our government would knowingly deceive us about something as sacred as the air we breathe," she said, her voice tightening in anger. "The air that our children breathe in schools, that our valiant first responders were facing on the pile."[21]

The Guardian
September 9, 2016

CALL TO LOVE

THE GLORIOUS LIGHT
Matthew 2:2-12

The little stable at Bethlehem was the place where the love of God broke through to humankind. The wise men out of the East followed the star and discovered the place of breaking in, where the mystery of love lay in the helplessness of a human baby, wrapped in swaddling clothes in the feeding trough of an animal. They discovered the place where God's love had come down.

That is the most important thing for each of us: to discover in our own time and hour the place where God's love has broken through and then to follow the star that has risen for us—and to remain true to the light that has fallen into our hearts.

------- ★ ★ ★ -------

Lord, allow us to always be the light for you. Help us break through to those who do not know you so that they may find the peace that passes all understanding. Amen.

Rev. Frederick A. Davie

THE HEART OF GOD
1 John 4:7-12

Today, please allow me to share a devotion from Henri Nouwen:

> Love unites all, whether created or uncreated. The heart of God, the heart of all creation, and our own hearts become one in love. That's what all the great mystics have been trying to tell us through the ages. Benedict, Francis, Hildegard of Bingen, Hadewijch of Brabant, Meister Eckhart, Teresa of Avila, John of the Cross, Dag Hammarskjöld, Thomas Merton, and many others, all in their own ways and their own languages, have witnessed to the unifying power of the divine love. All of them, however, spoke with a knowledge that came to them not through intellectual arguments but through contemplative prayer. The Spirit of Jesus allowed them to see the heart of God, the heart of the universe, and their own hearts as one. It is in the heart of God that we can come to the full realization of the unity of all that is, created and uncreated.[1]

God of Love, our world needs love now more than ever. We need unity against evil and hatred, racism and bigotry, extremism and apathy. Help us love one another, even when the other is the most difficult person to love. Help us see your Heart once again. Amen.

BLESSINGS ON THIS SABBATH!

Matthew 22:37-39

Jesus tells his followers that the first and greatest commandment is to love God completely with all our hearts, souls, and minds. Then he says the second is like the first—we are to love our neighbors as we love ourselves. In the first commandment, Jesus describes our spiritual core muscles as the heart, the soul, and the mind. These muscles enable us to love God wholly and completely. So how do we effectively exercise these spiritual core muscles?

Just as our physical muscles are connected—giving us the ability to stand, walk, sit, and run—our hearts, souls, and minds are also interrelated, and must be exercised if we are to be spiritually healthy. We have to focus on strengthening and growing all three muscles that make up our spiritual core, or we risk growing stagnant, complacent, and lukewarm, which would hinder all God wants to do in and through us.

Strengthening our spiritual core is not just for our benefit; it's also for the benefit of others. We must focus on developing each of these muscles, because only then will we have the capacity not only to love God but also to see ourselves as God sees us. This is crucial, because if we are commanded to love our neighbors as we love ourselves, then it is imperative that we actually love, value, and esteem ourselves.

We need to do more to support the families of service members and veterans. Service and sacrifice on the home front rarely gets the respect and recognition they deserve. The last decade has added only more strain on our military families, with long wars abroad and a tough economy here at home....Our veterans have done so much for us; now we need to do more for them.[2]

Hillary Rodham Clinton
November 11, 2015

---- ★ ⭐ ★ ----

Lord, being strong in our love for you and others will help us to truly conquer the challenges in our lives. Lord, once we are strong and vibrant from the core outward, then we can truly love those who are difficult to love. Amen.

CHOOSING LOVE

Romans 8:31-39

There's a woman in Burundi whose name is Maggy Barankitse. In the civil war between the Tutsi and Hutu tribes that tore apart Burundi, she was tied to a chair and made to watch as seventy-two family members and friends were brutally killed by a militia.

Somehow, miraculously, she was allowed to live. And afterward because of her love for God, she gathered 30 children, most of them orphaned, and said, "We're going to rebuild this community." They named it Maison Shalom, which means "house of peace." They built a school and a health clinic, and they started farming to feed the people.

When she was asked about transforming a place of brokenness into a place of extraordinary hope,

here's what she said: "Love made me an inventor." She has always been clear that her mission was not simply to build an orphanage or to help children. Rather it is to help raise them in God's love and to create a new generation that will break the cycle of violence in her country.[3]

She chose love. Nothing could separate her from the love of Jesus Christ no matter the atrocities she experienced.

We are above all things loved—that is what Jesus tells us over and over again. God loves us no matter what is happening all around us, and absolutely nothing can separate us from that love—not our own actions or the action of forces or institutions around us. Know you are loved by God and that there is absolutely nothing you can do about it.

------ ★ ★ ★ ------

God of all love and compassion, bless us with the courage and strength to face each day, any situation, and any trial with the grace that comes from being your child because you love us in spite of ourselves. Give us an everlasting hope; through Jesus and in his name. Amen.

LOVE ONE ANOTHER

John 13:34

Today is Maundy Thursday, and on this day, Jesus celebrated Passover with his disciples for the last time and gave them a new commandment: to love one another as he loved them. *Mandatum* is Latin for "commandment." The word has been shortened to *Maundy* (not Monday) to the confusion of Christians ever since.

We're not only baffled by the strange name but also by the surprisingly simple instruction. Mostly it's because we're confused about love. So often when we say "I love you," it means "I love the way you make me feel" or "I love what you do for me" or "I love the idea of being in love." See the problem? It's more about "me" than it is about "you."

Jesus didn't have that problem. Jesus's disciples did almost nothing for him, other than inspire headaches and heartbreak, yet he loved them. They demonstrated a remarkable capacity for missing the point and Jesus loved them. They grumbled, complained, and quarreled among themselves and he loved them. They fell asleep in the hour of his greatest need and Jesus loved them. The disciples betrayed, denied, and abandoned Jesus and he loved them anyway.

That should come as exceptionally good news since we are no different. And Jesus loves us. That should fill our hearts with a heavenly host of hallelujahs!

Now it's your turn to love like that, starting with yourself and concluding with that person who drives you bonkers. Love them anyway.

------ ⋆ ★ ⋆ ------

Lord Jesus, thank you for loving me anyway. By your grace, may I return the favor to everyone I meet today. Help me love those who are most difficult to love. Amen.

RESPOND WITH LOVE
1 Corinthians 13:1-13

Often we speak about love as if it is a feeling. But if we wait for a feeling of love before loving, we may never learn to love well. The feeling of love is beautiful and life-giving, but our loving cannot be based in that feeling. To love is to think, speak, and act according to the spiritual knowledge that we are infinitely loved by God and called to make that love visible in this world.

Mostly we know what the loving thing to do is. When we "do" love, even if others are not able to respond with love, we will discover that our feelings catch up with our acts.[4]

As the King James version states: "And now abideth faith, hope, charity, these three; but the greatest of these is charity."

------- ★ ★ ★ -------

Lord,

Because love does not delight in evil but rejoices with the truth . . . Help me stand up for what is right and good. May I defend the defenseless, and help the helpless. Show me how I can make a difference.

Because love always protects and always trusts . . . Help me to be a refuge for those around me. When the world outside is harsh and cold, may my heart be a place of acceptance and warmth.

Finally, because love always perseveres . . . Help my heart continually beat with love for You and others. Thank you for showing us what the word love really means. Amen.[5]

★ ★

FROM: Rev. Bill Shillady
SENT: June 17, 2015
TO: H

Dear Hillary,
I know that this is a very familiar passage to you based on your conversation with Rev. Frederick Donnie Hunt, pastor of First Calvary Baptist Church at the Main Street Bakery in Columbia, South Carolina, a few weeks ago. However, I was inspired to send it to you today based on these words on "Doing Love" from Henri Nouwen.
   May we do as Jesus did, love unconditionally.
Sincerely,
Rev. Bill Shillady

★ ★

JESUS WEEPS
Luke 19:41-44

In this nineteenth chapter of Luke, we read and watch as Jesus spends his last week on earth. After his triumphal entry into Jerusalem, we have this emotional scene as Jesus weeps over the city. I feel the same way as we weep over Brussels.

Terrorists have once again struck at the heart of Europe, but their campaign of hate and fear will not succeed. The people of Brussels, of Europe, and of the world will not be intimidated by these vicious killers. Today Americans stand in solidarity with our European allies. Our thoughts and prayers are with the families of those killed and wounded, and all the people of Belgium. These terrorists seek to undermine the democratic values that are the foundation of our alliance and our way of life, but they will never succeed. Today's attacks will only strengthen our resolve to stand together as allies and defeat terrorism and radical jihadism around the world.[6]

Hillary Rodham Clinton
March 22, 2016

Jesus teaches us what to do when tragedy strikes: accept our mortality, bless outcasts, seek healing, and keep doing what we are called to do—love God, love our neighbors, and love ourselves. As Jesus wept over Jerusalem, we weep for Brussels.

Today's bombings confront us with a stark reality: in the face of global terrorism, we are all vulnerable. Yet, like Jesus, we must continue on the path of peace and love.

What can we do to survive the darkness of terror? Along with so many, I will arise with hope and peace tomorrow morning. I will keep that journey towards Jerusalem and the darkness of the cross of Calvary that will grow deeper, and then, I will await the dawn of Easter morn and the promise of light and life that it means. I will lift up prayers on behalf of those who suffer because of the terrorists. I will keep my eyes focused on the ultimate goal, for the hope of new life, for the salvation poured out on the earth through Jesus's ultimate sacrifice for us.

------ ★ ★ ★ ------

Lord, we wake up to the news of another terrorist attack and lives changed forever. These places of attack seem so far away. But we are joined in our fear, our horror, our grief, our powerlessness. And yet, in this week, we remember that though there is evil in this world, there is a Love that is greater. There is a Love that overcomes even death. For those who suffer, send your comfort. For those who fear, send your presence. For those who grieve, send your healing love. Amen.

TWO BECOME ONE
1 Corinthians 13:13

I celebrate with you the ruling by the Supreme Court on marriage equality. I can think of no passage greater for this day than 1 Corinthians 13, the most read passage in all the weddings I've performed over the years. We are reminded that love is the priority.

Marriage in the Bible is a completely different institution from our modern image of a just, loving, equal romantic partnership. The guidance we find in Scripture for relating to our spouses comes from passages that refer to the ways in which we ought to relate to everyone, like 1 Corinthians 13.

God speaks to me constantly in Scripture about the inclusive and loving community. The theme of much of the New Testament is to be the beloved community, where those who are rejected by society find welcome (Mark 2:13-16; Luke 14:15-24), where people from diverse backgrounds become sisters and brothers to each other (Galatians 3:28), where the society's conventions of family and household are broken in favor of new kinds of unconventional and intentional families (Matthew 12:46-50).

------ ★ ★ ★ ------

Gracious God of love and grace, we give you thanks for a movement forward in our nation, where all people—regardless of their sexual orientation—can find an opportunity legally to share their love in marriage. For all those who have found love in their lives, we pray that they have the courage and the ability to make a life-long covenant. Amen.

"No longer may this liberty be denied," Justice Anthony M. Kennedy wrote for the majority in the historic decision. "No union is more profound than marriage, for it embodies the highest ideals of love, fidelity, devotion, sacrifice and family. In forming a marital union, two people become something greater than once they were."[7]

The New York Times
June 26, 2015

GIVE THANKS TO THE LORD
Psalm 105:1

When I was a kid I thought it the strangest thing that my mother invited the neighborhood drunk into our house on a Christmas morning. My mother was a relatively quiet, dedicated Presbyterian who loved people and rarely judged them. Only later in life did I come to understand that it was her faith that led her to show God's mercy to the village drunk.

My mother was crippled by arthritis and left by her husband to raise four children on her own. Even in the midst of her worry, she would often give thanks to God that life wasn't as bad for her and for us as it was for so many others. She would challenge us to be grateful for what we had, especially when we groused about not being able to afford the material comforts our friends enjoyed.

Little did we know then, but in each of her children, in each of us, she was instilling what has become an unshakeable faith in God's love and mercy. She proclaimed God's mercy by what she did as much as what she said. This crippled, little black Presbyterian woman made known the deeds, the goodness, of God. She encouraged us to do the same.

In this age of condemnation, belittlement, inter-ethnic rivalries, where mercy and love are seen as weaknesses, let us hear afresh the words of the Psalmist to give thanks, to call upon the Lord, to remember God's mercy, and to make known God's goodness to all the people.

God of infinite mercy, we thank you for your love and compassion that is often expressed in unexpected ways. May we always look to you on this journey, calling upon your name, giving thanks for all you do for us, and proclaiming your goodness and mercy from the streets outside the doors of our homes to the highways and byways of this world. We do it all in your name and for your sake. Amen.

Rev. Frederick A. Davie

THE FACE OF CHRIST
1 John 4:8

I t was probably St. Francis who first brought attention to the humanity of Jesus. Paintings of Jesus prior to the life of St. Francis largely emphasized Jesus's divinity, as they still do in most Eastern icons. Before the thirteenth century, Christmas was no big deal. The emphasis was entirely on the high holy days of Easter, as it seems it should be. But for Francis, for God to become a human being among the poor, born in a stable among the animals, meant that it's good to be a human being, that flesh is good, and that the world is good in its most simple and humble forms.

In Jesus, God was given a face and a heart. God became someone we could love. While God can be described as a moral force, as consciousness, the truth is, we don't (or can't) fall in love with abstractions. So God became a person that we could hear, see with our eyes, look at, and touch with our hands (see 1 John 1:1).

The brilliant Jewish philosopher Emmanuel Levinas says the only thing that really converts people is "the face of the other." When the face of the other, especially the suffering face, is received and empathized with, it leads to transformation of our whole being. It creates a moral demand on our hearts that is far more compelling than the Ten Commandments.

------- ★ ★ -------

Jesus, you taught us what God is like through your words, actions, and very being, making it clear that God is love. We give you all glory and praise for showing us what love is. Amen.

THE PIGPEN OF LIFE
Luke 15:20b

As the story goes in the parable of the prodigal son, the youngest one sets out and goes as far as he can to get away from his father and familiar surroundings. It doesn't take long for him to waste all his money and possessions and land in the pigpen of a foreigner feeding the swine.

What is the "pigpen of life"? I'm thinking that it is a pretty horrible place and represents our greatest fears. My guess is that most people will find themselves there in one way or another at some point in time. It doesn't matter whether we put ourselves there or someone puts us there; or circumstances of life just happen and one day we awaken to a new reality beyond anything we could imagine. It is a solitary place of ultimate vulnerability where our sensibilities about ourselves are diminished.

I love this passage because the father has been waiting and watching for his son. I know that surely must be what God does. God waits and watches for us. Nothing seems to catch God off guard, not even our rebellious ways. God sees our restless side, our need to go our own way, and does not hold it against us. No word spoken, no action taken, no thought is so horrible or sinister that God turns away from us completely.

------ ★ ------

How wonderful to have a God who watches and waits and who welcomes us back with gracious, healing love! Amen.

Rev. Dr. Cathy S. Gilliard

FROM: Rev. Bill Shillady
SENT: March 11, 2016
TO: H

Good Friday! I am still at Duke. I hope you had a good day in Durham yesterday. I will be lifting you in prayer today as you travel to Nancy Reagan's funeral. Blessings. Bill

★

FROM: H
SENT: March 11, 2016
TO: Rev. Bill Shillady

Thanks for this sermon on the Prodigal Son, one of my all-time favorites. She captures the essence of the message. I should go to hear her sometime (whenever that could be!).

WHO WE ARE

Matthew 3:13-17

Humankind's desperate yet conflicted need to understand Jesus as human and yet divine has been going on for a long, long time. No matter how we try to hang words around this idea, underneath all that striving is a fundamental and shared truth: we long for a God who knows what it's like to be us. We live with this longing in our hearts because human life is hard, and we struggle to know who we really are and who we're really meant to be.

Many of us begin to engage our faith not out of obligation but out of desperation, searching for God in the middle of life's questions and pain. Jesus did, too.

Despite all the challenges we face, I remain convinced that YES, the future is female.[8]

Hillary Rodham Clinton
February 7, 2017

We go out into the world and hear conflicting messages, names others assign us, and we find it hard to remember who we really are. Jesus did, too. What a relief.

Out in this cold, hard world we hear messages every single day, messages telling us who we are: not good enough, a failure, disappointing, unhappy, incapable of loving or being loved. But those voices are not calling us by our real names.

If we could ever pause, even for just a moment, to notice the divine spark of life and love placed in each one of us by our Creator, we might begin to discover who we are—who we really are. And once we know who we really are, we're bound to do audacious things.

Creator God, when the world sends me messages that make me doubt your goodness and grace, remind me of your love. Amen.

Rev. Dr. Amy K. Butler

SHALOM
Psalm 85:8-13

Today is the annual meeting of the United Methodist City Society, when member churches come together to celebrate and conduct our annual business. It is being held in Brooklyn at the New Jerusalem United Methodist Church, where I worked with two small congregations to merge them together, selling one of the properties to invest in the other church building, and to provide funds for ministry and mission.

The two small congregations are stronger as one and are growing with an enthusiastic pastor. They are ministering to their community, especially to teens and youth in trouble with the criminal justice system. The church partners with the police and other community to groups to help their neighborhood through a food pantry, Christmas gift giving, school backpacks, gang prevention workshops, health fairs, and so on.

The theme of our meeting is Shalom (Peace) for the City as we raise the major issues of racial justice and cultural diversity. To truly achieve peace in our city, we must have restorative justice, "justice and peace must kiss," as the New Jerusalem congregation does every day.

In Hebrew Scriptures, terms such as *shalom* (peace, wholeness, harmony, the community functioning in healthy ways) and *chesed* (steadfast love, faithfulness, compassion) are linked together with *mispat* (justice). When human community works right, it is characterized by peace, compassion, and justice, which leads to restoration, not retribution.

———— ★ ★ ★ ————

Shalom for our city begins with each of us restoring "our harmony" with Christ, and then seeking out our neighbor, our friend, and even our enemy to find the path to true peace. May the peace of Christ that surpasses our human understanding be with us all today and every day. Amen.

GOD OF PERFECTION
Hebrews 12:1-3

We live in a world in which there is little grace shown to those who mess up. We demand an effortless perfection from each other, from ourselves, and from the communities in which we invest our lives. But perfection is as much a fiction as it is an ongoing journey—never quite realized during this lifetime.

In our moments of weakness, disappointment, and falling short, we are called to look to Jesus as the one who lifts us out of our shame and offers us perhaps the most profound freedom of all—the freedom from having to be right all of the time.

Our turn towards Christ requires the relinquishing of pride that keeps us from true joy and peace available to all who are ready to admit their own shortcomings and utter the simple yet profound words, "I was wrong." When we offer this sacred confession

to God, we find ourselves enveloped in a thick blanket of grace, assuring us of our beloved status as children of God. When we cease succumbing to the temptation to always have to be right about everything, we feel our souls lifted up, no longer weighted down by a standard impossible to keep.

------- ★ ★ -------

May God's love—so free and refreshing—give us the strength to not lose heart and to admit our own shortcomings that we might find new and abundant lives. Amen.

Rev. Kevin K. Wright

STRENGTH TO LOVE
John 13:34

There were two people in a church I served who were about as different as any two people could be. I started to pay attention to their interactions with each other—the way they spoke and listened (or not), the body language the minute one or the other walked into a room or sat down at a table, how they almost always disagreed regardless of the issue at hand. It was clear that their shared history had been long and sordid.

One day, I overheard one of them blurt out through clenched teeth and a flood of tears, "I can't stand you! You get on my very last nerve!" It was jolting to hear her speak her truth out loud, and I reckoned that she had finally reached the end of her rope.

Sometimes, the reasons are obvious: the other person's point of view, attitude, personality, philosophy of life, way they engage the world, work or relationships are so very different from our own. Sometimes, the dislike is as subtle and as simple as the way people dress or wear their hair. We are most apt to say: "He (or she) doesn't like *me*," but more often than not, if left unattended, the dislike becomes mutual.

Perhaps we begin by acknowledging how difficult it is sometimes to love certain people and then take one step at a time, one day at a time, to see what might be possible through God's grace. It is good, hard work and no small task. It is the hard work of journeying with Jesus. It is also the path to freedom—to being truly free.

Lord, I am not always as loving as I like to think I am. Sometimes, it seems nearly impossible and yet, all things are possible with you. Give me the strength to love without condition. Amen.

Rev. Dr. Cathy S. Gilliard

PRINCE OF PEACE
Matthew 5:9-10; Quran 49:13

We awake this morning to the tragic news of lives lost once again to terrorist attacks. As we mourn the lives lost in the attacks on Beirut and Paris, let us consider these words about peace from two Scriptures.

"O mankind, indeed We have created you from male and female and made you peoples and tribes that you may know one another. Indeed, the most noble of you in the sight of [God] is the most righteous of you" (Quran 49:13).

"Blessed are the peacemakers, for they shall be called sons of God. Blessed are those who are persecuted for righteousness' sake, for theirs is the kingdom of heaven" (Matthew 5:9-10 ESV).

Both the Gospel of Matthew and Quran call us to work for righteousness. Both say righteousness is the work of peace and understanding. Both warn that we will be despised and persecuted for the work. We are told this will not be easy—but it will be blessed.

When the United States was hit on 9/11, our allies treated that attack against one as an attack against all. Now, it's our turn to stand in solidarity with France and all of our friends. We cherish the same values. We face the same adversaries. We must share the same determination.

After a major terrorist attack, every society faces a choice between fear and resolve. The world's great democracies can't sacrifice our values or turn our backs on those in need. Therefore, we must choose resolve. And we must lead the world to meet this threat.[9]

Hillary Rodham Clinton
November 19, 2015

------ ★ ★ ★ ------

God of peace, whose Son came to be our Prince of Peace, we can hardly find words to describe our anguish. Lord, we are called to pray for the perpetrators, for our enemies. Even though we are aghast at this brutal act of violence, as followers of the crucified and risen Lord Jesus Christ, we do not satisfy our desires with revenge.

We pledge our allegiance to the risen Christ, in whom you reconciled the world. He is our hope and peace for a broken world. Amen.

BROKEN BARRIERS
1 John 4:7-21

Let's face it, most of us inevitably will run across at least one person or two in our lives for whom loving seems nearly impossible. We will wonder, *How in the world can I possibly love this person in a godly way?*

This passage from 1 John is perhaps the foundation view of Christian faith. Love is the underpinning from which all our actions are to be judged. Abiding in God means to dwell in God's arms, to live in such a way that love is the driving force behind all we do and think and pray. There are so many definitions of love: love of friend, love of child, love of adventure, love of spouse, love of God. We lump them all together in one word. Yet, it remains an experience of who we are and what we do.

Love can conquer all. We see the presence of the divine in others only as we love them. To have fear, hatred, and animosity toward others dehumanizes them and shows that we have lost the essence of God's love in our thinking and in our actions.

———— ★ ★ ★ ————

God, you invite all people into your presence. In our diversity, unify us in your message of love in which you redeem your creation. Break into our hearts today. Create in us perfect love so that we may glorify your name as we love others, especially those who are most difficult to love! Amen.

This morning, Clinton spoke to the congregation of Mount Zion Fellowship Church in Highland Hills, Ohio. During her speech, she spoke about the importance of equality in the country and vowed to fight to break down barriers so everyone can take advantage of everything America has to offer. Clinton shared her favorite quote from former first lady Eleanor Roosevelt: "A woman is like a tea bag. You don't know how strong she is until she gets into hot water."[10]

Hillary Clinton Speeches
March 13, 2016

HEART OF THE LOVING GOD
John 20:15

Tears are the currency of love. A mother sobs next to her sick son late at night, pouring out prayers to God for healing and protection. A father's eyes well up as he longs for the sound of his daughter's laugh a continent away. Mary Magdalene weeps, waiting at the door of an empty tomb, each teardrop that falls from her eyes swimming in an ocean of love for the Rabbi who changed her life.

Our world does not always look kindly upon tears. Warped views of masculinity and femininity govern how we view those who cry, and that judgment is rarely charitable. And yet, Jesus's words to Mary in the garden convey no such judgment.

"Why are you crying? Who is it you are looking for?" (John 20:15 NIV). Jesus asks Mary, inquiring as to the reason for her distress.

There is no judgment, no condemnation, and no disdain. Jesus simply wants to know the reason behind Mary's tears. What is bothering you? What is troubling your heart?

As children of God, we can take comfort in knowing that in our moments of crying and heartache, our God seeks to minister to us in our distress. Our tears are not an inconvenience or an annoyance to our Creator; our tears are prayers flowing straight into the heart of our loving God.

———— ★ ————

Lord, let the tears come when they may. Christ will surely hear us and come to our aid. Amen.

Rev. Kevin K. Wright

THE GIFT OF LOVE
1 Corinthians 13:1-13

Paul's writings in 1 Corinthians 13 is a beloved passage. Paul had previously been speaking to the Corinthian church about spiritual gifts—prophecy, tongues, healing, miracles—saying they should not be the cause of divisiveness in the community of faith. Certain folks felt their gifts made them superior. No, Paul tells them, all Christians are parts of Christ's body, and each part in its own way is as necessary as every other.

The highest gift of all is *agape* love, he says. Without love, then faith, serving the poor, even martyrdom are mere illusions and even the greatest wisdom doesn't amount to a hill of beans. But *agape* love is the covenant love of God for humans as evidenced in Christ, and it is meant to be given to others.

Henri Nouwen said, "Our humanity comes to its fullest bloom in giving. We become beautiful people when we give whatever we can give: a smile, a handshake, a kiss, an embrace, a word of love, a present, a part of our life . . . all of our life."[11]

------ ★ ★ ★ ------

God, our prayer is but a response to your ceaseless outpouring of love. When we awake to a new day, you are already there to greet us. When sleepless nights and anxious moments toss us, you are there to comfort us. When difficult choices confuse us, you are there to guide us. You love us before we even turn to you. You are here now and gratitude swells within us.

We place before you our lives—fragmented, busy, tired. Teach us to love as you have loved us. Help us to give that love to others. We place before you our friends and family—the hurting, the sorrowing, the struggling child, the frustrated parent, the fragile relationship. We place before you our world—broken and fighting, yearning for justice and freedom, suffering drought and greed. Teach us the path of peace, the ways of sharing, the brighter vision, the greater gift.

Ever-present and ever-loving God, be with us this day and astound us with grace. Amen.

KINDNESS OVERCOMES DARKNESS

Romans 12:14-21

It's not easy to repay evil with kindness, but I know how much lighter my burden can be when compassion and forgiveness are my guiding lights. Compassionate words and actions are food for the soul, and our kindness may mean the world to someone living in a dark place.

Here are Henri Nouwen's comments on these Scripture passages:

These words cut to the heart of the spiritual life. They make it clear what it means to choose life, not death, to choose blessings not curses. But what is asked of us here goes against the grain of our human nature. We will only be able to act according to Paul's words by knowing with our whole beings that what we are asked to do for others is what God has done for us.[12]

Bullying has always been around but it seems to have gotten somehow easier and more widespread because of social media and the Internet. People can say something about somebody without having to look them in the eye or see them walk by, and so I think we all need to be aware of the pain and the anguish that bullying can cause.[13]

Hillary Rodham Clinton
December 23, 2015

What has God done for us? What has God done for me? For starters, God sent Jesus to show me the way I must live, the truth of life, and to give me abundant life. He loves me and our world so much that he was willing to go to the cross. God was willing to sacrifice his child for the world. God gave God's all . . . can we do less?

Loving others completely whether they love or like me is not to be questioned. If others talk about me or hurt me, I cannot take revenge. Love must come to the forefront. And through that love, I pray others will find God.

------- ★ ★ ★ -------

Lord, thank you for loving the world so much that you sent Jesus to show us the way, the truth, and the life. Through him, we find your Spirit in our hearts so that we can be your compassionate, loving presence and overcome evil with good. Amen.

SOURCE OF LOVE
John 15:12

The "Love Commands" come in three different forms in the New Testament. The first is "Love your neighbor as yourself" (Matthew 19:19).

The second is found in John 15:12, where Jesus says, "Love each other just as I have loved you." Jesus goes on to say that he is laying down his life for the disciples and expects them to do the same for each other. The Greek word for "love" in this passage is *agape* and can be translated as "self-giving" or "self-sacrificing" love.

The third command can be found in the Sermon on the Mount. Jesus says, "You have heard that it was said, You must love your neighbor and hate your enemy. But I say to you, love your enemies and pray for those who harass you" (Matthew 5:43-44).

Loving our enemies is really challenging. This is especially true if our enemy has harmed us or seeks to harm those we love. However, this love of enemies illustrates the uniqueness of Christian love: it doesn't depend on our feelings—it depends on our willingness to *act* in love. Another way of saying this is that Christian love is "blind."

Who are the persons you find it challenging to love? How can you act in their best interests?

—— ★ ★ ——

Source of Love, you call us to love as you have loved us. Sometimes this is so very difficult. Give us the strength and resolve to love all of your children. Amen.

Robert Martin Walker

"I am talking about love and kindness," Clinton told Buzzfeed reporter Ruby Cramer in January 2016 when Cramer asked her what motivated her to run for office. This was just before the long and grueling primary season began, and Clinton became mired in a battle for the endorsement that extended all the way to the convention itself. "What she wants to talk about hinges on a simple question of how we can, as humans, better treat one another," Cramer reported. "To Hillary Clinton, this is politics. She's talking, literally, about 'going back and actually living by the Golden Rule.'"[14]

Cosmopolitan
July 28, 2016

UNITED BY LOVE

1 John 4

Love unites all, whether created or uncreated. The heart of God, the heart of all creation, and our own hearts become one in love. That's what all the great mystics have been trying to tell us through the ages. Benedict, Francis, Hildegard of Bingen, Hadewijch of Brabant, Meister Eckhart, Teresa of Avila, John of the Cross, Dag Hammarskjöld, Thomas Merton, and many others, all in their own ways and their own languages, have witnessed to the unifying power of the divine love. All of them, however, spoke with a knowledge that came to them not through intellectual arguments but through contemplative prayer. The Spirit of Jesus allowed them to see the heart of God, the heart of the universe, and their own hearts as one. It is in the heart of God that we can come to the full realization of the unity of all that is, created and uncreated.[15]

------ ★ ★ ★ ------

God of love, our world needs love now more than ever. We need unity against evil and hatred, racism and bigotry, extremism and apathy. Help us to love one another, even when the other is the most difficult person to love. Help us to see your heart once again. Amen.

* *

FROM: Rev. Bill Shillady
SENT: September 23, 2016
TO: H

Dear Hillary,
I am praying fervently for you to be true to yourself as a child of God. With all the shootings in these last few days, and the raising of the ugliness of racism in our society, I am praying for both Black Lives Matter and Blue Lives Matter. I have to go back to an old devotional for such a time as this. Our favorite spiritual writer, Henri Nouwen, helps us to move in another direction with our feelings.

Sincerely,
Rev. Bill Shillady

* *

COMMUNITY
Ruth 1:15-19

Naomi and Ruth did what they were supposed to do, yet the system still failed them. The land turned inhospitable for them. They had nothing but each other. They used the combined wisdom and tenacity of old and young, of Moabite and Judean, of mother and daughter. Because they went together, they survived, even thrived, and built something new that eventually changed the world.

When we, like Naomi and Ruth, find ourselves in a land turned inhospitable, in a system that wants to push us out, what hope do we have? Where do we find the courage and wisdom to try a new way?

God builds us for community. God gives us ears to listen to other voices, eyes to see the talents of others, feet to walk the path together, hands to serve one another, backs to bear each others' burdens, tears and laughter to share life, ferocity to fight for what is right for another's well-being.

Today, give God thanks for those who have traveled with you along treacherous and barren roads and the communities of which you've been a part throughout your life.

------- ★ ★ ★ -------

Ever-present God of love, I offer to you my gratitude to the saints who have been my companions through life. In your wisdom, you gave us each other to travel rough roads hand in hand, even to carry each other at times. Today and each day, make me mindful of those for whom I am called to be a traveling companion and of those who are emerging to travel with me. Most of all, guide me in the way of Jesus, revealing the path that he would travel and giving me the courage to embark on the journey each day. Amen.

Rev. Laura Patterson

GOD'S BLESSED FAMILY
Genesis 33:1-4

The Jacob and Esau story is about twins who, throughout their lives, battle each other for their father's blessing. But eventually they are reconciled. In overcoming their rivalry, they find peace.

Jacob and Esau is a modern story. It reminds us of the extremes to which jealous brothers or sisters can go in hurting each other to find recognition and their niche in life.

We spend our lives in competition with others. We want the best seat. Just look at the disciples fighting over who will sit on Jesus's right hand and left hand when he comes into his kingdom.

We need God's help and insight more than ever. Perhaps, if we felt the security of our love in God, we would not need to put others down, to compete, to measure ourselves by others' achievements, to seek our good over everyone else's.

This Jacob and Esau story is about forgiveness and hope. We can live with older brothers and sisters, and we can live with other members of the holy, cherished human family as sisters and brothers, all. Catholics and Protestants, Jews and Palestinians, blacks and whites and Hispanics and Asians—we all can see ourselves as part of God's blessed family and work together for the good of society.

------- ★ ★ -------

May God forgive us for the ways in which we betray God's love with jealousy, pride, and greed. May God deliver us from demonizing those who are different, from the path of revenge and "eye for an eye" mentality, and to the road of reconciliation and renewal. Amen.

BEAUTY FROM ASHES

1 John 4:7-12

Born in Spain in 1542, John of the Cross joined the Carmelite order after experiencing poverty and suffering from his work caring for hospital patients with incurable diseases and madness. Out of this poverty and suffering, John learned to search for beauty and happiness not in the world, but in God.

We are already great but we can be greater. And we will be greater. I love our country and I believe in the American people, and I know there is nothing we can't do when we make up our minds. Throughout our history, generations of Americans have risen together to meet the tests of their time. They defended democracy. They built the greatest middle class the world has ever known. They marched for civil rights and voting rights, for workers' rights and union rights, for LGBT rights, rights for people with disabilities. And now, now we've got to come together and we have to prove we can meet the challenges of our time.[16]

Hillary Rodham Clinton
November 7, 2016

After John joined the order, Saint Teresa of Avila asked him to help with her reform movement. John supported her belief that the order should return to its life of prayer. But many Carmelites felt threatened by this reform and kidnapped him. He was locked in a cell with only one tiny window. He was beaten three times a week, yet in that unbearable dark, cold, and desolation, his love and faith were like fire and light. After nine months, John escaped. He devoted his life to sharing and explaining his experience of God's love.

John's life of poverty and persecution could have produced a bitter cynic. Instead it gave birth to a compassionate mystic who lived by the belief that "Where there is no love, put love—and you will find love."

His words and writings have a profound understanding of how love works and how true love changes us at a deep level.

------ ★ ★ ★ ------

A Prayer of St. John of the Cross:

Let your divinity shine on my intellect by giving it divine knowledge, and on my will by imparting to it the divine love, and on my memory with the divine possession of glory. Let us so act that by means of this loving activity we may attain the vision of ourselves in your beauty in eternal life. Amen.

COMPLETE DEVOTION
Revelation 19:6-8

I could write entire volumes about the Book of Revelation. However, I simply write about this wonderful image of the church as the bride of Christ. It's about devotion. God wants relationships with us that are heartfelt, spontaneous, vibrant, alive, and reciprocal. It's little wonder that Jesus said the greatest commandment is to love the Lord our God first and foremost with all our hearts. Jesus longs for authentic relationship with his bride, not simply religious obligations or empty rituals. God is not at all impressed by empty words or heartless platitudes.

I believe when we embrace this purpose wholeheartedly, it is easier to stay passionate about our faith, our spiritual disciplines, and every other aspect of our spiritual walk. All of our actions and activities flow from a relationship of love with God rather than from an obligation to fulfill our Christian duty.

When God is first and foremost in our hearts, souls, and minds, all our other relationships will fall into place.

Prayers this day for the church and for those who were killed in South Carolina.

———— ✦ ★ ✦ ————

Into my heart, into my heart,
Come into my heart, Lord Jesus. Amen.

Harry D. Clarke

"On that terrible evening and every day since, Americans across the country have joined our hearts with the people of Charleston and South Carolina. Millions of Americans are still walking with them—in grief, solidarity and determination."[17]

Hillary Clinton Speeches
June 17, 2016

TRANSFORMING POWER OF LOVE
1 John 4:18

L ove is a word that we talk about as if it is something easy and cheap. We talk about how we love our favorite soft drink or our favorite baseball team. When we hear the word *love*, we don't necessarily think about the sacrificial, incarnational, Christ-like sort of love that the letter-writer John is talking about.

The letters were probably composed sometime in the early second century. The author is addressing an internal conflict in the Christian community, as some of the members of the church had departed from the traditional beliefs about Jesus. These folks didn't believe that Jesus was fully human, and so the community had become divided over who had the truth and who didn't. As a result, they weren't practicing love or respect toward one another.

John, who had come under attack, was not feeling very loved by this community, but he did not respond to their rejection with angry words or vengeance. In the face of hatred and anger and division, John preached to this church about the transforming power of LOVE.

John says that we are called to pour out love on others. Because of God's love, we are called to live in transformational ways. We are not called to love just the people who are easy to love. We are called to love the people we would prefer to hate, ignore, or reject. We have never seen God, but if we love one another, that love is a clear sign of God's love in us and our love for God. For if we can't love our brothers and sisters whom we have seen, how can we love God whom we have not seen?

Lord, help us push past our disappointment and anger and continue to love one another, even in the face of differences. We can love one another as God has loved us. Amen.

ENDURES ALL THINGS
1 Corinthians 13:7

In his famous hymn to love, the apostle Paul says that love "endures all things." Endurance is not one of the stimulating spiritual virtues. Endurance usually involves a lot of work, and not always pleasant work at that.

By comparison, faith can sound glamorous. After all, you can make a leap of faith. Why, it's almost dashing! Love sounds grand. There are songs written about love. In fact, it's hard to find a song that isn't written about love. Courage sounds gallant. Hope sounds, well, hopeful.

But endurance? It doesn't sound glamorous or grand or gallant. It just sounds like a lot of work.

I have come to think of endurance as love with its work clothes on. When Paul says, "Love bears all things . . . endures all things," it is another way of saying that love endures because it puts up with a lot.

I was speaking with someone who reflected the challenge of continually having to relate with someone who is difficult. "It's an endurance test. That's what it's like to be her friend." *What a great description*, I thought. After all, "to endure" means to put up with a lot and to make it last. Two different meanings, and yet, when love has its work clothes on, the two are inextricably related. Love endures all things.

-------- ★ ★ ★ --------

Thank you, God, that there are people whose love for me endures. In some ways, they put up with a lot, but that also means that their love for me is lasting. What a gift. Amen.

THE GREATEST COMMANDMENT
Matthew 22:34-40

I was very proud and thankful for your answer at the town hall meeting in Knoxville, Iowa, when you were asked a question about your faith. Your witness to the Greatest Commandment was right on target.

My study of the Bible, my many conversations with people of faith, has led me to believe the most important commandment is to love the Lord with all your might and to love your neighbor as yourself.... There is so much more in the Bible about taking care of the poor, visiting the prisoners, taking in the stranger, creating opportunities for others to be lifted up, to find faith themselves. And I think there are many different ways of exercising your faith.[19]

Hillary Rodham Clinton
January 25, 2016

For us, as disciples of Jesus, sanctifying grace leads us to become more and more the persons whose every thought, word, and deed is motivated by love of God and love of neighbor.

Jesus's commandments, particularly in Matthew, are more than a ceremonial, moral adherence or an otherworldly rule of life—they are love of God and neighbor. Jesus commanded love for one's neighbor, a combination of compassion with justice in a life of faithful works that help one's neighbor.

A few years ago, Pope Benedict said: "Love is the only thing that can fill hearts and bring people together. God is love. When we forget God, we lose hope and become unable to love others. That is why it is so necessary to testify to God's presence so that others can experience it."[18]

----- ★ ★ ★ -----

God of love and grace, we praise you with our whole hearts. Today, we ask for the strength to love you with all our hearts, souls, minds, and strength and, with that love as our source, to love our neighbors as we love ourselves. Amen.

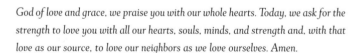

THE LOVE OF A FATHER
Matthew 4:21-22

My father was a gentle, kind person. I experienced his anger only once or twice as a child—at times when I had done something terribly wrong.

To this day, his words continue to ring in my conscience: He would say, "Remember who you are!" For my Dad, Christian faith and being a child of God were the most important moral guides for life. His constant words, "Remember who you are!" helped me to be a responsible human being.

James and John were disciples of our Christ, but they were forever the sons of their father and their mother. The lives they chose when

they dropped the nets and followed Christ took them far from their families and the shores of Galilee. But deep down inside, they were still the sons of Zebedee.

Our parents have helped to mold us into the children of God we have become. For that, we are grateful. God—like a loving father—calls to us to come home and nourish the relationships that bind us one to another.

------- ★ ★ ★ -------

Faithful God, we thank you for our earthly fathers and father figures in our lives, especially those who have given us a glimpse of your love and essence. Bless, encourage, and strengthen all fathers this day that they may hear your voice and walk closely with you. Give them love, wisdom, and guidance as they care for their families and those within their influence. Lord, where fathers are missing or lacking in the lives of children, bring healing and restoration. We pray especially for those today who need to know your love and care. Amen.

DIVINE LOVE
1 John 4:18

Today I want to talk about divine love. Hope-filled love. Love that casts out all fear. Agape love. Agape is love that is of and from God, whose very nature is God's spirit itself. "God is love."

Agape love is a determined act of the will. It is God's love put into action among human beings. It is you and Senator Tim Kaine making conscious decisions to put the welfare of others above your own. This is a hard thing to do. This type of love does not come easily or naturally to us.

If we are to love as God loves, that love must flow through us from its true source. We are vessels through which God's love is poured into the world. Because it is God's love and not our own that has been poured into us, we are able to follow the command of Jesus who said to love one another.

Jim Wallis wrote an excellent reflection of the atmosphere of fear and hate that has been generated by your opponent. Here is a part of Wallis's thoughts: "But the polarized and divisive political culture we are seeing is also about something else. The anger, fear, and visceral reactions of many Americans . . . come from deep feelings about how 'their' country is changing. Anger and fear leads to blame and even hatred for those they hold responsible."

Wallis goes on to ask: "For those of us who are people of faith and moral conscience, how do we lift up love over hate in this angry election season? . . . And if our faith traditions also tell us that a society is ultimately judged by how it treats its most vulnerable people, how do we best vote for the concerns of the most vulnerable in this coming election?"

------ ⋆ ⭐ ⋆ ------

God of love and grace, help us accept each other with the agape love you have given us. Amen.

GOD'S NATURE AND OURS

1 Thessalonians 5:13b-22

God's nature is love, mercy, and justice. An illustration of God's tenacious, loving nature is found in this parable shared by the Christian theologian and spiritual writer, Henri Nouwen:

> One morning, after he had finished his meditation, the old man opened his eyes and saw a scorpion floating helplessly in the water. As the scorpion was washed closer to the tree, the old man quickly stretched himself out on one of the long roots that branched out into the river and reached out to rescue the drowning creature. As soon as he touched it, the scorpion stung him. Instinctively the man withdrew his hand. A minute later, after he had regained his balance, he stretched himself out again on the roots to save the scorpion. This time the scorpion stung him so badly with its poisonous tail that his hand became swollen and bloody and his face contorted with pain.
>
> At that moment, a passerby saw the old man stretched out on the roots struggling with the scorpion and shouted: "Hey, stupid old man, what's wrong with you? Only a fool would risk his life for the sake of an ugly, evil creature. Don't you know you could kill yourself trying to save that ungrateful scorpion?"
>
> The old man turned his head. Looking into the stranger's eyes he said calmly, "My friend, just because it is the scorpion's nature to sting, that does not change my nature to save."[20]

If God's nature is to love and save, what is our response? Paul spells it out for us: "Be cheerful no matter what; pray all the time; thank God no matter what happens. This is the way God wants you who belong to Christ Jesus to live" (1 Thessalonians 5:16-18 MSG).

------ ★ ★ ------

God of love and grace, we praise you with our whole heart. Thank you for loving us unconditionally. O Lord, you have asked us to continue to love one another, for love comes from you. Forgive me for those times when I have not loved you or others in the same depth of the Love that Jesus shared and taught. Amen.

Rev. Matthew T. Curry

REMEMBER

MILESTONES
Luke 8:4-15

On April 7, we passed a milestone. It has been one year since we began this daily routine—365 devotionals.

Writing these devotionals (or gathering from my fellow clergy who love and support you) has become an ingrained part of my daily routine. Though some mornings I may be dry like the desert in the message for the day, I hope you are as blessed as I am by these words each morning.

It is my sacred honor and privilege to be a pastoral friend to you and Chelsea, Marc, Bill, and Charlotte.

Rev. Bill

------- ★ -------

"I get a scripture lesson every morning from a minister that I have a really close personal relationship with. And, you know, it just gets me grounded. He gets up really early to send it to me. So, you know, there it is in my inbox at 5:00 a.m. I have friends who are rabbis who send me notes, give me readings that are going to be discussed in services. So I really appreciate all that incoming. And the final thing I would say, because again, it's not anything I've ever talked about this much publicly, everybody knows I have lived a very public life for the last 25 or so years. And so I've had to be in public dealing with some very difficult issues and personal issues, political, public issues. And I read a treatment of the prodigal son parable by the Jesuit Henri Nouwen, who I think is a magnificent writer of spiritual and theological concerns. And I read that parable and there was a line in it that became just a lifeline for me. And it basically is practice the discipline of gratitude. So regardless of how hard the days are, how difficult the decisions are, be grateful."[1]

CNN
February 4, 2016

OLD AND NEW: NEW YEAR'S DAY
1 Corinthians 5:17

January gets its name from the two-headed Roman god Janus, who looked back to the past and forward to the future—also known to the Romans as the god of gates and doors. He is commonly depicted with two faces, one regarding what is behind and the other looking toward what lies ahead. Thus, Janus is representative of contemplation on the happenings of an old year while looking forward to the new.

In his role as the guardian of exits and entrances, Janus was also believed to represent beginnings—as one must emerge through a door or gate to enter into a new place. Therefore, the Romans considered Janus an obvious choice for the first month of their year.

I know that, from my experience as a lifelong Methodist, how important my own church community has been to me.[2]

Hillary Rodham Clinton
July 11, 2016

My favorite saying is, "God doesn't close one door without opening another." But I add, "It can be hell in the hallway." So, as we close the door on this year, with a fresh beginning in the new year, I hope many doors will open for you.

I pray as we enter this new year, we do so as a new creation in Christ Jesus our Lord. May he be the door through which we pass to a life centered in discipleship and love.

———— ★ ★ ————

God, as I celebrate the past and what I have accomplished, I do so with an eye toward the future filled with hope in Christ Jesus. For he is one standing with me no matter the journey between doors closing and opening in my life. Amen.

OUR FUTURE: EPIPHANY DAY
Matthew 2:1-12; 18:5 ESV

Today is Epiphany. An epiphany is an unusual manifestation or perception of the essential nature or meaning of something huge. Often it is an encounter with God. The magi announced to the leaders that there had been an epiphany in the birth of a king—Jesus Christ. And the leaders were scared. A new kingdom was coming, a new ruler. It meant losing all they had . . . because of a child.

Matthew says these events happened during King Herod's reign of tyranny and death. He ordered two of his sons and one of his wives to be murdered. Herod was filled with fear of losing his power and was especially afraid of the power of children.

Children represent the future. Herod feared the future and wanted to deny the ending of the old order. Why fear the power of children? Taking a child in his arms, Jesus said, "Whoever receives one such child in my name receives me." We should not fear children, because they are our portal to the kingdom of God.

I heard a story of a couple's three-year-old daughter asking several times if she might be left alone with her new baby brother. Afraid of the possibility of sibling rivalry, the parents consulted a therapist. After being assured that the child wasn't aggressive and was well adjusted, the therapist indicated it was okay. She did, however, suggest that the parents might want to listen to the baby monitor, so they could go to the baby in a second if there were any difficulty. The parents left their three-year-old daughter with the new baby and went to their own bedroom to listen.

They heard the child close the door to the nursery and walk over to the crib. After a moment, they heard her say, "Baby, baby, tell me about God. I think I'm forgetting."

Let's not fear our children; let's ask them to tell us about God.

------ ★ ★ ------

Wise and wonderful giver, for all your gifts we are grateful. Provide us with a star for our own lives, so that we are always pointed in your direction, finding the treasure of the Christ child with each step we take. Amen.

FROM DUST AND ASH: THE SEASON OF LENT
Genesis 2:7; 1 Peter 1:23

I am invested in what the world thinks of me. Before company comes, I race around vacuuming, cleaning, and committing telltale dust bunnies to the hand vac.

When we're trying to convince the world that we're clean, it's not only our homes that are on display. With family, friends, and co-workers, we strive to show others our pristine lives, lives that are whole, upright, and free of dirt and dust bunnies. But with the imposition of ashes, the secrets of dust are dragged into public light.

Ash Wednesday is one of the only public displays of repentance in our faith that is visible for others to see. We can leave our singing, our prayers, and our tithing behind in the house of God, but the ashes placed on our foreheads that begin the Lenten season are front and center.

The truth about dust and dirt mixed with the waters of baptism is the good news of Christ: "You have been born again, not of perishable seed but of imperishable, through the living and abiding word of God." We are made whole in Christ.

------- ⋆ ★ ⋆ -------

Righteous God, we recognize our humanity this day. Grant us the courage to accept the healing you offer and to turn again toward the sunrise of your reign so that we may walk with you in the promise of peace you have willed for all the children of the earth. May we be made whole and holy once again in Christ Jesus. Amen.

During her three decades in politics, Clinton has been quite willing to talk about how her work has been inspired by her Methodist faith. She traces some of her political positions, particularly concerning children and the poor, directly to Christ's commandment to care for "the least of these."[3]

CNN Politics
October 31, 2016

A TIME OF REFLECTION: SEASON OF LENT
Philippians 3:17–4:1

L ent has never been one of my favorite times of the year. A somber and sober season, Lent is when we are to concentrate on death and sin. It is often perceived as a time of self-sacrifice, discipline, and repentance.

It is during the season of Lent that we often learn lessons of life, because it is the rare time for us to consider the darker aspects of our faith. It is the season when we face our mortality and when we concentrate on our personal needs for repentance. Confronted by the cross, we take stock of our spiritual selves and ask the tough questions about the states of our souls.

Lent also asks us to look at the world and declare the time of repentance has come. Death is too evident in our world. As Jesus was crucified for crimes he did not commit, countless people die each day, simply because they are in the wrong place at the wrong time or born in the wrong place at the incorrect time. War, violence, famine, and disease take a terrible toll in our so-far-from-perfect world.

Lent puts this right up in our faces and forces us to examine it. May we find a way to make Lent a powerful, meaningful time of spiritual renewal as we learn lessons of life from the death of Jesus Christ.

God of the covenant, in the glory of the cross, your Son embraced the power of death and broke its hold over your people. In this time of repentance, draw all people to yourself so that we who confess Jesus as Lord may put aside the deeds of death and accept the life of your kingdom. Amen.

TRIUMPH: GOOD FRIDAY

Luke 23:46

G ood Friday is a reminder that life is filled with difficulty and, yes, even tragedy. It is a reminder to us that darkness, death, and unexpected tragedies reign only temporarily. The cross of Good Friday is a signpost that points to Easter morning and God's glorious power—that death cannot conquer life.

Easter morning is a reminder that God's power of love and life always triumphs. Holy Week tells us that we can turn our tragedies into triumphs. Now, I am not going to say that you can turn every blow in life into an asset, but your *spirit* can become a *new asset*. Your personality can change. With God's triumphal power, we can change.

------ ★ ★ ★ ------

Merciful God, as we remember how your son, Jesus, bore our sins in his body on the cross, how seven times he spoke, seven words of love, we ask you to bless our remembrance this day. Almighty God, we ask you to help us to understand the mystery of your love and make us into a people who are ever more worthy of it. Amen.

FROM: Rev. Bill Shillady
SENT: March 25, 2016
TO: H

Dear Hillary,
It is hard to keep up with your schedule. I don't know how you do it! If you are going to be in Chappaqua for Easter, I wanted to extend the invitation again, to you and Bill, Chelsea and Marc and Charlotte, for Easter Brunch. It would be great to catch up if you are going to be at church.
Blessings this day,
Rev. Bill

★ ★ ★

FROM: H
SENT: March 25, 2016
TO: Rev. Bill Shillady

We would be delighted to join you for lunch after church, accompanied by Chelsea, Marc, and Charlotte. Looking forward to seeing you at church. Happy Easter!

EMPTY TOMB: EASTER

John 20:1-18

The Rev. Bill James had a ministerial career that spanned over seventy years, and his legacy continues to be felt by churches and pastors. He wrote more than fifty hymns, but "Easter People" is the most well-known. My favorite line is, "Every day to us is Easter, with its resurrection song."

I have always cherished the Methodist church . . . because it gave us the great gift of personal salvation but also the obligation of social gospel.[4]

Hillary Rodham Clinton
September 13, 2015

What does it mean to be "Easter People"? How do we make sure that Easter is not just an isolated day on our calendars but a life-changing message of life and hope? Are you living your life as a pre-Easter person or a post-Easter person?

Jesus's death and resurrection is the central theme of our faith. We find in this narrative God's love for us, God's affirmation of creation, and God's preference for life. In the story of the empty tomb, we find that our own deaths and fears have been vanquished. Does your life reflect this awesome truth?

Lord, help us to be faithful in making an impact in the lives of those around us and around the world. Help us to remember we are Easter people living for you. Amen.

Rev. Matthew T. Curry

CHRIST IN US: ST. PATRICK'S DAY
Ephesians 6:10-17

The part of my Irish heritage has me wearing a wee bit of green this day. So what better way for us to begin than with a prayer attributed to St. Patrick? It captures the wonderful spirit that made him Ireland's patron saint and one of the Church's most beloved missionaries.

St. Patrick faced his share of resistance, but he was so successful in preaching the gospel and organizing the church in Ireland that he is largely credited with converting the Irish to Christianity. His emblems are the snakes, which legend claims he drove out of Ireland, and the shamrock. He used an image of the three leaves of the clover, being part of one shamrock, to explain the three distinct entities of the Father, the Son, and the Holy Spirit that constitute one God.

-------- ⋆ ★ ⋆ --------

Prayer for the Faithful

May Christ be with us!
May Christ be before us!
May Christ be in us,
Christ be over all!
May Thy Salvation, Lord,
Always be ours,
This day, O Lord, and evermore. Amen.[5]

Saint Patrick

Speaking from a Methodist pulpit on Sunday morning, Hillary Clinton explained her political vision with a reference to the classic Sunday school song "This Little Light of Mine."

"Too many people," she said, "want to let their light shine, but they can't get out from under that bushel basket. It is way too heavy to lift alone. And that's where the village comes in."[6]

The Washington Post
September 13, 2015

HOLY HUMOR SUNDAY
Genesis 18:1-15

Humor is found in the Bible from beginning to end. There are puns and images that provoke smiles—and we come to see that God has a sense of humor too. Ecclesiastes 3 reminds us there is a time to laugh and a time to mourn.

Many American churches are resurrecting an old Easter custom begun by the Greeks in the early centuries of Christianity. For centuries in Eastern Orthodox, Catholic, and Protestant countries, "Bright Sunday" (the Sunday after Easter), was observed with parties and picnics to celebrate Jesus's resurrection. Churchgoers and pastors played practical jokes on each other, drenched each other with water, told jokes, sang, and danced.

So we laugh. The laughter of knowing that God is good. The laughter of the wonder of all that God does. It's the humor of those who know love. It is not nasty or cruel. It focuses on our failings, our pride, our silly habits. Laughter is healing and transformative.

------ ★ ------

Loving God, glorious Creator, we praise and thank you and rejoice on this day that you have made. We remember not only the cross but the joy of Resurrection; we sing of Christ's victory and praise you for bringing life out of death, hope out of despair, and laughter out of sorrow—and granting them to us as part of our wonderful inheritance in him. Amen.

Democratic nominee Hillary Clinton gently skewered GOP opponent Donald Trump on Thursday—and joked about herself—in a tense joint appearance at a charity dinner that has been a lighthearted presidential campaign tradition. Both candidates spoke at the Alfred E. Smith Memorial Foundation Dinner. . . . A few of Clinton's zingers:

* "Getting through these three debates with Donald has to count as a miracle."

* "Trump looks at the Statue of Liberty and sees a 4."

* "Donald is as healthy as a horse. You know, the one Vladimir Putin rides around on."[7]

Huffington Post
October 20, 2016

EARTH DAY, APRIL 23

Psalm 8; 118:24 ESV

Psalm 8 is the perfect song for Earth Day and for every day because "this is the day the LORD has made; let us rejoice and be glad in it!" (Psalm 118:24 ESV).

Here is a prayer for Earth Day:

------ ★ ★ ★ ------

Gracious God, we have taken the fruits of your creation and your merciful abundance for granted. We have uttered prayers of thanksgiving without true gratitude. Meanwhile, we have failed to recognize the suffering of the earth and of the people who have produced our

food. Ignoring our connection to the rest of your creation as we reap nourishment, we move further away from your vision of your beloved community. Forgive us, O God, and transform us. Open us to the richness and beauty in connecting our food—at the Lord's Table and at our individual tables—to all the natural and human resources who have brought it to those tables. Help us to give thanks not just for our food but for all those who have brought it before us and to work that they might also flourish. Encourage us to work for justice for all, so that all may give you thanks and be fed. In Christ Jesus we pray, Amen.[8]

CHAMPION OF STRENGTH: MOTHER'S DAY
Matthew 12:46-50

Celebrate this day as a daughter, mother, grandmother, friend, or as a champion of all women. I am honored to share a Mother's Day prayer with you.

------ ★ ★ ★ ------

Lord of love, we give you thanks and praise for the women who have nurtured us through the years. We thank you for the women who struggled to give us birth. Thank you for the women who showed us the meaning of forgiveness and faithfulness. Thank you for the women who expected great things of us and helped us discover our strengths. Thank you for the women who showed us how to pray and trust in Jesus Christ. Thank you for the teachers whose motherly attention helped us grow into productive, capable adults. Whether our experience of being mothered came through one woman or many, we owe our thanks and praise to you, O God, for the blessings we received through them. Today, we honor all those women. Help us be gentle towards those who have done the best they knew how, even if sometimes we wish they had done differently. Help all of us to become bearers of your redeeming love to all your children on this globe. Challenge us, O God, to be like the mother hen who gathers her chicks under her wings, to be representatives of your safety, and to care for those around us. Amen.

Of all the titles she's held, "Grandma" is the one that Hillary Clinton cherishes most. . . . "I arrange my campaign schedule around seeing Charlotte, and one of the highlights of the last year was getting the chance to have Chelsea, Marc and Charlotte on the campaign trail with me."[9]

Us Weekly
April 22, 2016

TRINITY SUNDAY
Deuteronomy 6:4-7

This ancient confession from Deuteronomy is foundational to all that we say about God—God is one in unity, being, power, holiness, and purpose. As we celebrate Trinity Sunday, we remember these ancient words from Deuteronomy. And we need to remember that the Father, Son, and Holy Spirit are three portions of the one reality we call God.

Yet this one God has revealed himself to us in three different ways: Creator, Redeemer, and Sustainer. God is not an unchanging monad, but a lively dancing, creating, and relating being—becoming, constantly growing, evolving, and inspiring.

The Trinity reminds me that God is for and with us; God is in and among us. One God—the God revealed to us in Jesus Christ. The God who, in the waters of baptism, makes us disciples. The God who meets us at table to give us the bread of heaven and the cup of salvation. The God who is in us and among us, using us to share the good news of love and purpose for all the world.

Be grateful for being a human being, being part of the universe. Be grateful for your limitations. Know that you have to reach out to have more people with you, to support you, to advise you, listen to your critics, answer the questions. But at the end, be grateful. Practice the discipline of gratitude.[10]

Hillary Rodham Clinton
February 3, 2016

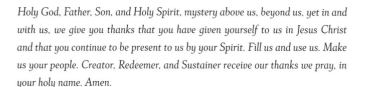

------ ★ ★ ★ ------

Holy God, Father, Son, and Holy Spirit, mystery above us, beyond us, yet in and with us, we give you thanks that you have given yourself to us in Jesus Christ and that you continue to be present to us by your Spirit. Fill us and use us. Make us your people. Creator, Redeemer, and Sustainer receive our thanks we pray, in your holy name. Amen.

A TIME TO REMEMBER: MEMORIAL DAY
Psalm 31

Memorial Day began after the Civil War as an effort toward reconciliation between the families of veterans in the North and the South. May 30 was carefully chosen because it was not the anniversary of a specific battle and would be a neutral date for both sides.

But human beings hold onto their wounds, and reconciliation takes time, grace, and mercy. So initially, as the holiday spread, it was an occasion for both sides to give angry speeches about the wartime atrocities inflicted by the other side and to expound the righteousness of their own.

Eventually, Memorial Day became a time to remember all veterans and the lives of all family and friends while visiting their graves.

Recognition and remembrance can bring healing, as we ponder what we have done in war and as we move toward a peace that is truly everlasting.

Lord, on this day, we pray for comfort for all those who have lost a loved one to the ravages of war. May the peace of Christ, which passes all human understanding, knit together this weary and war-torn world. May God's mercy pour out over all God's children, with no respect for the borders of nation states, which—from the perspective of eternity—are awfully temporary. Amen.

NEW CREATION: PENTECOST

2 Corinthians 5:16-17

Pentecost is the birthday of the church, when the Holy Spirit empowered the early followers to be bold in proclaiming the good news in Jesus Christ. On that day, this small, fearful band of followers (huddled in Jerusalem, unsure of what to do without Jesus guiding them) became the bold ones proclaiming salvation to all the nations gathered. And the church was born as a new creation!

Paul says to the church at Corinth, if you are "in Christ," you are being made into a "new creation." Resurrection—the bringing of life from death—is in you and in me as we find ourselves in Christ.

Paul is referring to a transformation from the inside out. It occurs over the journey of a lifetime. Indeed, it is not the destination that is important but the journey itself.

In place after place after place, the Methodist Church and my fellow Methodists have been a source of support, honest reflection and candid critique.[11]

Hillary Rodham Clinton
September 13, 2015

Each day I say to myself, *God isn't done with me yet!* God is drawing us nearer, refashioning us, restoring us. God keeps doing a "new thing." That newly-created, renovated-from-top-to-bottom being is you. As Charles Wesley puts it in "Love Divine, All Loves Excelling": "Finish then thy new creation, pure and spotless let us be . . . perfectly restored in thee."

------ ★ ★ ★ ------

Lord, I open myself up to your creating and creative power on this day of Pentecost. May the Holy Spirit empower me to be a new creation in Jesus Christ. And may I be empowered to transform the world by your creating power in my life. Amen.

FREEDOM IN CHRIST: JULY 4
Galatians 5:13-14

Paul's letter to the Galatians is one of his most passionate epistles. His views on Christianity were being challenged by two groups. On the one hand were the legalists, who said that Christians must follow every aspect of the Jewish law. On the other hand were the libertarians, who believed that Christ had liberated them from following the Jewish law in every respect.

Paul rejects both of these positions. To the legalists, he says the law in itself cannot bring salvation. To the libertarians, Paul argues that freedom in Christ doesn't mean "doing whatever you please."

The "third way" advocated by Paul was that Christ liberates us to live a life of love. When we love our neighbors as ourselves, we are fulfilling God's intention for our lives.

Christian freedom was never intended to be liberation from our responsibilities to others. True freedom is to be tied to others by the bonds of love. This kind of freedom is radical submission of ourselves to a life lived in the spirit of God.

--------- ★ ★ ★ ---------

Liberating God, help us to experience the genuine freedom you offer. Open us up to the gift of being free from the oppression of our egos and to being free for a life of self-giving love. Amen.

Robert Martin Walker

* *

FROM: Rev. Bill Shillady
SENT: July 4, 2015
TO: H

Dear Hillary,
Happy Independence Day!
    At our camp that City Society operates, Camp Olmsted, the children are divided into small groups. They have chosen presidents for their small group names. I thought you and Bill would enjoy they chose "the Clintons" as their name.
Rev. Bill

* *

SPIRITUAL GROWTH: FALL
Matthew 7:18–20

A few weeks ago after a clergy meeting near upstate New York, I joined some of my colleagues who wanted to visit an orchard for an "apple picking" outing. It was a gorgeous, beautiful, sun-shining afternoon. We all were very excited! In the huge orchard, countless apple trees, all different kinds, were lined up endlessly.

While I was filling up a bag with the golden crispy apples, I was thinking, *In order to be a well-ripened apple, how much time, how much pain and agony (chilly wind, scorching heat, cold rain, etc.) does an apple have to go through? Wow!* Then, each individual apple looked so precious and valuable to me that I was reluctant to take even a bite.

Not only fruits and vegetables have to bear so much suffering to be ripe but also our human souls have to endure an enormous distress, affliction, and anguish to be mature. It's not an easy task to harvest the fruit of the Spirit— love, joy, peace, patience, kindness, goodness, faithfulness, gentleness, and self-control. However, as the disciples of Jesus Christ, bearing the spiritual fruits is our bounden duty and ultimate goal to move toward the "perfection" of our lives and faith journeys.

Oh gracious God, we often forget and we sometimes are careless to give thanks to you for all the gifts so freely bestowed upon us. In our everyday lives, help us to recognize your blessings, and help us to be humble to receive your grace and love. With this thankful attitude, our spiritual fruits are ripened little by little every day. Amen.

Rev. Dr. Constance Y. Pak

TOGETHER AS ONE: WORLD COMMUNION
John 6:35

The First Sunday of October is observed by many as "World Communion Sunday." This day is a call for all Christians—of whatever background and theological tradition—to recollect that we are one in Christ and that the table at which we receive communion is God's table, not our own.

I am captivated by the image of men, women, and children of every language, color, and nationality gathering in fields, straw huts, brick schools, wooden shacks, and stone cathedrals, praising God and entering into both a physical and spiritual communion with one another.

Who better than Henri Nouwen to summarize this sacred meal?

> Jesus is the Word of God, who came down from heaven, was born of the Virgin Mary through the power of the Holy Spirit, and became a human person. This happened in a specific place at a specific time. But each day when we celebrate the Eucharist, Jesus comes down from heaven, takes bread and wine, and by the power of the Holy Spirit becomes our food and drink. Indeed, through the Eucharist, God's incarnation continues to happen at any time and at any place.
>
> Sometimes we might think: "I wish I had been there with Jesus and his apostles long ago!" But Jesus is closer to us now than he was to his own friends. Today he is our daily bread![12]

Lord, we remember you today, our daily bread. Let us be as one today. Let us be the hands and feet of Christ, serving others as you have served us. Amen.

JUSTIFICATION: THE ANNIVERSARY OF THE BEGINNING OF THE REFORMATION
Romans 1:16-17

It was at the door of Wittenberg's Castle Church where Martin Luther reportedly posted his Ninety-Five Theses on October 31, 1517, launching the Protestant Reformation. It was the genesis of the Reformation.

So, on the anniversary of the beginning of the Reformation, I celebrate the key doctrine of "justification by faith" begun 498 years ago.

Martin Luther came to believe that Christ justified humans by faith alone, a theological insight that put him on a collision course with church leadership. In the sixteenth century, the Roman Catholic hierarchy taught that people could get right with God through external means. The practice that really irked Luther was the sale of indulgences—certificates indicating the remission of sins and sometimes marketed as a way out of purgatory.

Luther saw this as corrupt and unbiblical. He challenged the practice by posting his "Disputation on the Power and Efficacy of Indulgences," better known as the Ninety-Five Theses. What Luther intended as a conversation starter ended up doing far more. It launched the Protestant Reformation and transformed western Christianity.

Luther also taught that every person—butcher, baker, or homemaker—is called by God. So when United Methodists say that every person—whether lay or clergy—is called to ministry, they are echoing Luther.

With recognition of the birth of the Reformation, I remind myself and you that our salvation comes by the grace of God in Christ Jesus. Happy Reformation Day!

------ ★ ★ ★ ------

"O Lord! Help me! O faithful and unchangeable God! I lean not upon man. It were vain! . . . Thou hast chosen me for this work. I know it! . . . Therefore, O God, accomplish Thine own will! Forsake me not, for the sake of thy well-beloved Son, Jesus Christ, my defence, my buckler, and my stronghold. . . . Amen." (Martin Luther)[13]

THANKFUL FOR OTHERS:
ALL SAINTS' DAY, NOVEMBER 1
1 Corinthians 1:1-9

Some days everything goes right. Some days everything goes wrong. Some days it's, "Good morning, God." Other days it's, "Good God, it's morning."

One day you wake up to sunshine and blue sky, commuter traffic flows along like a river, you get to see Charlotte for a whole day, and you feel that your work that day was a huge success. You go to bed convinced that you are a truly blessed, fine, upstanding human being.

> *Whether your family just arrived or has been here since before the United States even existed . . . you make our nation stronger, smarter, and more creative. You belong.*[14]
>
> **Hillary Rodham Clinton**
> November 8, 2016

Then there are days that dawn in gloom and end in disaster. You spill coffee on your favorite shirt, fog delays your flight, people glower at you and reject everything you do and say (sort of like a congressional committee hearing). You go to bed convinced that you are a truly cursed, wretched human being.

If it is true that we are all saints, it is also true that we are all sinners who have fallen far short of the goals of God.

Of course, nearly all the days of our lives fall somewhere in between these two extremes—thankfully.

On this day, the church remembers all the saints. Let's take a moment to remember the great people in our lives and strive toward the perfection that the Scriptures call us to achieve through our spiritual pocket of God's grace and love in Jesus Christ.

------ ★ ★ ★ ------

Lord, on this Day of the Saints, we thank you for those whom we name in the stillness of our hearts. Merciful God, we thank you for the saints. Amen.

OUR GREAT LEADER: VETERANS DAY
2 Timothy 3:16-17

A Special Prayer for Veterans Day:

O holy God, great physician, lover of all people, we are astonished by your amazing grace. We are captivated by your power and awed by your mercy. In the heart of our hearts, we long to know you more deeply, to touch even the fringes of your cloak, and to know peace and healing. We pray for the faith that can make us whole.

We pray for those in need of your healing this day:

For the sick, the injured and hospitalized, and those whose illness has isolated them. Give them a spirit of healing and hope.

For the outcasts, and those whom we have cast out through our actions or inaction. Shine a light on our prejudices, soften our hardened hearts, and transform us for loving service toward every Christ we meet.

For those who mourn and weep. Let them stand firm in your promises, buoyed by your strength and care. Give them the comfort and assurance that nothing can separate them from your love.

We give you thanks for the tremendous sacrifices of the 20 million men and women who are veterans. We pray for those working to serve veterans, that they will provide needed benefits and support. God grant veterans comfort, strength, and encouragement. We pray for those who have difficult memories to overcome or debilitating medical conditions to treat, that they will be healed. May we have a genuine spirit of gratitude for the sacrifices they have made for our freedom.

Loving God, we pray for healing and hope to reign in this world. Where there is conflict and war, let there be peace. Where there is hunger and poverty, let there be abundance. Where there is distress and despair, let there be light—warm and unquenchable.

We pray to hear your words, "Follow me," for they are words not only of discipleship, but of assurance—that as your disciples, we will never be forsaken. You will lead us, all of us, into unexpected places. Give us the courage to follow you each day of our lives. Amen.

BOUNTIFUL LIFE: THANKSGIVING DAY
Deuteronomy 8:6-18

Thanksgiving has its own set of symbols (turkeys, pilgrims, pumpkins, and Indian corn). But the symbol that best expresses the abundance of Thanksgiving is the cornucopia—an ancient symbol used in both Greek and Roman mythology.

The cornucopia, the horn of plenty, should sound the joyful noise of God's bountiful blessings, of the abundant, overflowing graciousness that God makes available in our lives. But this horn of plenty also sounds a warning, a note of judgment to shake us out of our self-preoccupied complacencies and selfish accumulations, a note to remind us that we must not forget God and to use our blessings to bless others.

In return for God's gifts—love and forgiveness, abundance and blessing—there is something required of us: that we love one another. And not simply those we find easy to love but those who are most difficult.

God is not an abstract theoretician. God is a dynamic, doing God—acting, creating, judging, and loving—in the lives of men and women. Jesus Christ himself is the best example of God's proactive involvement in human life.

------ ★ ★ ★ ------

God of peace and plenty, with awe and wonder we thank you for the beauty and abundance of our land and its people. You have freely blessed us with more than we could ever earn. Lead us to continue in thankful living and giving, for the sake of him who gave himself for us, Jesus Christ our Lord. Amen.

FROM: Rev. Bill Shillady
SENT: November 24, 2015
TO: H

Happy Thanksgiving to you and Bill, Chelsea, Marc and Charlotte!

★ ★ ★

FROM: H
SENT: November 24, 2015
TO: Rev. Bill Shillady

And, same to you and Judy and all your family and friends, among whom I count myself. Love from all of us to you, H

WORLD AIDS DAY, DECEMBER 1
Matthew 25:44-45

Today brings people together from around the world to raise awareness for HIV and AIDS and to demonstrate solidarity. It's an opportunity for public and private partners to spread awareness about the pandemic and encourage progress around the world in prevention, treatment, and care.

As people of faith, specifically United Methodists, we must live into our slogan of "Open Hearts, Open Minds, and Open Doors." So often our faith communities close their doors and hearts to people living with AIDS.

Today is a day with the word *hospitality* at its center. This word means a variety of things to different individuals, families, and cultures. We must truly practice radical hospitality to those who are still marginalized by this disease. While Christian hospitality might include serving others with a meal, it also must include righteous and just actions. Hospitality, in its broadest sense, is the basis upon which the United Methodist Covenant to Care program was founded. "If you are a person living with AIDS or a loved one of a person living with AIDS, you are welcome here."[15]

We do have the tools to end this epidemic once and for all, but we need to rededicate ourselves to fighting HIV and AIDS and leaving no one behind. That means continuing to increase research and expanding the use of medications like PrEP. . . . And let's reform outdated, stigmatizing HIV criminalization laws.[16]

Hillary Rodham Clinton
March 6, 2016

------ ★ ★ ★ ------

God of hope, all of us are affected by HIV and AIDS. We give thanks for signs of hope, for growing understanding, for medical advances, for changing attitudes and behavior, for greater awareness and concern in your church. Bind us together with strong ties of love, so that our church community may be a place where all can find hospitality and acceptance. May it be a place of welcome for all. Amen.

COME, LORD JESUS: ADVENT, WEEK 1

Luke 21:25

All hell is breaking loose. That's how we'll know that God's kingdom is near and Jesus will be returning for the Second Coming. That hardly puts us in a festive mood, does it? And we might want to duck our heads because it surely seems that Jesus will be returning any day now, right?

How often does it seem like "all hell is breaking loose" in our world and personal lives? When nothing seems to make sense and we are feeling overwhelmed by the challenge of it all, it's easy to shake our heads and wonder whether the whole world has gone mad and where God is in the midst of the chaos that surrounds us.

But perhaps that is the point of the Advent season—or at least one very significant point. During these chilly days of winter, we are warmed by the light of God's love breaking in on the madness, and somehow—miracle of miracles—God continues to be born, providing rays of light and hope.

"When all this starts to happen, up on your feet. Stand tall with your heads high. Help is on the way!" (Luke 21:28 MSG)

------ ★ ★ ★ ------

Come, Lord Jesus, come and be born again in me. In us. Amen.

Democratic presidential candidate Hillary Clinton courted members of the nation's first black sorority Wednesday by highlighting a number of issues where there is disparity between white people and people of color.

"Something is wrong when black women are more than three times more likely to die in this country in this century from complications due to childbirth," Clinton told members of Alpha Kappa Alpha Sorority Inc. "Imagine if a white baby here in South Carolina were twice as likely to die as an African-American baby. Imagine the outcry and the resources that would flood in."[17]

The Post and Courier
February 23, 2016

THE GREAT MYSTERY: ADVENT, WEEK 2
2 Corinthians 5:18-19

One of the most beautiful chants in the Christmas Mass is "O Magnum Mysterium," translated: "O great mystery, and wonderful sacrament, that animals should see the new-born Lord, lying in a manger! Blessed is the Virgin whose womb was worthy to bear our Saviour, Jesus Christ. Alleluia!" Each Advent as I move closer to Christmas Eve, I am more convinced that Anglican Bishop Geoffrey Rowell got it right when he described the Christian faith as "a revelation and a mystery—a revelation to be received and a mystery to be lived out." He went on to say that "notes of awe, wonder, reverence and reserve" are "essential characteristics of Christian believing."

There is a time and a place for intellectual analysis, skeptical debate, and academic research around the doctrine of the Incarnation—but Christmas Eve is not the time, and the manger is not the place. Here, the only appropriate responses are awe, wonder, reverence, and humility as we celebrate the mystery of the Word becoming flesh among us.

And here's the thing: Whatever else the Incarnation means, it means that the great mystery of God's love in Christ is alive among us in the complex, conflicted, confusing mess of our ordinary lives and our broken world. The great mystery is not an esoteric flight from reality, but a present experience in our very real world.

In fact, followers of Christ are called to be the continuing agents of God's reconciling love and grace, not just on Christmas Eve but also on the other 364 days of the year.

When it comes down to it, the great mystery is not only that God came among us in Jesus but that God intends to go into the world in the lives of people like every one of us. Now, that's a great mystery![18]

Rev. James A. Harnish

-------- ★ ★ --------

God of Wonder, may I accept the call to be an agent of your love, not just today but every day. Amen.

DIVINE PLANS: ADVENT, WEEK 3
1 Chronicles 28:1-8

Jesus comes to us in so many ways, at so many times. But do we see him? Do we recognize him? Or do we go on with business as usual? Are we ever prepared for what God is going to do? Because God's business is not the usual.

We see God's unusual business today in the story of King David. David has always been an ambitious guy with big plans, and now many of those plans have been accomplished. He has just been crowned king over all Israel.

David figures it is time to do something nice for God. He is going to build a temple almost as big as his own palace, a temple that will gain as much glory and renown for the king who built it as for the God to whom it is dedicated.

God's response: "No." God will not be a part of David's plans. But David can be a part of God's plans. God will create from David a house, a dynasty, through which salvation will come to all people. David's plans for God are really centered on David himself. God's plans are for all creation. God's business is not usual.

We're often surprised by God's unusual plans. Who would have thought that God would manifest God's presence in this world through the birth of a baby to a young woman named Mary and her husband, Joseph? No, God's business is not typical but divine.

God of joy and exultation, surprise us again with your divine plan that seems totally opposite our usual expectations. Keep us faithful in your service until the coming of our Lord Jesus Christ, who lives forever and ever. Amen.

BIRTH OF CHRIST: ADVENT, WEEK 4
Isaiah 9:2-7 ESV

When we read the wondrous vision of Isaiah 9:2-7, it can seem like an impossible dream. The end of war? A world in which the oppressor's rod is broken? How can that be?

The wondrous good news is that "the zeal of the LORD of hosts will do this" (v. 7). Healing the cosmos is God's intent, as fourteenth century mystic Julian of Norwich saw: "All manner of thing shall be well."[19]

How will God heal this broken world? Through Incarnation. The Potter becomes the clay. A child is born whose life, death, and resurrection launch the making of all things new. Jesus—Yeshua—whose name means "salvation," is called four names in Isaiah 9: Wonderful Counselor, Mighty God, Everlasting Father, and Prince of Peace. The awareness of who he really is only emerges over time, for initially he seems only to be the child of a young Jewish couple living under Roman occupation.

And so it is with us, the body of Christ, who bear his name and participate in his making of all things new.

------- ★ ★ ★ -------

Lord, in this holy season of Advent in which we await and then celebrate the birth of Christ, may we commit ourselves anew to our incarnation of the divine will, to becoming the good news of God's love in our neighborhood, workplace, and larger world. Amen.

Rev. Dr. Elaine A. Heath

Hillary and Bill Clinton basked in the Christmas spirit Saturday night at the United Methodist Church of Mount Kisco, shaking hands and sharing "Merry Christmas" greetings and hugs with their fellow church-goers.

"This is our blessing this night every year in this church," said Bill Clinton, the two-term 42nd president of the United States as he smiled and greeted other church members.[20]

Lohud

December 24, 2016

MIDNIGHT CLEAR: ADVENT, WEEK 5
Luke 2

The Rev. Dr. Edmund Sears wrote the lyrics to the beloved Christmas carol "It Came Upon the Midnight Clear" in the winter of 1849. The U.S. was a mess. We had just ended the Mexican-American War, leaving veterans impoverished and broken. The fight over slavery was heightening daily. The recession of the previous year left much of his town impoverished. Where could he possibly find hope?

Rarely do we see the third stanza of this hymn—which is unfortunate, because it's the most honest:

> Yet with the woes of sin and strife
> The world has suffered long;
> Beneath the angel-strain have rolled
> Two thousand years of wrong;
> And man, at war with man, hears not
> The love-song which they bring;
> O hush the noise, ye men of strife,
> And hear the angels sing.

It's not just 2016, or 1849, or 1492 that were terrible years for some people. Even on that midnight clear, people were afraid. Mary, Joseph, and the shepherds—all afraid. But better yet, all serenaded by angels.

In the darkness, God is composing. In the darkness, angels are singing. May you be blessed by their song.

------- ★ ★ ★ -------

Singing God, there are times where the darkness cuts so deep it's hard to remember that angels may be surrounding even me, even now. May you open my ears to the songs of hope in our weary world, to the voices around me singing your melodies. May I, too, learn the tune and join in the song. Amen.

Rev. Allie Scott

CHRISTMAS EVE AND CHANUKAH
Isaiah 9:2

This year (2016), we celebrate both Chanukah and Christmas Eve. One of the most important connections between these two holidays in our faith traditions is the celebration of light and life amid the barren darkness and cold of winter. This is so clearly reflected in the symbols of both holidays—the kindling of light representing God's presence.

The most ancient symbol of Judaism, the menorah, represents God's presence and creative power, embodied in light. Christian tradition shares God's presence in the light that is represented in the birth of the Christ child. The lights of the Advent wreath—five candles representing hope, joy, love, and peace—culminate tonight as the Christ candle is lit to remind us of God's presence in our world.

Chanukah and Christmas ultimately affirm the miracle of redemption, of liberation and salvation, of God's love and of the deliverance of all people. We yearn for light, the light of the miracle of the oil and the light of Christ.

May we all know and walk in the greatness of the light that God has given us.

In the thirteenth chapter of First Corinthians, St. Paul extols the virtues of faith, hope, and love for our fellow human beings. He says we need them all in this life, because of our imperfections: we "see through a glass darkly" and only "know in part." He proclaims love the greatest virtue, necessary to keep faith and hope alive and to give us direction.[21]

Hillary Rodham Clinton
July 11, 2016

------ · ★ · ------

God of light and life, ruler of both light and darkness, send your love and grace upon our celebrations of Christmas and Chanukah. We who have so much to do to push back the darkness seek your voice each day. Come and penetrate our dark world once more, as we seek to be a light of inspiration to others. Amen.

AN INTERRUPTION: CHRISTMAS EVE
Luke 2:8-10

B eing a parent of young children means being interrupted—while cooking, while working, while on the phone, while sleeping . . . no task is ever completed without an interruption. The most exasperating interruptions are those that go something like this:

> Child: "Daddy, Daddy, Daddy!"
> Parent: "Just a minute."
> Child: "Daddy, it's important!"
> Parent: "OK, what is it?"
> Child: "Um, I forgot."

Not all interruptions are created equal. As Christians, we are part of a story of interruptions, especially when we consider the Christmas story.

Mary's life is interrupted by an angel and then by an unplanned pregnancy. Joseph's life is interrupted by this pregnancy and by the requirement to travel to Bethlehem for the governor's census. Shepherds are minding their own business (and their sheep) when the angels appear before them and announce the news that a savior is born. The magi find an interruption in the night sky they are studying and follow that astronomical anomaly to Jesus. King Herod is threatened by the news of this newborn king, so he seeks to destroy him.

Over and over, this is a story about interruptions, which should not be surprising as Jesus's birth is the biggest interruption in human history—God, in the form of a vulnerable newborn, breaking into our world and our lives.

------- ★ ★ ★ -------

Dear God, may the interruptions of this Christmastime be like the star of Bethlehem, pointing in the direction of Jesus Christ. Amen.

Rev. Matthew T. Curry

COME BACK!

Luke 2:1-14

 One of my favorite traditions on Christmas Eve is my congregation's children's nativity drama. Last year, a young man was given the part of the innkeeper and his one line was "No room!" That evening, with a packed sanctuary, a very pregnant Mary and her dutiful husband, Joseph, stood beside a very lopsided donkey, played by twins nonetheless. When it was time, the youth very clearly and loudly shouted, "No room!" As the holy couple turned to walk away, the boy's face changed into a look of sheer and desperate concern. Suddenly he shouted, "Come back! There's room!"

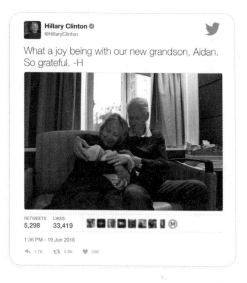

On some level we all wish things would have been less complicated for Mary and her baby. Giving birth in a stable must have been scary. Scripture says she was a young girl, maybe fourteen or fifteen. In the dark of night, in a place far from home, Mary gave birth to God. And this young mother wrapped her baby in the only clothes she had, lying him in the only bed available—a manger filled with scratchy hay.

The eternal Son of God was born to a woman in a cold and dark place, in a forgotten and out-of-the-way part of the world. May we never forget the great humility of our Lord and Savior as we walk in his ways and seek after his will for our lives and the lives of all who live in the world—especially in the forgotten places.

------- ＊ ★ ＊ -------

Holy Jesus, help me glorify your breathtaking lowliness as I seek to serve you in the world. Amen.

Rev. Danyelle Ditmer

MAKE ROOM FOR ALL

AUTHENTIC LOVE
John 20:13b

Whenever I hear people on national television talking about Jesus, I typically cringe. The picture of Jesus promulgated by individuals perched behind cameras on cable news shows or at political rallies rarely aligns with the image of Christ presented to us in the Gospel accounts.

It is an old and dirty tactic for people to try to take hold of Jesus for their own agendas. Throughout history Christ has been used to justify everything from the Crusades to the institution of slavery. Time and time again, people have tried to take Jesus away from the dispossessed and use him for their own heinous and selfish ambitions and desires.

The only Jesus who exists is the Son of God, the one who teaches us what it means to authentically love God and love each other. This Jesus commands us to give cold water to strangers, visit those in prison, and love our enemies. This Jesus cannot be contained or held within our narrow perception of who he is. No one can take Jesus away from us no matter how hard they try. Thanks be to God.

------- ⋆ ★ ⋆ -------

May the Lord bless you and keep you. May the Lord shine his face upon you and be gracious to you. May the Lord lift up his countenance upon you and give you peace! Amen.

Rev. Kevin K. Wright

Clinton voiced support for criminal justice policies that give people who are incarcerated "second chance, third chance and fourth chance programs" once they're released back into society. . . .

Clinton got a warm welcome by the pastors at all three African American churches.

"This campaign cannot be about insults. It has to be about results," said the Rev. Solomon Kinloch Jr., pastor at Triumph Church.[1]

The Detroit News
March 6, 2016

BREAK BREAD TOGETHER
Mark 2:13-17

One of the great things we overlook about Jesus is how he often ate with those whom the first-century elite did not let near their doors. Jesus practiced an open and inclusive table.

Jesus having a meal with tax collectors and sinners had socio-political significance. Sharing a meal represented mutual acceptance. His open-table, grace-filled meals challenged the philosophy and politics of holiness, which was a closed-table fellowship.

Jesus embraced a vision of an inclusive community reflecting the compassion of God. Jesus loves both the saint and sinner—a radical egalitarianism, an equality that denies any discrimination between people and ends the hierarchical system.

So as you go forth to Iowa and beyond, I know you will invite everyone to the table for the important conversations that need to take place for the healing of our nation. Just follow our Savior's lead.

It's been a hallmark of Hillary's campaign—and her career—to engage directly with and listen to families and communities, to voice hard truths about systemic racism, and to focus on solutions that can bring people together and lift people up.[2]

Maya Harris
Clinton's senior policy adviser
October 1, 2016

------ ★ ★ ★ ------

Lord, we thank you for the many lessons we learn from the life of Jesus and especially from whom he invites to the table. Help us to build the welcoming table of your kingdom here and now, not relying on some future glory. Amen.

TUMBLING DOWN
Hebrews 11:1-3, 29-30; Joshua 6:20

The Israelites had finally crossed the Jordan. Now they were ready to begin the conquest of the Promised Land—to claim the land that flowed with milk and honey. But like most things in life that are worth having, it wouldn't come without sacrifice and lots of work!

Jericho, with its imposing, impenetrable walls towering over it, a fortified city, armed with all the sophisticated weaponry of that day, was staring Joshua in the face. Jericho was standing between Joshua and the people of God, preventing them from taking over and occupying the land God had promised them.

Put yourself into the shoes of the Israelite soldiers. Jericho was the first city they had ever seen that was surrounded by huge walls. It must have looked like an absolute impossibility. But they listened to the Lord's instructions, and they saw those massive walls fall down flat.

Walls are tumbling down because of your vision, faith in God, and energy. So my sister, excelsior! Always upward!

------ ★ ------

Lord, we thank you that you are always with us. We will continue to march against the walls that divide our nation and sound the trumpets of equality, justice, and compassion. Amen.

"We don't need to be building walls, we need to be building bridges," Clinton said to applause, seemingly referring to the president's proposed plan to build a wall on the U.S.-Mexico border.
"And the best bridge to the future is a good education, my friends," she added during her appearance at LaGuardia Community College.[3]

The Hill
April 12, 2017

BUILDING BRIDGES
Hebrews 13:1-2

The verses from Hebrews refer to the story of Abraham welcoming three strangers (Genesis 18:1-11). Without knowing who they were or where they were from, he offered them hospitality: food, drink, and rest. They brought him a message: Abraham and Sarah would have a promised son. So these strangers turned out to be messengers ("angels") with a divine message.

Isn't it interesting that Abraham's hospitality to these visitors resulted in his receiving a great gift?

In our current national debate about immigration, we sometimes forget to see the gifts that migrants bring to our

nation. In one sense, all of us are immigrants. We are here as the result of our ancestors coming from another part of the world.

There are voices in our immigration debate that tell us to look upon migrants with fear. They want to erect barriers to restrict or even stop certain nationalities from immigrating to America. We need to help these persons to overcome their fears and to understand that our ancestors were once welcomed to this country.

What overcomes fear is love. Love builds bridges, not walls. Love tears down barriers; it doesn't erect them.

------- ★ ★ ★ -------

Welcoming God, you send us messages through the voices of those who come to us as strangers. Open our ears to listen with compassion to their pain and anguish. May we welcome them as you welcome us: with unconditional love. And let us gratefully receive the gifts they bring. Amen.

Robert Martin Walker

GREAT DIVERSITY
Galatians 5:1-26

Chapter five of Galatians is worth a good long read. It is about Christian freedom, which Paul imagines to be a kind of slavery to love. It is about the difference between the law and God's grace. Paul uses circumcision as an example, concluding that it matters little if we are or are not circumcised. Instead it matters a lot how we talk about the subject to each other.

This passage deals with cultural issues and division in the church—about tolerance and intolerance, how to talk about right and wrong, and cultural customs.

The Galatian church had been led down a path of division, led by an unidentified leader who was using the law to separate people and build walls in the Christian community, creating a spirit of intolerance, of difference. It categorized people and, rather than celebrating diversity, it used the law to alienate people from each other.

However, as we read this chapter, we learn what it means to be in love with each other—to be slaves in love with each other. We are to live by the fruits of the Spirit: love, joy, peace, patience, kindness, generosity, faithfulness, gentleness, and self-control. There is no law against such things.

Let us fall in love with the great diversity of the church and our nation. Think less about circumcision, ancient or modern, and more about love.

------ ★ ★ ★ ------

O God, we pray that we can be a little yeast that leavens the entire dough of community. Help us to truly love one another, as you have loved us. Amen.

RELIGIOUS LIBERTY
Romans 10:12-13

I found this statement by our first president, George Washington, from August 1790. Washington's letter to the Hebrew congregations of Newport, Rhode Island, is small in size, but its impact on American life is immense. In 340 well-chosen words, the letter reassures those who had fled religious tyranny that life in their new nation would be different, that religious "toleration" would give way to religious liberty, and that the government would not interfere with individuals in matters of conscience and belief.

Paraphrasing the Bible's Old Testament, Washington wrote, "Every one shall sit in safety under his own vine and fig tree, and there shall be none to make him afraid."

Washington continued: "For happily the Government of the United States gives to bigotry no sanction, to persecution no assistance, requires only that they who live under its protection should demean themselves as good citizens, in giving it on all occasions their effectual support."[4]

In his writing to the tiny Jewish community in Rhode Island in this new nation, his theme was that we will no longer speak of mere "toleration," because toleration implies that minorities enjoy their inherent rights "by the indulgence" of the majority.

Let this be a reminder to us of the diversity of peoples and faiths in our great nation.

You, my sister, can lead us to continue to heal our land of racism and divisiveness. Keep courage on the journey that God is unfolding for you.

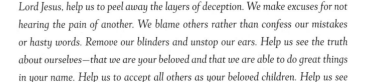

Lord Jesus, help us to peel away the layers of deception. We make excuses for not hearing the pain of another. We blame others rather than confess our mistakes or hasty words. Remove our blinders and unstop our ears. Help us see the truth about ourselves—that we are your beloved and that we are able to do great things in your name. Help us to accept all others as your beloved children. Help us see the hurt around us that we can help heal. Amen.

LIVE COMPLETE
Matthew 3:2

Unconscious living . . . alienation—from neighbor and from self . . . clinging desperately to stereotypes and presumptions that have long since failed us. "All we like sheep have gone astray. Everyone has turned to his own way" (Isaiah 53:6 KJV).

The words of John the Baptist in Matthew 3:2 are a radical call to a new era of awareness. Heralding the advent of Jesus, he calls us to a repentance that says turn around from our alienated living that has taken us astray. The Greek word is *metanoia*—turn around. Take a different look at yourself, your neighbor, and your world.

If ever we needed a call to this kind of repentance, it is now. If ever John, Jesus, and the Gospel writer's words need to arrest us and point us to another way of being, it is now. The nation is changing, and people are flailing around and failing. The myths of national and racial superiority are no longer working. Our individual and collective souls ache for new lives, new ways forward.

------ ★ ★ ★ ------

Gracious God of the ages, we humbly present ourselves before you as we seek to repent of our own unconscious and alienated living. As we turn around daily to live more complete lives, empower us with the courage and wisdom to call others to do the same, imbuing us with humility, love, and patience in the process. This we ask in your name and for our sake. Amen.

Rev. Frederick A. Davie

Hillary Clinton made an appearance on Power 105.1's The Breakfast Club this morning, where she spoke to the trio about gun violence, police brutality . . . "It's something that we have to be honest about. We have to face up to systemic racism. We see it in jobs, we see it in education, we see it in housing. But let's be really clear; it's a big part of what we're facing in the criminal justice system. African American men get arrested, charged, convicted, and incarcerated far more often and for far longer for doing the same thing that white men do," Sec. Clinton said.[5]

NBC News
October 26, 2016

WE NEED EACH OTHER
1 Corinthians 12:12-27

This passage is about the body of Christ being so connected that we can't get along without each other. The apostle Paul calls us to a better way of dealing with our differences. "I need you. And you need me." Despite our differences, we should have "equal concern for each other" (1 Corinthians 12:25 NIV).

In the United Methodist Communion ritual, we talk about being a part of one loaf. Even as the loaf is broken and given away, we all are still a part of that one loaf. If we mean what we say in partaking of the body of Christ, then our connection to each other should be more than symbolic. We are interdependent and interconnected.

> We have to replace the school-to-prison pipeline with a cradle-to-college pipeline, because in America, every child should have a good teacher and a good school, no matter what ZIP code they live in.[6]
>
> **Hillary Rodham Clinton**
> April 13, 2016

Holy Communion requires an investment in one another that moves beyond the surface. By taking Communion together, we commit to a process of healing because we need each other. We ask for forgiveness from God only as we forgive others.

Maybe we can promise to take the same risk around a Holy Communion table and move forward with our conversations, our commitments, and our challenges to solve racism and bigotry together in our churches and our nation.

------- ★ ★ ★ -------

Lord, give us grace to lay aside our differences and celebrate our diversity. Prince of Peace, take away all hatred and prejudice and whatever else may hinder us from being the inclusive body of Christ on this earth, nurtured by the Spirit, and called to be your hands and feet of love in this world. Amen.

TRUE FREEDOM
Deuteronomy 10:17-19

The Scripture today reminds us that we came to this country as strangers: "You shall also love the stranger, for you were strangers in the land of Egypt" (Deuteronomy 10:19 NRSV).

Most of today's Americans were not the original inhabitants of this land. Our ancestors—parents, grandparents, or older generations—came seeking freedom from oppression; some came under its yoke as slaves. Others are descendants of those who were already here.

Hatred and revenge are two emotions that can enslave us to evil, and recent immigration issues have challenged America. Legislation has sought to control if not eliminate immigration—and fear of foreigners is not unusual in our post-9/11 world.

Jesus teaches us to "Love your enemies and pray for those who persecute you" (Matthew 5:44 NIV). Loving our enemies has everything to do with our total freedom.

As long as people are in bondage, as long as there are widows and orphans who are oppressed, as long as there are immigrants who are unwelcome, as long as there are women and men without jobs, as long as there are children who die from hunger, we are not truly free.

------ ★ ★ ★ ------

God who has a deep heart of love and mercy for our world, we give you thanks for our nation. Thank you for those who have sacrificed their lives for our freedom. Help us welcome and greet those who come to this land for freedom, and help us respect all people. We pray for peace, safety, and that all our neighbors may be free. We ask this through Christ Our Lord. Amen.

OUR LAMENT
Psalm 44:1-8

My heart is broken yet again! There are simply no words. What does one say when people's lives have been turned upside down? We continue to cry for peace—peace in our city, our country, and the world. We need healing.

On Sunday in Baton Rouge, three more police officers were shot dead, several people were injured, and some churches went on lockdown or cancelled services. Our world and our nation are in need of healing.

We lament and simply pray that God hears the words of our heart. We need to accompany those prayers with acts of compassion, mercy, and love. Could this be a defining moment for our nation? Can we take our place in history to change our narrative?

The Psalmist reminds us that weapons will not defeat our enemies; we must trust in God, who will turn our enemies into friends. The best weapon to change this nation is to give God thanks for all that God has done for us. With a grateful heart, we can find our hearts strangely warmed to the love of God and to our neighbor.

★ ★ ★

Lord, hear our prayers. Heal our hearts and this nation. Help us be instruments of change for you. Amen.

With the circumstances of the shootings unexplained Sunday night, a community already numbed found itself searching for new words to describe its horror and despair.

"Stop this killing. Stop this killing. Stop this killing," said Veda Washington-Abusaleh, the aunt of Alton Sterling, the 37-year-old man killed by Baton Rouge police on July 5.

"That's how this all started, with bloodshed. We don't want no more bloodshed. . . . Because at the end of the day, when these people call these families and they tell them that their daddies and their mommies not coming home no more, I know how they feel, because I got the same phone call," she said, breaking down in tears during an interview Sunday by a Baton Rouge TV station.[7]

The Washington Post
July 18, 2016

LABORERS FOR GOD

Matthew 20:1-16

In this parable, Jesus wants us to know that in the face of our limited, worldly understanding of what is fair and what is unfair, God works with a different reality, in a different direction, and by different standards.

God wants us to work in his vineyard with happy hearts and willing bodies. We are reminded that working and serving in God's world is a great privilege and opportunity. The reward is the joy of knowing that we are part of a great adventure that gives meaning to our lives. The reward for serving others is found in knowing that we are part of a Christian process of laboring to leave the world a little better than when we entered it.

> I believe that when unions are strong, families are strong—and when families are strong, America is strong. And I will always stand with workers in protecting their rights to organize, bargain collectively, be safe on the job and retire with dignity.[8]
>
> **Hillary Rodham Clinton**
> November 4, 2016

This parable is about the overwhelming authenticity of God's love in this world. Each life, each worker, is valued the same. Like in the parable, most of us show up around quitting time. Thus, we don't want justice; we want mercy. We don't want fairness; we want grace. And that's what this parable promises: a God who gives us not what we deserve but what we need.

------ ★ ★ ★ ------

God of grace and mercy, whether we are lifelong laborers or new arrivals in your vineyard, we know you value us just as we are. God of the last, the first, and all those in between, we seek your presence in our lives as we work to make the world a better place. Amen.

HELPING HANDS
Luke 10:25-37

When Jesus said to love your neighbor, a lawyer who was present asked him to clarify what he meant by neighbor.

In ancient Jewish culture one's family, tribe, and those who live with you are your neighbors. Not your enemies or foreign people. But Jesus clearly extends the idea of neighbor to everyone.

In the good Samaritan story, Jesus takes a different twist on the subject—not about who is

our neighbor, the lawyer's question, but about how to be a good neighbor.

I love how Henri Nouwen describes our neighbors:

> When Jesus tells the story of the good Samaritan . . . to answer the question "Who is my neighbor?" he ends by asking: "Which . . . do you think proved himself a neighbor to the man who fell into the bandits' hands?" The neighbor, Jesus makes clear, is not the poor man lying on the side of the street, stripped, beaten, and half dead, but the Samaritan who crossed the road, "bandaged his wounds, pouring oil and wine on them . . . lifted him onto his own mount and took him to an inn and looked after him." My neighbor is the one who crosses the road for me![9]

------- ★ ★ ★ -------

Holy God, your son, Jesus, invites us to hold the needs of our sisters and brothers as dear to us as our own needs. Loving our neighbors as ourselves, we pray for our world and for those who cross the road to be good neighbors to all in need. In my time of need, send me a good neighbor. Amen.

PEACEABLE KINGDOM

Isaiah 11:6

The peaceable kingdom beckons. Let us respond with urgency.

This metaphorical language is intended to shake us out of our complacency—to compel us to imagine a world where the predator and the prey actually live in peace, all under the command of a benevolent authority. The language encourages us to live beyond the boundaries and dictates of this world and to be summoned by the beckoning light of a more perfect order. It not only spurs the imagination, but it is a catalyst for action. The beloved community signals us to consider a new order; it pulls at the very core of our being and demands a response.

What should this response be? If we consider the moral arc of ancient Scripture and the recurring words of the prophets over the ages, the response has to be to commit ourselves to the pursuit of peace, righteousness, joy, and holiness, not just for ourselves and our clan but for all of God's created order.

The peaceable kingdom is the beacon that lights our way when times are dark and uncertain. In times such as these, the glory of the peaceable kingdom shines brightly, reminding us that extreme income inequality, the killing of unarmed citizens by agents of the state, suicide, and drug addiction need not enshroud us with dark clouds of hopelessness.

------ ★ ★ ★ ------

Gracious Creator, may the eternal words of your sacred texts keep us inspired to follow the light of your love, promise, and hope, ever committed to creating that kingdom of peace, where the vulnerable will cease to be prey for the powerful. Amen.

Rev. Frederick A. Davie

* *

FROM: Rev. Bill Shillady
SENT: January 20, 2016
TO: H

Good morning,
I am leaving for the airport in an hour or so to head to the Pre-General Conference briefing in Portland, Oregon. Keep our church in your prayers. This is the first gathering of heads of delegations before the GC in May.
Blessings,
Your Preacher Friend

* *

WHEN DISASTER COMES
Micah 6:8

Once again, a senseless and violent killing in Orlando, Florida, has left fifty people dead, fifty-three injured, and countless others stunned.

The words of Micah, major words from the minor prophet, to "do justice, embrace faithful love, and walk humbly with your God," were originally spoken in the midst of emerging chaos and conflict. This, Micah said, was the requirement of God. It should be our requirement as well.

To "do justice" in the midst of this latest tragedy is to commit ourselves to the hard but necessary work of advocating for those who suffer from the misguided and prejudiced viewpoints of others—and to work tirelessly to fulfill the requirement of God to love our neighbor.

To "embrace faithful love" is to establish a daily passion for everything that is good, right, and holy in the way in which we treat one another, respond to sinful acts all around us, and lead others into an awareness of what a love for kindness can accomplish.

To "walk humbly with your God" is a clear acknowledgement that when we do not have adequate words or actions in the midst of senseless acts of violence, all we can do is turn to our God with prayers of compassion. In the wake of this latest disaster, we place the lives of the victims in the precious hands of our loving God.

In the midst of our daily routines and ongoing lives, let us do these things.

------ ★ ★ ★ ------

O God, we claim your promise that when we do not know how to pray, your Spirit intercedes on our behalf with sighs too deep for words. Our minds recoil from the violence that ended lives prematurely and injured a multitude physically, emotionally, and spiritually. Be with those who have no words, those who are clinging to life, those whose lives have been shattered by loss, and those who are working to save lives and mend bodies and spirits. We offer this prayer in the name of the One whose love is infinite. Amen.

WHOLE BEING

1 Timothy 2:1-7

This pastoral letter is traditionally attributed to the apostle Paul and consists mainly of advice to his younger colleague and delegate, Timothy. Paul instructs Timothy to care for the church at Ephesus while he goes on to Macedonia. Here is a community of faith that has the time and space to reflect on the order of society and to value prayer for all people, but especially for those in authority. This is an expansion of the values of our Lord; all people matter and all need to be held up as valuable in prayer before God.

Our lives as the Scriptures suggest must be about more than living quietly and peaceably. They must include that element of responsibility that creates and sustains the safe space for people to engage with each other and with God. But it's not just about individuals pursuing a personal piety consisting of little more than a certain morality and a focus on a world beyond this one. Our prayers must be with the disturbance of God, where power is abused and love not lived out for all. We cannot abuse the fundamental teachings of Jesus to love God, to love our neighbor, and to love ourselves with our whole beings.

------ ★ ★ ★ ------

Lord, provide the place where people can come together to find the common thread of our humanness so that love and kindness may prevail. Amen.

The problem of poaching elephants, said W.C.S. president Cristián Samper, is not merely an ecological threat. The illegal ivory trade fuels terrorist and criminal syndicates throughout Africa that wreak havoc on local populations and threaten security abroad.

Chelsea and Hillary Clinton made the issue a priority of the Clinton Global Initiative. Chelsea produced a news documentary on the ivory trade for NBC News, and Hillary gathered intelligence . . . to assess the issue.

They launched "The Partnership to Save Africa's Elephants," a campaign to convene nongovernmental organizations and governments to ban the ivory trade, increase dwindling elephant populations and publicize the links between the ivory trade and poaching.[10]

Politico

June 13, 2014

GOD'S PERFECT LOVE

John 15:1-11

Between the devastation of the earthquake in Nepal and the painful situation in Baltimore after the tragic and senseless death of Freddie Gray, there's been more than enough suffering and brokenness to go around. It's easy to wonder where God is in natural disaster and injustice and why we humans have such a hard time loving one another.

This Gospel text reminds us of the source of all life, hope, and healing—the love of God as revealed in our Lord Jesus Christ. In this Scripture, part of the discourse at the Last Supper, Jesus is preparing his closest followers for his impending humiliation and death at the hands of an unjust political and social system.

In a world so broken and bruised, this love of God made real in Jesus and extended to us is the only antidote to

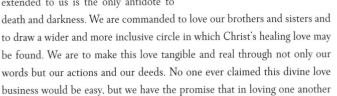

We have allowed our criminal justice system to get out of balance, and these recent tragedies should galvanize us to come together as a nation to find our balance again.[11]

Hillary Rodham Clinton
April 29, 2015

death and darkness. We are commanded to love our brothers and sisters and to draw a wider and more inclusive circle in which Christ's healing love may be found. We are to make this love tangible and real through not only our words but our actions and our deeds. No one ever claimed this divine love business would be easy, but we have the promise that in loving one another God lives in us and God's love is perfected in us.

Gracious God, bring healing to our streets and correct the injustices felt by so many. Heal our nation! Help us to bear the fruit of love in every action we do. Amen.

BE TRANSFORMED
John 15:12-17

Jesus called his disciples "his friends," and his friendship changed their lives. The first followers of Jesus were transformed from using nets to bring fish into their boats to using the net of love to bring everyone into the kingdom where they could experience the amazing, unconditional love of God. They were altered from fearful followers to fearless leaders who were willing to lay down their lives for the Christian faith.

The truth is that when we allow Jesus to become our friend, our confidant, our constant companion in this journey through life, we are transformed. We become passionate, compassionate, visionary, and loving followers.

The most important thing about our friends is that they are there for us in our times of challenge and need. Imagine Christ is present to you as an even closer friend. He is as real as the air we breathe and as near as the people next to us.

------ ★ ★ ★ ------

Lord, I thank you that you are my friend. Today I open my heart and life and allow you to come in and bless me with your presence, grace, and love. Thank you for laying down your life that I might have life abundantly. Help me to share your love with all those around me. Amen.

MESSENGERS OF PEACE
Acts 2:1-8

In the Book of Acts, we read about the early Christian community overcoming the language barrier that impeded the early church to evangelize—Pentecost. We remember how the power of the Holy Spirit broke down the walls of language, culture, and race.

During the building of the early church, the Holy Spirit provided for the "good works of God" to be heard in all the known languages of the world. Language, culture, and race were overcome by the Good News in Jesus Christ, as the power of the Spirit caused all to hear in their own language, in their own context, in their own hearts. The walls that divide were shattered by the revelation from that early community on Pentecost Day.

Today we remember how the difficulties of language and culture can cause a breakdown in unity—and how divisiveness and lack of toleration have too often caused war and heartbreak.

It is time to recognize how the church, if truly committed to the cause of Christ and to the power of the Holy Spirit, should be working to break down the barriers of language and culture that divide and cause war. We must live in an interfaith world where acceptance and tolerance of another's journey of faith is just as true and real as our own.

------- ★ ★ ★ -------

Lord, allow the Spirit of the living God to empower us to overcome our misunderstandings and to find the common language of love for others— especially our enemies. Help us to be messengers of peace in our conflicted world, to build community through acceptance and toleration, and to work for the unifying power of our common humanity. Amen.

Muslims across America showed an outpouring of support for victims after the deadliest shooting spree in U.S. history left 49 people dead in an Orlando, Fla., nightclub. . . . The American Muslim Community Centers, a mosque in Longwood, Fla., said the mosque stands with Americans and "senseless violence has no place in our religion or in our society."[12]

USA Today
June 12, 2016

GOD BE GLORIFIED

Luke 18:35-43

The famous songwriter Fanny Crosby wrote more than 9,000 songs, including "Pass Me Not, O Gentle Savior," "Blessed Assurance," and "To God Be the Glory."

When Fanny was only six weeks old a minor eye inflammation developed. The doctor who treated the case was careless, though, and she became totally and permanently blind. Fanny Crosby harbored no bitterness against the physician. She felt that God had made her blind so she could see clearly in other ways and become a guide to people of faith.[13]

Henri Nouwen wrote:

> Jesus, the Blessed Child of God, is merciful. Showing mercy is different from having pity. Pity connotes distance, even looking down upon. When a beggar asks for money and you give him something out of pity, you are not showing mercy. Mercy comes from a compassionate heart; it comes from a desire to be an equal. Jesus didn't want to look down on us. He wanted to become one of us and feel deeply with us.[14]

------ ★ ★ ★ ------

Lord, fill our hearts with mercy so that our compassion can help us to see clearly all those who need our love and your grace. Help us see with the eyes of the Spirit all those around us so that we can hear their stories, see their journeys, and walk hand in hand with them. Amen.

FROM: H
SENT: May 28, 2015
TO: Rev. Bill Shillady

Did you see press today about my conversation with a gentleman in South Carolina who was studying Corinthians for his Bible study that night? If not, I will send to you.

★ ★ ★

FROM: Rev. Bill Shillady
SENT: May 28, 2015
TO: H

I missed it. I would love to see it!

OUR DEEPEST LONGING
John 4:7

The woman comes to draw water and leaves transformed. Her encounter with Jesus would have been unheard of in those days, as Jews had little or no engagement with Samaritans at all; and the male and female public display would have been scandalous.

Jesus meets her in the place of deepest longing—that special place that yearns for truth, where grace is received and where life takes on new meaning. The woman finds freedoms she had not anticipated: freedom to be fully known and accepted, freedom to stretch beyond her wildest dreams, and freedom to share the good news of her experience and be taken seriously.

The image of sitting at a well and being nourished by living water is powerful. I have been fortunate to sit with people who have offered radical grace when I needed it most. They accepted me as I am, challenged me to be my best self, and convinced me that the person they encountered is good enough just the way I am.

Today, let us be grateful for those who sit with us by the well, offering life-giving water.

-------- ★ ★ ★ --------

Lord, my soul is thirsty; give me living water. Amen.

Rev. Dr. Cathy S. Gilliard

* *

FROM: H
SENT: May 28, 2015
TO: Rev. Bill Shillady

Hillary Clinton wins over a voter - CNNPolitics.com
With scripture, Hillary Clinton wins over a voter:
*http://www.cnn.com/2015/05/27/politics/hillary-clinton-2016-election
-faith/index.html*

* *

SADNESS

1 John 4:18

Seeing the horrendous images of the slaughter in the Bataclan Concert
Hall in Paris, the first things we feel are sadness, sorrow, and pain. We
hear the groaning that is too deep for words from a world that longs for God's
redemption (see Romans 8:22-23). Our hearts are broken with the things
that break the heart of God.

And then, with good reason, we instinctively feel fear. It's a normal,
healthy human emotion. But it's also a dangerous one. Fear can awaken us
to real and present danger. But fear can also ignite flames within us that,
if not balanced by wisdom and compassion, feed the destructive fires of
xenophobia, racism, prejudice, injustice, and violence.

So what does the love that drives out fear look like in this sad time? For
one thing, it looks like hospitality to refugees. Christian leaders have called
for our nation's leaders to continue, with careful screening, to welcome
refugees who are fleeing from the same violence we are trying to defeat.

For followers of Jesus, the real "weight of this sad time" is the weight of
love, which is nothing less than the weight (and foolishness) of the cross.[15]

Rev. James A. Harnish

------ ★ ⭐ ★ ------

*Lord, help us to not be fearful but instead have your heart, your love for others.
Let us be the voice of reason in these times of trouble. Amen.*

NEVER GIVE UP
Galatians 6:9-10

Paul is giving advice to a divided community in this letter to the church in Galatia. If there are rifts in relationship, restore one another with a "spirit of gentleness" (Galatians 6:1 CEB). Bear one another's burdens. Be a new creation!

In June of 1955, Sir Winston Churchill, near the end of his life, was asked to give a commencement address at a British university. Physically infirm, he had to be helped to the podium. Holding onto the podium, head bowed for what seemed an endless amount of time, the voice that years before had called Britain back from the brink of destruction sounded publicly for the last time in history: "Never give up. Never give up. Never give up." With that, Churchill turned and went back to his seat.

I read that there was silence, and then the whole audience, as if one person, rose to applaud him. During the darkest days of World War II, when country after country was being swallowed by the Nazis, when German planes were bombing English cities into piles of rubble, when the threat of invasion seemed imminent, when even the hardiest of souls was giving up hope, Churchill never lost hope and never gave up. In addition, on three different times, his career was apparently over and he was sent off to oblivion. Three times, he came back to lead his country. Here was a man who never gave up.

Whenever we are tempted to do less than our best or perhaps to quit completely, we ought to remember this verse and the truths that it contains. Whenever we find ourselves getting tired or burned out or losing enthusiasm for doing right and speaking truth, we need to remember the words of this text. If we are doing the right things in our faith and our lives, then we will reap a wonderful harvest of love.

So, my sister, keep doing all the good you can, whenever you can. Do not grow weary. Feel the many prayers that are meant to lift you up—to keep at it. In other words, "Never give up."

------- ★ ★ ★ -------

Lord, give us the strength that we need to never give up. Develop within me a compassionate heart towards everyone. Help me to work for peace in this world. No matter what is happening, help me to never give up. Amen.

OPEN EYES
Psalm 137; Matthew 25

The famous theologian Karl Barth once advised Christians, "Take your Bible and take your newspaper, and read both. But interpret newspapers from your Bible."[16] The image of three-year-old Aylan Kurdi, the young Syrian Kurdish boy whose body washed ashore on a Turkish beach after a failed attempt by his family to escape Syria, brought to my mind the need to see world events through the lens of the Bible.

That tragic photo of Aylan's lifeless body focused needed attention on the plight of the four million refugees who have fled war-torn Syria to the surrounding countries and the seven million who have been displaced within Syria. Many have called this tragedy the worst humanitarian disaster of our time.

From this news story, I can't help but think of the story of Exodus, in which a huge mass of Hebrew refugees fled the tyranny of slavery and began a long, dusty, and miserable trek through the unforgiving sands of the Sinai Peninsula. Or the events of 2 Chronicles, in which the Israelites in the Northern Kingdom of Israel were defeated by the Assyrians and scattered throughout the empire, never to reassemble or return. Or Joseph, Mary, and Jesus—displaced refugees fleeing the wrath of a tyrannical ruler.

I find myself praying for God's presence to guide these brave Syrian migrants and reading the haunting words of Psalm 137 as a prayer for all refugees.

--------- ★ ★ ★ ---------

God of all people, but especially of refugees, help me to see this world through the lens of Biblical history and teaching. As I do so, help me to see the presence of Jesus in the least, the last, and the lost. May I respond with love and assistance to all who are in need. In your love, grace, and mercy we pray for peace. Amen.

Hillary Clinton said Tuesday that closing the door on refugees fleeing Syria would undermine "who we are as Americans."

"We have always welcomed immigrants and refugees," Clinton said. "We have made people feel that if they did their part, they sent their kids to school, they worked hard, there would be a place for them in America."[17]

CBS News
November 17, 2015

BEACON OF HOPE
John 13:31-35

Although we can make radical and prophetic statements about accepting people who are different than we are, we often struggle to extend lavish welcome in our faith communities and even in our lives. Sometimes we're unable or unwilling to do the hard work of reaching just across the aisles to bridge ideological, political, religious, or cultural gulfs that can undercut our community and prove to the world what it has always thought about us: *Those Christians can't even accept each other. How could they ever accept me?*

It never hurts to stop and take stock of our practice as the community of Christ, whether in our churches, in our homes, or in the widening world. Building the beloved community takes work and attention and commitment so that here, among this group, we truly and honestly reflect the radical inclusion and welcome that was Jesus's intent for the whole world.

------ ⋆ ★ ⋆ ------

Lord, soften my heart today and help me be open to someone who makes me uncomfortable. Challenge me in everything I do to model your lavish welcome in my life. Amen.

Rev. Dr. Amy K. Butler

A GENTLE REMINDER
Matthew 25:40

A few years ago, a woman approached the church custodian and me to ask if we had a coat that might fit her. She had seen the New York Cares coat drive box in the narthex and wanted to take a look inside. We heartily said, "Yes!"

She often attended the morning midweek worship service and had never expressed a need of any sort. I suggested she take two coats. "No," she said, "but I'll get one for my daughter."

A few minutes later, she found what she said was a "perfect fit!" A perfect fit—though it seemed to me too short in the waist, the sleeves way too long hanging over her hands, and the hood almost swallowing her tiny face.

I can hardly describe the joy on her face at having found that coat that someone else had discarded for whatever reason. Here was a person working every day but unable to afford a coat to keep warm on a frigid 27-degree day; a mother who, like me and every parent I know, wanted to make sure her child was cared for.

Sometimes, God brings people who really need our care up close to remind us of our real business.

------- ★ ★ ★ -------

Dear Lord, open our eyes to see those most desperate for our help. Amen.

Rev. Dr. Cathy S. Gilliard

A LOT LIKE HIM

John 13:35; Galatians 5:23

Not long after Mattie, our adopted grandchild, was born, her then ten-year-old cousin, Julia, asked her own mother, "Will Mattie grow up to look like Aunt Deb and Uncle Dan?"

That's an intriguing question because Mattie's birth parents are African American. Deb and Dan are Caucasian.

Julia's mother wisely answered, "Mattie won't look like Aunt Deb and Uncle Dan, but as she lives with them, she will become like them in other ways."

We don't have a clue as to what Jesus actually looked like. Most paintings of him end up

looking a lot like the artist. But as we live with him, as we grow closer to him, as we surrender our way to his way, we can become like him in lots of other ways.

Jesus told us what that life looks like when he said, "This is how everyone will know that you are my disciples, when you love each other" (John 13:35 CEB).

Paul told us what it looks like when he wrote, "The fruit of the Spirit is love, joy, peace, patience, kindness, goodness, faithfulness, gentleness, and self-control" (Galatians 5:22-23 CEB).

------- ★ ★ ★ -------

O God, by the power of your Spirit, enable us to grow into your likeness, so that through our lives, your love and grace will be made known in this world. Amen.

Rev. James A. Harnish

YOUR HEART'S ZEAL
Revelation 3:20

This verse in John's vision of the Book of Revelation is written to the seven churches of Asia Minor. This section is part of the message to the church of Laodicea, one of the wealthiest cities in the ancient Roman world.

Some say the verse is written because that fellowship had lost its zeal. It's addressed to the indifferent Christian, whom the Lord urged to open his or her heart's door and to invite Jesus Christ in for intimate fellowship. I believe this verse expresses a truth taught elsewhere in Scripture, namely, that Jesus Christ desires intimate fellowship with all people.

Henri Nouwen's interpretation is one I truly love. He writes: "Jesus is the door to a life in and with God. 'I am the gate,' he says (John 10:9). 'I am the Way; I am Truth and Life. No one can come to the Father except through me' (John 14:6). Still, many people never have heard or will hear of Jesus. They are born, live their lives, and die without having been exposed to Jesus and his words. Are they lost? Is there no place in the Father's house for them?

"Jesus opened the door to God's house for all people, also for those who never knew or will know that it was Jesus who opened it. The Spirit that Jesus sent 'blows where it pleases' (John 3:8), and it can lead anyone through the door to God's house."[18]

I think Jesus can open any door he wishes. He can even appear behind locked doors according to the accounts of the Resurrection. So I believe all have the opportunity, in this life or beyond, to welcome God's presence and love into their hearts.

------ ★ ★ ★ ------

Lord, I open my heart to your son, Jesus. Each day may he enter in so that I may be the beacon of light of your love to this world so all may know of your grace and mercy. Amen.

LET THERE BE DIFFERENCES
2 Kings 10:15

I understand that you will be speaking to the National Baptist Convention this week. It got me to pondering what our good old theologian John Wesley says about the big tent of Christianity. Wesley uses this obscure biblical passage to begin what many consider one of his most important sermons, "A Catholic Spirit," in which he speaks of the many differences in Christianity. By *catholic*, he means the universal church.

Wesley admits such differences in thinking and worship are proper grounds for meeting as different congregations. He understands that we will not see eye-to-eye and that gathering together in like-minded communities is natural. But he thinks these differences in thinking and worship should not prevent us from being united in affection for one another.

Further, he says, none of us can be assured that all of our own opinions, taken together, are true. None of us is omniscient. Given our inherent limitations, the wise Christians will allow others the same liberty of thinking that they desire. And for me, the essence of Wesley's sermon is the quote, "If your heart is as my heart, then give me your hand."[19]

-------- ★ ★ ★ --------

Lord, may this message become so for our church and for all who believe. Amen.

FROM: Rev. Bill Shillady
SENT: September 4, 2016
TO: H

Good Sabbath Morning,
Home in Brewster, refreshed and renewed.
    I hope you are strengthened and encouraged by all the prayers coming your way.
Blessings!
Rev. Bill

THE BLESSEDNESS OF UNITY
Psalm 133:1-3

What a beautiful yet very sad Psalm! Where is the unity among the people of God? Where is the unity among groups in our society? In place of unity in this world, we see a fractured and divided society, splintered into economic gaps, racial discrimination, sexual orientation bias, male and female inequity, and a host of divisive issues.

In these times of conflict and disunity, Psalm 133 is like water on parched ground. People who are divided and estranged from one another need to be reminded of God's call and grace to "live together in unity." May this Psalm offer us hope and the promise of kinship as all God's children. And for all people who suffer scarcity in everything from food and housing to justice and love, may we be the messengers of God's love and the agents of transformation to bring about true unity.

Now America is once again at a moment of reckoning. Powerful forces are threatening to pull us apart. Bonds of trust and respect are fraying. And just as with our founders, there are no guarantees. It truly is up to us. We have to decide whether we will all work together so we can all rise together. Our country's motto is e pluribus unum: *out of many, we are one. Will we stay true to that motto?*[20]

Hillary Rodham Clinton
July 29, 2016

Creator of the universe, you made the world in beauty and for unity. Lord, we wish to restore all things to you and hope to rebuild our relationships as one people on this earth and especially in our nation. Wherever harmony is disfigured by racism, sexism, poverty, sickness, selfishness, war, and greed, help us build that new creation in Jesus that is justice, love, and peace to the glory of your name. Amen.

OUR DIRECTION

Psalm 86:15

I was a junior in college when Martin Luther King Jr., was shot. In Indianapolis, the assassination led to one of the most amazing speeches in American political history.

Robert F. Kennedy was running for president. He was scheduled to rally his supporters in a predominantly black neighborhood in Indianapolis. When word came of the assassination, local police warned him they might not be able to provide protection if there was a riot. Kennedy insisted that he make the announcement. He spoke from his heart, without notes or written text, on the back of a flatbed truck.

Although other major cities faced riots, Indianapolis remained calm. Sixty-three days later, Kennedy's voice was also silenced by an assassin's bullet.

Forty-eight years later, we need to hear his voice again, as we are still called to make the same choice he offered the crowd that night.

> In this difficult time for the United States, it's perhaps well to ask what kind of a nation we are and what direction we want to move in. . . . We can move in that direction as a country, in greater polarization— black people amongst blacks, white people amongst whites, filled with hatred toward one another.
>
> Or we can make an effort, as Martin Luther King did, to understand, and to comprehend, and replace that violence, that stain of bloodshed that has spread across our land, with an effort to understand, compassion, and love. . . .
>
> What we need in the United States is not division; what we need in the United States is not hatred; what we need in the United States is not violence and lawlessness, but love and wisdom, and compassion toward one another, and a feeling of justice toward those who still suffer within our country, whether they be white or whether they be black.[21]

------- ★ ★ ★ -------

O God, even as you calmed a troubled time with the words of Bobby Kennedy, so speak and work through me to calm these troubled times and lift the vision of a better day. Amen.

Rev. James A. Harnish

PRAY WITH HER

After the Democratic Convention, I was contacted by
Dr. Emily A. Peck-McLain, a clergy member of the New York
Annual Conference and professor of Christian Formation, Preaching, and
Worship at Eastern Mennonite Seminary in Virginia regarding
the foundation of the We Pray With Her group.

This online community of young United Methodist Clergy
Women watched as, for the first time in our country's history, a
woman would accept a major political party's nomination
to be their candidate for president.

As young clergy of United Methodist churches, there
was little they could do financially to support their fellow United
Methodist in her calling to run for president. They could not post signs
or make statements from pulpits, but they could support Secretary
Clinton by praying, encouraging, supporting, and
challenging her to live out her faith.

During and even after the campaign, more than 115 young
clergy women joined to pray and send devotions as Hillary Rodham
Clinton worked to shatter that glass ceiling of the office of President
of the United States. As United Methodist clergywomen, "We realize
appreciatively that we stand on the shoulders of women who have come
before us and worked, just as Secretary Clinton has for her whole adult life,
to advance women's rights and participation in our society and church."

These extraordinary women sent devotions to me that were
posted for the members of their private Facebook group, allowing me
to also share them with Secretary Clinton. Every day they prayed the
devotion for her, as I'm sure Secretary Clinton prays for them as
they all continue to work to shatter stained-glass ceilings.

* *

ALL SAINTS
Numbers 27:1-7

Today is All Saints' Day, a day that makes me think of our spiritual inheritance, of the people who have gone before us and reached back to take our own hands to help us along the way.

The story of the daughters of Zelophehad is a story of inheritance—spiritual and otherwise—and of women who have gone before us, fighting for us. These five women had a lot of gumption. They went before Moses to ask him to change the law. It seems impertinent—how dare these women question Moses? How dare they question God? But they knew something about God that Moses had overlooked. They knew God takes the side of the poor and the oppressed. Those like Hebrew slaves, or those like five poor, fatherless, brotherless women with no money and no leverage but with a deep faith in a God of justice.

Mahlah, Noah, Hoglah, Milcah, and Tirzah stood up for themselves and all the women who followed them so that they might receive their birthright same as the men. On All Saints' Day, we remember them, just as we remember the saints we have known in our lives and just as we remember the saints of history.

-------- ★ ★ --------

O God, my strength and my redeemer, I give thanks for a day to reflect on those saints who have taught me faith. I pray that I and my fellow Christians may learn to be saints ourselves. Amen.

Rev. Shannon E. Sullivan

* *

FROM: Rev. Bill Shillady
SENT: November 1, 2016
TO: H

Dear Hillary,
It has been five years since your mother passed. I am sure during this campaign her spirit and love has been such a guiding force for you.

I awoke this day thinking of my two brothers. It is from the memories of their lives that I find comfort and hope.

Blessings on this day. May the words of this young woman, who found an obscure passage in Numbers that provides a wonderful inheritance for this All Saints' Day, be a blessing.

Blessings. You and your team are in my prayers.
Rev. Bill

* *

HE STILL LOVES US
Ephesians 3:16-19

In Ephesians 3, Paul offers truth that keeps us rooted and grounded in love through the messiness that is life. The depth of God's love for us is so great that our minds cannot comprehend it. Let that sink in for a minute.

When others seek to hurt us, God still loves us. When we are our own worst enemies, God still loves us. When we turn away from the very one who loves us most of all, God still loves us and welcomes us back again.

God is already in every circumstance we might encounter: from our greatest achievement to our lowest moment. What a powerful truth to let take root in our lives. I wonder how different the world might be if the people of God began to live as though they believed it? Could it be that it is not us who are waiting on God but God who is waiting on us?

* ★ *

God, may I be confident in your love for me, and may this knowledge root me, ground me, and fill me this day and every day. May I have the power to dwell in the length, width, height, and depth of your love; and may I plant this seed wherever your Spirit leads me until the world is overflowing with the fullness of God. Amen.

Rev. Leslie Stephens

Hillary Clinton said Tuesday that she hopes to soon see a "wave of young women" run for office.

"Let us hope there is a wave of young women running for office in America," Clinton said, accepting an award at a New York luncheon for the nonprofit organization Girls Inc. "And let's be sure we support them in every way we can. Let's help them shatter stereotypes and lift each other up."[1]

Politico
March 7, 2017

GROWING WITH GOD
Psalm 65

I have always been drawn to the teachings of Hildegard of Bingen, a medieval mystic and doctor. She believed strongly that, like nature, each person has a life force within them, gifted by God, which possesses a greenness or *veriditas*. When we submit our spirits to God, God's Spirit enlivens and awakens that greenness in community with the created world and with other people.

Like the psalmist writes, we can see the glory of God in the majesty of mountains and in the grain of the field. But we are also called to recognize God's creation with us and within one another. Be on the lookout for God's greenness, not just in nature but in the faces and spirits of God's beloved children whom you meet today.

I'll never forget what it was like to be a mom at work. It wasn't easy. And I was lucky: I had financial security, a supportive employer, and affordable childcare. Too many families don't. I've met so many parents stuck in impossible situations, at their wits' ends trying to make it all work. It just shouldn't be this hard to work and have a family.[2]

Hillary Rodham Clinton
September 29, 2016

-------- ★ ★ ★ --------

God, keep me reaching toward the light. Keep me well watered and flexible enough to bend with the winds. Keep me growing beyond fences and keep me budding and blooming, fruiting and yielding, so that I may be a blessing to others. Amen.

Rev. Anna Guillozet

POWER OF STRENGTH
Exodus 1:15-20

In the midst of a story about ruthless oppression, infanticide, and heartbreak, Shiphrah and Puah show the power of quiet resistance and the capacity we all have to affect change. They used their jobs as midwives to work against systems that sought to harm others. It could not have been an easy thing to disobey and lie to the king; it required courage. This resistance to oppression and violence is noticed by God and the biblical authors as a holy act.

While Shiphrah and Puah are not well-known biblical heroines, their actions had great impact, not only for their lives but for the lives of Hebrew children and their families. Their examples show us that working against forces of violence, oppression, and evil are acts of faith and devotion to God, whether it be at the feet of the birth stool or on the world stage.

Holy God, give me the courage and resolve of Shiphrah and Puah that I too will stand up to injustice, greed, and violence in all their forms. Thank you for these examples of courage and strength; help me emulate them and be an example for others. Amen.

Rev. Katie Goss Pearce

CLOTHED IN DIGNITY
Proverbs 31

Proverbs 31 does not serve as a to-do list for the perfect woman, as many interpret it to be; indeed, this chapter clearly demonstrates how women are using their God-given creativity and energy to provide for families, for neighbors, and for all of God's creation. As the writer states in verse 25, we have been clothed in strength and dignity to help us in our work, in our loving, and in our playing.

When we take on our God-given strength and dignity in all we do (whether that is to raise children, to preach the gospel, or to lead a country), we are filled with laughter and joy as we fearlessly look forward to the future, knowing that God is with us every step of the way. In addition, when we allow God's strength and dignity to flow through us, we creatively and passionately live into God's calling for us in the world, making the world stronger and more dignified. Therefore, my prayer for us today is that we will experience laughter and face the future without fear as we take on the strength and dignity with which God clothes us.

------ ★ ★ ------

God of us all, I give you thanks for your word and the truth that I am fearfully and wonderfully made. Whatever chaos the world throws at me today, I pray that you clothe me in dignity so that I may be filled with laughter looking forward to the future unafraid! I pray this in the name of Jesus Christ our Lord. Amen.

Rev. Emily Scales Sutton

She noted, too, that the problems of equality are not limited to the developing world. "Because if America is going to lead, we need to empower women here at home to participate fully in our economy and our society," Clinton said. "We need to make equal pay a reality. We need to extend family- and medical-leave benefits to more workers and make them paid. We need to encourage more women and girls to pursue careers in math and science."[3]

The Daily Beast
April 5, 2013

GREATER CALLING AT HAND

Ecclesiastes 11:6

I t's hard to know what's working and what's not. But, we keep at it, keep plugging away, because we know that there is good to come. The days are long. The nights are long. There is hardly a moment to stop for a meal, to stop for a break, to even stop to breathe. But there is a reason for it all. There is a greater purpose, a greater calling at hand. It's not about what *you* can do, the headlines *you* can make, the great deeds *you* can accomplish in our country and across the world. It's about God. A calling to serve the people, a calling to lead. Keep moving. Keep going. Keep scattering. The calling is true. The seeds are planted. And there is good fruit growing.

> *Let's be real. We still have a long way to go. Our policies just haven't kept up with the challenges women and families face today.*
>
> *Too many women still aren't paid fairly. On average, women earn 20% less than men do for full-time, year-round work. Women of color earn even less.*[4]
>
> **Hillary Rodham Clinton**
> September 29, 2016

O God, you have called me to great work in this world. Give me strength to continue on this difficult road. Help me to see the fruit of the seeds I scatter, the good that has come, and keep my heart focused on the good that is to come. Amen.

Rev. Kristin Heiden

CLOTHE YOURSELF IN RIGHTEOUSNESS
Colossians 3:12, 14; Psalm 72:6 ESV

As women, the way we look, the garments with which we are clothed, are under constant scrutiny. Clothing communicates something about us to the world whether we want it to or not. Yet clothing also works on us from the outside in, so that when we change our clothes, we are changed. When you put on a coat, you eventually warm up inside. When you put on pajamas, you eventually get sleepy. When you put on a business suit, you eventually feel confidence, assurance, and courage.

So what happens when you clothe yourself with the things of God? What happens when you put on compassion, kindness, humility, meekness, patience, and—above all—love? Of course the world sees you differently, but more importantly, you are different. You are the kind of person who boldly brings people together, who works for the common good, who seeks the welfare of all, who welcomes strangers as friends, and who loves in a world that desperately needs it.

God of love, you have clothed me in Christ through my baptism. Empower me this day to be for the world someone who is wrapped in compassion, kindness, humility, meekness, patience, and—above all—love. Amen.

Rev. Brandi Tevebaugh Horton

FROM: Rev. Bill Shillady
SENT: November 6, 2016
TO: H

After watching your joy and smile in the rain yesterday, Psalm 72:6 came to mind. "May he be like rain that falls on the mown grass, like showers that water the earth." This is a prayer for the king. I would make it my prayer for you this day and in the future.
Rev. Bill

EXTRA BANDWIDTH
Luke 5:15-16

During a planning session for a major event, our leader asked a simple question: "Do we have the bandwidth for that?" He wasn't talking about our technology but about our spiritual, physical, and emotional capacity to take on a new project. We didn't, so we let it go.

When we need extra bandwidth for technology, we pay for upgrades to the system. But what can we do in our everyday lives?

Martin Luther writes, "I have so much to do that I shall spend the first three hours in prayer." We should turn to practices that ground our work. They expand our capacity by reminding us we are not alone and the world rests in God's hands, not ours. I find that, during busy seasons, setting aside time for devotion before bed allows me to sleep without the list of tasks looming.

We have to set limits on our bandwidth by creating boundaries. Every "yes" means a "no" somewhere else. If we are not paying attention to our bandwidth, we cannot protect those things we are unwilling to sacrifice to other demands. And we need someone in our lives who is not afraid to hold us accountable to the boundaries we have set.

The demands of power and position are great, and the need never ends. But even Jesus knew his bandwidth, set limits on his time, and turned to things that would expand his ability to serve.

Holy One, when the weight of the world is on my shoulders, ease my burden. When there are not enough hours in the day, give me rest. When the demands of the crowds are overwhelming, help me to retreat and renew so I can serve ever more fully. Amen.

Rev. Katie Z. Dawson

BE TENACIOUS
Genesis 32:22-32

I wonder what the exact moment was like when Jacob realized he was wrestling with the One who could bless him. There had to have been a flash of insight when he knew this wasn't some mugger or a soldier from his brother's camp—that it was a manifestation of God's own self. The fight didn't get easier with the truth, but his purpose became focused and the morning's light seemed closer. Jacob didn't let go and neither did God. In the end, Jacob's name changed from one that meant "supplanter" to Israel, which means "triumphant with God." How stunning would the transformation be if you no longer heard the worst of who you are when people say your name and instead were reminded that you are a precious and tenacious child of God?

Every first fight women have fought—from the first Methodist clergywomen to the first female president—has felt like a battle that's shrouded in a lonely night. Your night may feel long, and you don't have the benefit of the concealing darkness as you fight. At times, it seems like the wrestling threatens to tear us all apart. We are all feeling a different piece of this season's deep faith wrestling. Despite that, we hold on with determination, demanding a blessing of peace, so that it doesn't slip away altogether. God reminds us that we are created for a transforming goodness. It isn't work that is easily done, but it is the truest manifestation of our abundant blessing.

------- ★ -------

Gracious Creator, you formed me to be tenacious as I hold on to your promise. Make me tireless as I wrestle with my own doubts and fears. Grant me courage to overcome the obstacles created by those who don't see your blessing in me. Pour your peace into my heart and lead me in your wisdom. I give thanks that you are present in the midst of the struggles and the overwhelming joys alike. Amen.

Rev. Janessa Chastain

HE HOLDS OUR FUTURE
3 John 1:2

Julian of Norwich lived a mostly isolated, monastic life, putting her spiritual life at her center. When she was about thirty, in the 1300s, she grew very ill and had a near-death experience. Last rites were even administered. During this time, she had several revelations from God, one of which was Christ telling her, "It was necessary that there should be sin; but all shall be well, and all shall be well, and all manner of things shall be well."[5]

This is the reassurance Christ offers all of us. The world is not as it should be. We see people suffering close to home and far away. People we know and love and those we will never meet struggle with healthcare costs, chronic pain, mental illness, and myriad other difficulties. What we also know is that our God holds the future and that the new creation where all the wrongs are made right has already begun in Jesus Christ. That vision is what guides us in our daily actions, to build toward that new creation and to participate in it. It is the vision that whispers to the present, "This is not all there is" and calls it forward into the possibility of change. All shall indeed be well.

------ ★ ------

Holy God, convict my heart of the truth that you hold the future in the palms of your loving and caring hands. Inspire me to work toward your future of justice, joy, hope, and peace. Amen.

Rev. Dr. Emily A. Peck-McClain

"Let resistance plus persistence equal progress for our party and our country," said Clinton, referring to the catch-all term for the protests and for Senate Majority Leader Mitch McConnell's criticism of Sen. Elizabeth Warren (D-Mass.)—"she persisted"—which had immediately been adapted into a rallying cry.

Clinton also told Democrats to be proud of the "progressive platform" they had drafted after the 2016 primary, suggesting that it had put the party in sync with protesters.[6]

The Washington Post
February 24, 2017

A TABLE FOR ALL
Matthew 15:21-28

The Canaanite woman wasn't reverent; she was yelling, refusing to take no for an answer. For me, this past Sunday at Communion felt similar. We were blessing the animals, and we have little kids. It was messy. A family came for Communion, and one child ate his bread before he could dip it, so I gave him another piece. He ate that too and refused juice. His little sister refused both. Their baby brother, two years old, was told to dunk his bread, and he did—like he was dunking a basketball. (This is why we have grape juice–colored carpet.)

Afterward, someone told me that they wished Communion was more reverent now, like it was in their day. I think what we're doing now is as reverent as ever. Did you know United Methodists were the first ones to include the phrase "he ate with sinners" in the Communion liturgy? Now, serving Communion to reserved adults and future basketball stars alike, I can't think of anything more reverent than to allow everyone to have a place at the table.

God, who sets every table, help me to be reverent toward you by opening up your table, your church, and my heart to everyone. In the name of Jesus, who ate with sinners, I pray. Amen.

Rev. Monica Beacham

FROM: Rev. Bill Shillady
SENT: October 16, 2016
TO: H

Hope you saw the AP article on the daily devotionals. I hope you were pleased with the focus. Of course, the devotionals have become part of my spiritual exercises each morning. As I write or edit them, I am praying for you and our nation.

So blessings on this day. May you find a few moments of Sabbath.
Rev. Bill

STAND UP

Esther 4:14 NRSV

Women have long played an important role in government, even when we haven't talked about them. They have been the women behind the men. The Bible tells us the story of one woman who stepped forward and stepped up for her people. When Queen Esther learned that a decree had been made for the Jews to be killed, her uncle Mordecai encouraged her, saying: "Perhaps you have come to royal dignity for just such a time as this."

For just such a time as this. It is the rallying cry of women—we step up when we are needed the most. And in no other time have we needed a leader who will stand up for all the people—both those who worship like her and those who do not; those whose lives are being threatened by broken and damaging systems and those who hurt themselves and others by perpetuating those systems. This is just such a time.

> I know this isn't easy. I know that over the past week a lot of people have asked themselves whether America is the country we thought it was. The divisions laid bare by this election run deep. But please, listen to me when I say this: America is worth it. Our children are worth it. Believe in our country, fight for our values, and never, ever give up.[7]
>
> **Hillary Rodham Clinton**
> November 16, 2016

------ ★ ★ ★ ------

God, you want the world to be better than it is, and you call each of us to participate in that transformation. Help us each day to live into our baptismal vows to accept that freedom and power. Give us the strength we need to step up and step forward when you call us to and to be your co-workers for the kingdom at "just such a time as this." Amen.

Rev. J. Paige Boyer

COMMIT TO PRAY
1 Samuel 2:8

Hannah's story is one that touches many lives. Disappointment, rivalry, maybe even fear were parts of her reality. As a leader today, these words may be on your heart. As women, our lives are heavy with this burden. We are often hardest on ourselves.

Yet this is not what God wants for us. You may see yourself as dust, as needy, yet God sees you as loved. As you have committed so much of yourself and your life to leadership, so Hannah committed so much of herself to her community as she sought a child. This prophetess changed history as she lived out her calling faithfully and fully. She was blessed with a son, Samuel. In fact, she committed her long-awaited child to God.

In all things, Hannah continued to pray. Her determination was a part of her faith. From her, we can learn the power of committing to pray. In all things and at all times, pray. Hold tight to your determination and know that you are not alone in your commitment to this country, your community.

------- ＊ ★ ＊ -------

God almighty, I pray, seeking your direction and committing once again to the community which I serve. I pray, O God, for your will to be done. Fill me with your strength and help me to trust you in all my days, especially when I need most to hear you. Amen.

Rev. Catherine Christman

"When I looked up and saw a woman by my table, she gently asked me what was I studying. I said. '1 Corinthians 13,'" says [Frederick Donnie] Hunt, an associate minister at First Calvary Baptist Church in Columbia. "And what happened next I'll never forget. She said, 'Love is patient, love is kind,' and went on to recite the rest of the verses by heart."...Hunt was the only patron in the bakery when Clinton sat down across from him and had a conversation about faith, a topic that Clinton is passionate about but rarely addresses in public.[8]

CNN Politics
May 28, 2015

YOU ARE CHOSEN

Luke 24:9-11

Mary Magdalene and the other women were commissioned to tell the good news of Jesus's resurrection to the others. They were chosen. Jesus didn't come first to Peter or James or John. He came to the women.

Throughout the Gospels, we see that Jesus is a supporter of women. Remember, in this difficult season when people are over-analyzing every word you say, Jesus has called you to this place. Just as Jesus took the women seriously and gave them great and important tasks, so too have you been taken seriously for this great and important task.

As a young clergywoman, I understand the struggle of knowing I deserve to be taken seriously while breaking into a male-dominated profession. The whole world is watching. When things get ugly, remember *who* you are and *whose* you are. Remember that you are a beloved child of God, called and commissioned to make a difference for the better in our world.

Gracious God, who has always called and supported women, help me to hear your voice today. Give me the strength to respond. Build in me the courage to continue to break into spaces where I may not be welcome but am called to go and so very needed. Bless me in my work today so that I might remind others that they too are your beloved ones, just as I am. In your son's name, I pray. Amen.

Rev. Julia Singleton

WONDERFULLY MADE
Psalm 139:1-14

Birthdays are the perfect times to pause and remember our beginnings. They are also the perfect times to consider that God knew us even before we began. In the darkness of our mothers' wombs, the Creator of the universe was doing what creators do best—making something new. It truly is knowledge too wonderful to grasp that the God of all that is has been intimately involved with our lives from before our beginning and will be long after our end.

Today, remember that you are "fearfully and wonderfully made" (v. 14). There are many ways to understand the word *fearfully*, but I find power in rendering it as a synonym for "reverently." Sometimes it's easier to remember that of others—surely you remember the first time you saw your daughter's ten fingers and toes. You remember the first time you saw your granddaughter's eyes. We don't remember our own first cry or first smile or first step. But God does. God was there. God is always on all sides of you, hemming you safely in with love and steadfast presence.

-------- ★ ★ ★ --------

Holy creator God, on the day I celebrate my birth, remind me that you have always been with me and will always be. As I look at my own fingers and toes, the ones that you knit together as I was being shaped in my mother's womb, help me to see them with reverence and wonder, just as you do. In your name, I pray. Amen.

Rev. Dr. Emily A. Peck-McClain

* *

FROM: Rev. Bill Shillady
SENT: October 26, 2016
TO: H

Happy birthday to you!
May you be blessed in all you do this day in celebration, in hope, in joy, and in God's love.
　　Dr. Emily Peck-McClain, the coordinator of the "We Pray With Her" group has written you a special devotional for this day.
Rev. Bill

* *

NO MATTER WHAT
Romans 8:38-39

I t's so easy to beat myself up, to feel ill-equipped, to think the critical voices inside my head and around me are right—that I don't have what it takes or can't get everything done that I need to. I wonder if you might have some of those voices in your head too.

But then I remember.

Nothing can separate us from God's love. No matter what we do, no matter what we don't, God's not going anywhere.

I remember the times God has been there for me, turning up in the midst of mistakes and failures and shortcomings, and saying, "I'm still here." I remember the people who saw me in the depths of despair and said, "You matter to me." I remember, in spite of everything, I am a beloved child of God.

------ ★ ★ ★ ------

Holy and loving God, the way you love us is incredible. Remind me of who you are. Speak to me this day, so the promise and abundance of your love can carry me through. Amen.

Rev. Allie Scott

REMEMBER TO LAUGH
Proverbs 31:25-26 NRSV

Scripture doesn't say much about laughter. Jesus doesn't share parables about the best jokes he ever heard. But two very important women in the Old Testament meet the circumstances of their lives with a laugh: Sarah, who uses laughter to overcome her heartbreak in Genesis, and this "woman of valor" described in Proverbs 31.

Laughter is an incredibly powerful force. It dispels darkness, challenges our fears, and fortifies the laugher. The Proverbs 31 woman is hardworking and prosperous, wise and virtuous, and blessed through her work. She is confident that God sees and loves her, and she trusts in God's grace and bounty. No matter what "the days to come" have to offer her, she can laugh in defiance and meet her challenges head-on.

When we move along the path to which God calls us, we are guaranteed to face challenges. People will question our motives, our abilities, and even the values that we hold closest to our hearts. On those difficult days, think of the Proverbs 31 woman—the "woman of valor"—and clothe yourself with the strength and dignity that God provides. Then, remember to laugh.

------- ★ ★ ------

El Roi, God who sees me and is seen, thank you for your unending love and guidance as I try to live faithfully into the call you have placed on me. Grant me the continuing strength to face my adversaries with grace. Let your peace descend on me in moments of challenge, so I may continue to place my trust in your holy direction and truly "laugh at the days to come." Amen.

Pastor Shannon V. Trenton

ON SOLID GROUND
1 Samuel 2:1-10

While Hannah's appearance in the Bible is brief, she had a pivotal role in Israel's history and was an example of a woman of strong faith. Hannah was one of two wives to her husband. The other wife mistreated Hannah because she was unable to have children, to the point Hannah felt degraded and distressed. But by the grace of God and Hannah's strong faith in the Lord, God granted her a child who became one of Israel's greatest leaders.

In Hannah's prayer, she praises God for being a strong rock when her life became unsteady. By her example, we know that when we feel slandered and mistreated, to the point of being degraded and distressed, we need to turn to the One who gives us strength and who will bring good out of our trials. We can stand firm on the solid ground of God, our rock and our strength.

———— ⋆ ★ ⋆ ————

Lord, my rock and my strength, help me place my faith and trust in you when I feel discouraged and distressed. Remind me of your grace and love for all those who call on your name. In Jesus's name, I pray. Amen.

Rev. Elizabeth R. Taylor

"Remember, you are the heroes and history makers, the glass ceiling breakers of the future. As I've said before, I'll say again, never doubt that you are valuable and powerful and deserving of every chance and opportunity in the world," Clinton said.[9]

USA Today
February 7, 2017

LEAD WITH BOLD ACTIONS

2 Kings 22:18-20

I n the days of the Kings of Judah, Josiah was a teenager ruling a kingdom far from the ways of God. Though he had not been raised to know God, he took steps that seemed right and just and subsequently found a lost book of Scriptures in the Temple. When Josiah heard God's teachings and love and laws for the first time, he knew something needed to change.

So he sought the wisdom of a follower of God, a prophetess named Huldah. In a male-dominated culture, she brought the words of God to their present circumstance, explaining why the people found themselves in a destruction they invited and how God would bring redemption through those who sought holiness. This woman, loving her Lord and embracing her role as encourager and leader, spoke a new narrative to the generations of vengeance that defined the kingdom. She invited Josiah—and by extension, the nation—to embrace a way defined by love, mercy, caring for neighbors, and seeking peace in their relationships and alliances.

No one has all the answers. We need to find them together. Indeed, that is the only way we can find them. . . . We must do better, together. Let's begin with something simple but vital: listening to each other. For Scripture tells us to "incline our ears to wisdom and apply our hearts to understanding."[10]

Hillary Rodham Clinton
July 11, 2016

Josiah followed the prophetic words of Huldah, with her invitation to the people to repent, renewed a covenant with God, and removed their sources of temptation to be swayed away from God. While we do not live in a theocracy as Josiah led, we do have the ability to lead with humble hearts, bold actions, and peaceful ways.

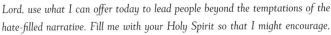

Lord, use what I can offer today to lead people beyond the temptations of the hate-filled narrative. Fill me with your Holy Spirit so that I might encourage, speak boldly, and invite people to a new narrative of mercy and grace. Amen.

Rev. Casey Ann Irwin

RAW HEARTACHE
John 11:38-44

A nd then it grew silent. The fervent motion toward the finish line, the dignified expression, and the gracious conciliatory remarks—it had all been said; there were no more words. Life had entered the pause.

The pause of life, the place between places, the time of transition. The raw heartache of loss is temporarily eased by the rush of adrenaline. It helps us simply to get through it. But then, weeks later, it grows silent. Where does life go from here?

When Jesus enters the pause following the death of a person, a relationship, a career, or a vision, he calls us by name. "Come out!" He unbinds the trappings of an old life, those ritually mandated wrappings that are simply too restrictive for the new life to which he calls

us. The tattered remains of a fallen dream shed from our form, released by Jesus's call to be free and unburdened for a new call. There is work to be done. You don't belong trapped behind some rocky site of mourning. The silence is broken. Come out; you are free. Life steps out of the pause.

———— ★ ★ ★ ————

Lord of the Resurrection who calls us by name, help us to be bold. When we hear your call, allow us to shed the remains of any past loss and heartache in order to follow you into new life. Heal us, revive us, and renew us for your service. Amen.

Rev. Nicole de Castrique Jones

ORDINARY PEOPLE, ORDINARY STORIES
Hebrews 11:1, 31, 39-40

Much of the time, we humans feel very ordinary. We go through our day-to-day routines, and no real difference is made. Yet ordinary people are exactly the ones who change the world.

The Bible is full of stories of ordinary people doing extraordinary things. Hebrews 11 lists these ordinary folks. They were shy, powerless, childless, prostitutes, women, men, and children, who, by faith, changed their own lives, the lives of those around them, and the world. They followed God and believed in something better.

Even though they did extraordinary things and were commended for their faith, they did not receive what was promised because "God provided something better for us so they wouldn't be made perfect without us." Their story is not complete without us. Their story is our story.

Our stories are interconnected. Our stories build upon those from ancient times, from yesterday, and tomorrow. We may not feel our contribution is much. We may believe we are too ordinary to make a difference. We may not see how the story continues. But it does continue. The story of God's world continues, and it includes each of us—ordinary, extraordinary us.

------ ★ ★ ------

Gracious God, we are all ordinary people called to be part of something extraordinary. You have provided something better for us all. Help us boldly continue our story, continue your story. Remind us that our ordinary contribution creates an extraordinary story. Amen.

Rev. Sarah A. Slack

FIERY WOMEN
Judges 4:4-9

Deborah served as the judge, the highest public office in her community. She is called "wife of Lappidoth," which can also be read in Hebrew to mean "woman of flames." This "fiery woman" was called to lead a divided people, and she led them into forty years of peace. The text above notes her military commander's hesitation to follow her orders to fight their Canaanite foes. Did her gender cause him to doubt her judgment? Was his demand for her to go with him into battle so that if they failed she would take the blame?

It isn't easy being a strong female leader. Too often we feel isolated. Others around us may verbalize doubts about our decisions. In the verses following this text above, we learn that Deborah's prediction comes true when a woman named Jael secures victory for the Israelites by killing a Canaanite general who ran away from battle. Though Deborah may have felt alone as she led, she wasn't alone. God's wisdom and strength guided her, and God called other women to serve and support her leadership.

------ ★ ------

God, through the ages, you have called fiery women to lead nations. Grant me strength and courage for this day so that I may trust your guidance. Please continue to provide other women who support my efforts to lead. By your grace, I pray. Amen.

Rev. Sarah Harrison-McQueen

Invoking the role of women in the Arab Spring and Egypt and the brutal rape in India that awakened that country to its problem of sexual violence, Clinton called this moment in history a "remarkable moment of confluence" between political activism and technology, in which "there is a powerful new current, a grassroots activism . . . We need to seize this moment." But, she cautioned, "we need to be thoughtful and smart and savvy."[11]

The Daily Beast
April 5, 2013

PEOPLE OF STORY

John 1:1-5

We are people of story. As people of faith, we see how our stories fit in the larger story of God's redemption and hope. In the beginning, when the earth was a formless void and darkness covered the face of the deep, God spoke. There was a Word. Through that Word, all things came into being.

In God's perfect time, that Word became flesh and dwelt among us as Jesus. These are dark days. We feel defeated. We're lost and depressed. We're anxious about the future of our country. We worry about our children and grandchildren. We're afraid of what comes next.

Author and speaker Brené Brown has said that our job isn't to deny the fear or to disengage from tough emotions, but rather it is our job to rumble with the truth of our stories. We are to defy the endings and remind ourselves and our communities that our stories don't end in darkness and defeat. The story doesn't end with the cross of pain and suffering. The story ends with Resurrection and new life. The story ends with a light that shines on in the darkness, and the darkness has not overcome it.

> We don't all have the same gifts and blessings, but that's okay. In fact, it's good. That's Paul's message in Romans 12. Because together, our contributions add up to something greater than anything we could offer on our own.[12]
>
> **Hillary Rodham Clinton**
> September 13, 2016

------- ★ ★ ★ -------

Light of the world, continue to speak into my darkness. Help me to own my emotions as we co-write a new ending to my story, one filled with new life and new hope for all people. In your holy name, I pray. Amen.

Rev. Lisa Schubert Nowling

LET US WEEP

Jeremiah 31:15

I didn't realize that I had been crying, but my chest was soaked. As I sat on the beach watching my son frolic in the waves and the sand, I was overwhelmed by fear and grief. This glorious, sunny day and picturesque moment was overcast by the news of yet another Black young man killed in the streets by those who swore "to protect and to serve" him. In that moment, I joined the chorus of weeping mothers.

Across this country there are mothers weeping. We are weeping for our children, both dead and alive. We are weeping because there seems to be no safe space for them to grow and simply be. We are weeping because the systems are built to entangle instead of preparing them to flourish. We are weeping because our children lose their innocence way too soon. We are weeping.

Join the powerful chorus of weeping mothers! Our tears water seeds of change and flood city streets with shouts of revolution. Our cries of lament disturb the privileged and awaken the comfortable. Join the powerful chorus of weeping mothers because you too are a mother.

------ ★ ★ ★ ------

Lord, in all the ways you nurture and love your children, I give thanks. I pray for weeping mothers across the world. Hold them close and grant them moments of peace. I pray to always hear the cries of your people and to be moved to faithful action. Amen.

Rev. Dr. Theresa S. Thames

Hillary Clinton stood before a crowd gathered to celebrate the 200th anniversary of the African Methodist Episcopal Church on Friday evening and addressed a week of stunning violence around the country that included the shootings of two black men by police officers in Louisiana and Minnesota as well as a deadly attack on police in Dallas.

"We know there is something wrong in this country," said Clinton. "There is too much violence, too much hate, too much senseless killing. Too many people dead who shouldn't be."[13]

Philadelphia magazine
July 8, 2016

THY ROCK
1 Samuel 7:12

Literally meaning "stone of help" or "rock of grace," Ebenezer is mentioned only a few times in Scripture. In his hymn, "Come Thou Fount," Robert Robinson penned, "Here I raise my Ebenezer; hither by thy great help I've come."

As a college chaplain, I was charged with taking first-year students on a hike from the tallest point in Georgia into the "enchanted valley" of our campus. I asked them to find a rock on their hike down, which I kept during their four years on campus. During their last days, they hiked up and out of the valley, preparing for graduation. I then gave their rocks back, reminding them God had brought them that far.

I challenged them to go forth, prepared to use that rock to mark where God had called them to be servants to the world.

Our lives of faith are marked by these stones of grace. The testament of our faith is our willingness to respond to God's call with thankfulness.

Thankfully, this task is never in solitude. We travel with community and the abiding presence of God. The last remark I made to my students at that highest point is that the hike down and up was never a venture by one's self. By thy great help we've come.

------- ★ ★ ★ -------

God of the mountains and valleys, call me daily to be your servant. With every joy and challenge, continue to guide me to be thankful as I raise my Ebenezers. My rock and my help, I pray. Amen.

Rev. Blair Tolbert

AS WE WORK TOGETHER
Genesis 21:16-17

This particular moment in history feels like an impossible setback for women. But I am reminded that Scripture is filled with the stories of hurting women who were loved, sought after, and empowered by God.

Genesis records the story of Hagar, Sarah's maid who does what she is told, producing a child for Abraham and Sarah. A slave to those in power, she is later cast off—sent into the wilderness with her child to die. The good news is that God finds Hagar in the wilderness. Like Hagar, so many women among us have been used, abused, and abandoned, our needs forgotten and our voices ignored. But God hears our cries. With God's help, we are transforming the world.

May the God of gentleness and strength, break open our hearts to see our sisters in the desert, to hear their cries for justice, and to join our voices with theirs. Let this be the moment we awaken, to work together with God's help to change the world.

------ ★ ★ ★ ------

Empowering God, open my eyes even when looking is hard. Empower me to be a builder of bridges and doorways that provide ways out of places of suffering. Make me into an instrument of love, creating wells of grace in situations where all that seems possible is more death and tears. Let me be a protector and nurturer for those whom you put in my path, much as you are to Hagar, who is still in our midst. Amen.

Rev. Katie Trinter

I feel pride and gratitude for this wonderful campaign that we built together, this vast, diverse, creative, unruly, energized campaign. You represent the best of America and being your candidate has been one of the greatest honors of my life.[14]

CNN Politics
November 9, 2016

THE RISK

Matthew 15:21-28

The Canaanite woman understands something in this story that the disciples of Jesus are just not quite grasping yet. Jesus is not just the hope for Israel. He is hope for the entire world. Her persistence and insistence that Jesus can help her daughter strikes Jesus as nothing but vulnerability and courage. It is courageous for this woman to take the risk to ask. Again and again, she asks. It could not have been easy, especially with the disciples glaring in the background.

Her faith brings healing. Her persistence and willingness to be vulnerable, believe in something that she cannot quite see is honored by Jesus. Today, take the risk to be vulnerable—even when the world tells you it is less than courageous to show trust and take risks, be vulnerable. God will lead you in the riskiness.

------- ★ ★ ★ -------

God, today I am called to vulnerable, to trust you and take risks. Help me know that you are near as I do so. Amen.

Rev. Emily L. Stirewalt

FROM: Rev. Bill Shillady
SENT: October 7, 2016
TO: H

Good morning, my sister,
Prayers for your debate preparation. Prayers for peace in our nation and world. Prayers for you, Bill, Marc, Chelsea, Charlotte, and Aidan.

Also, I missed the feast day of St. Francis of Assisi three days ago, so blessings on your dogs! Lilly, our golden, is also a blessing to us.
Rev. Bill

STAY GROUNDED

Psalm 1:1-4

S ome days, it feels as if the "wicked" have all the luck, as if the "disrespectful" are the ones who get the most air time, as if standing "on the road of sinners" would be a lot easier than working for peace with justice. Yet the psalmist assures us the wicked are like dust the wind blows away, while the one who meditates on God's Word will be like a tree planted by a stream. He or she will bear fruit at just the right time, when it's most needed. And his or her work will have a lasting impact, like leaves that don't fade.

Perhaps the task for each of us, then, is not to convince the masses that the wicked will blow away like dust or that the disrespectful simply will not last. It's certainly not to take the easy road of vying for power by pitting people against one another. Rather, it's simply to stay grounded in what we know to be true and right and good: to keep meditating on God's word until the season when it does bear fruit—fruit that will last and prosper for generations. Instead of defeating the voices of evil, some days it seems our call is simply to stay grounded, to remember who we are, and to let God's Word bloom in us.

------ ★ ★ ------

God, help me stay grounded in your Word, not swayed by the wicked nor exhausted by adversaries; instead, help me plant myself in your living water, knowing that such devotion will yield justice and peace in due time. Amen.

Rev. Elizabeth Ingram Schindler

SPINNING PLATES

Psalm 46:10 NIV

Have you ever seen the trick where the juggler balances several spinning plates, each on the top of a thin stick?

Modern life, especially for women, can feel a bit like this. We have lots of plates in the air to keep spinning: work, school, soccer games, church, and the piles of laundry that never seem to go away. The list of commitments is long, varied, and demanding.

I wonder: *Will I be able to do all of this?* In those moments, I hear the psalmist say, "Be still, and know that I am God."

The Hebrew translation for *be still* means to "let drop" or "become slack." Stillness in the presence of God is a comfort. We can rely on God's everlasting presence with us through all things, even when we drop a plate or two.

I have to admit I don't like dropping plates. I have become a proficient juggler. But this passage is a necessary reminder for all of the jugglers among us. As the number of plates multiplies, know God is with you in the craziness and in the stillness.

Find time in your schedule to truly enjoy this moment—this day. May God's words, "Be still, and know that I am God," bring you peace.

------ * ★ * ------

God, there are a lot of plates spinning right now. I lift up the plates to you. Give me wisdom to choose my plates carefully and to carve out time to be still in your presence. Amen.

Rev. Sara M. Nelson

SPEAK UP
Esther 4:14 NRSV

Last week I was on a prayer walk with George, an eighty-year-old male parishioner, when we came across a couple of young girls selling handmade bracelets. They were, rightfully, very proud of their work.

But that pride was nothing next to what we saw when George informed them that I, a thirty-two-year-old clergywoman, was his pastor. The surprise and joy that quickly washed across their faces are gifts I can't imagine duplicating, as they excitedly responded with wide eyes, "Really!?" Certainly, we could see them thinking that George should be *my* pastor—not the other way around.

Their excitement only continued to heighten into wide eyes of hope as they readily accepted an invitation to have me offer them a prayer.

I share this story because I know it is only one example of how, if I had been alone, I might have missed an important opportunity. I would likely have shied away from telling them I was a pastor, even if I had told them about my church that I love. Fortunately, this hesitancy never occurred to George as he spoke the truth of who I am, shattering the limited ceiling of these young girls, who may never have imagined they could ever be pastors.

These are the moments we hope you live for, moments of seeing impossible hopes and dreams shift into possible realities.

What hopes or dreams may perish if we do not live into the truth of proclaiming boldly who we have been created to be? What hopes and dreams are we called to embody not just for our sakes but for the generations of women who will stand on our trailblazing shoulders?

Raising our voices in this way is not always easy—few things worth doing ever are. Yet we have to return to the hope of stories like these. We retell these stories not because we are perfect or because we always feel like we are well equipped for the tasks before us; we retell these stories because we are assured in these moments that, indeed, God has brought us to where we are "for such a time as this."

Awe-inspiring God, for the work you have set before me and for the strength and abilities you give me to do it, I give you thanks. This day and in the days ahead, may you also provide for me the humility and grace to do this work with care and the courage and confidence to do it with boldness. In Jesus's name. Amen.

Rev. Jen Tyler

TESTED BY FIRE

Loving God of the universe and of all humanity:
You are the God who believes in new beginnings.

You are the God who calls us to aim high in our dreams and hopes.

You are the God who forgives us when we miss the mark of your high calling.

You are the force that helps to break the glass ceilings of sexism, racism, and ageism—really any "isms" that exist that create barriers to keep people down.

You are a God who calls all people to love each other, even to lay down their lives for one another.

Lord God, this evening, one of the most divisive and unpredictable presidential races in modern memory has reached its end.

We need a new beginning. God, bring order out of the chaos of these last few months. Set us free from the turmoil.

We need your healing to end the hate and fear, to challenge us to be stronger together as we work for the progress of all people in our beloved country. Because united we stand and divided we fall, may our nation serve as a shining beacon of unity, freedom, and hope around this world.

We are grateful that your child Hillary Rodham Clinton was willing to take on this challenge of making our nation better, of moving forward and not backwards, of bringing hope and equality to all people. We are grateful for a leader who celebrates diversity and sees it as a blessing and not a curse. We are grateful for a leader who lives out her faith daily and joins other faiths in the common thread of respect for others and helping the least, the last, and the lost.

Empower her and us, O God, to bring our nation together for the common good of all your children.

We are thankful that Hillary and Tim have placed themselves in this race to guide our nation—as they respect and implement your call to seek mercy and justice.

Help them to continue to lead us in showing kindness and compassion to our neighbors.

They will need to help us love those who are difficult to love. They will help us to express empathy and empowerment to the widows and the fatherless and the poor. And they will help our nation to offer hospitality and justice for the sojourner and the immigrant.

They will continue to lead us in reconciliation with hope for the future—regardless of today's outcome.

Send your spirit of healing, peace, justice, and freedom upon us. Break down the walls of political partisanship, help us build bridges for the future, and make us one.

One nation under God, indivisible, with liberty and justice for all. Give us wisdom to walk in your ways, courage to speak in your name, and humility to trust in your providential ways. Amen.

---- ★ ★ ★ ----

FROM: Rev. Bill Shillady
DATE: November 8, 2016, 6:00 AM
TO: H

Good morning,
I will be there tonight. I hope to see you. I have a few devotionals for this day that have been written. I will send you periodic ones throughout the day. Here is my prayer for this day. Love trumps hate.
Rev. Bill

THE DAWN OF THE ELECTION
Zechariah 7:9-10

Hear our prayer, Lord:

Loving God of the universe and of all humanity, you are the source of life and creation and every blessing, the judge of every nation, and the hope of earth and heaven. We pray to you on the dawn of this day for this important and historic election. We call to mind the best that is within us: that we live under God, that we are indivisible, that liberty and justice encompass everyone in our nation.

We acknowledge the sin that runs through our history as a nation: The displacement of native peoples, racial injustice, economic inequity, and regional separation. We acknowledge the division and hate that has reared its terrible head in these months leading up to this day. The gospel compels us to respond as faithful citizens in our community. We ask for eyes that are free from blindness so that we might see each other as brothers and sisters—one and equal in dignity.

We confess a deep and abiding gratitude for the goodness of ordinary people who have made sacrifices, who have sought opportunities, who have journeyed to this land as immigrants strengthening its promise in successive generations, who have found freedom on these shores, and who have defended this freedom at tremendous cost.

May our decisions on this day reflect your call to seek mercy and justice. May we vote to show kindness and compassion to our neighbors.

Be with us on this day and in the days and weeks that follow this historic moment in our nation's history. Be with your daughter Hillary and your son Tim and their families and team today and everyday henceforth. Remind us that your ways are not necessarily our ways, that your wisdom can transcend our human plans and those plans of every nation, leader, and judge, and that your foundations of truth and grace shall not be destroyed.

Let those of us who follow your Son, Jesus Christ, be a peaceable people in the midst of division. Let us show your love to all people regardless of their race, their religion, their culture, and their political attitudes.

Give us wisdom to walk in your ways, courage to speak in your name, and humility to trust in your providential ways. Amen.

SPIRIT OF THE LORD 6:30 a.m. prayer
Isaiah 61:1-4

*O*n this day, God, and into the future, may Hillary know that you have brought her to her position of leadership and influence. Help her to help the rest of us to be the people who build, restore, heal, and transform communities that have suffered for generations. May your spirit rest upon her in power. May your anointing be upon her. Amen.

Rev. Dr. Elaine A. Heath

* *

WILL NOT BE WEARY 8:24 a.m. prayer
Isaiah 40:31

O God, enfold your precious daughter Hillary in your loving, empowering, protective arms this day and every day. Continue to embolden her and use her as your instrument for healing your people.

Let this prayer be her prayer:

> *Before me in the planned shape of this day I look for unexpected surgings of new life. Around me in the people whom I know and love I look for unopened gifts of promise. Within me in the familiar sanctuary of my own soul I look for shinings of the everlasting light. Before me, around me, within me I look for your life-giving mystery, O God, before me, around me, within me. Amen.*[1]

Bishop Jane Allen Middleton

------ ★ ★ ★ ------

Hillary Clinton ✓
@HillaryClinton

This team has so much to be proud of. Whatever happens tonight, thank you for everything.

RETWEETS   LIKES
138,289   364,348

5:55 PM - 8 Nov 2016

↩ 14K   ↻ 138K   ♥ 364K

SIGNS OF HOPE 10:30 a.m. prayer
Revelation 21:5

Merciful God, you are the one who brought order out of chaos and created all things. This day, bring moments of order in the chaos. Bring signs of hope and beauty in the midst of poll results and news. Bring reminders of your presence in all things, even here, even right now. Amen.

Rev. Anjie Peek Woodworth

* *

STAND FIRM 11:30 a.m. prayer
Joshua 1:9

Gracious God, will you stand close by Secretary Clinton's side in this moment and shower her with wisdom, courage, and a holy calm during this momentous day? Grant her a steady assurance of your loving presence as she moves through the next few hours and encounters whatever lies ahead. Be her strength, resolve, and shield. In your holy name, we pray. Amen.

Rev. Kevin K. Wright

------ ★ ★ ★ ------

CREATOR OF ALL THINGS 12:30 p.m. prayer
Revelation 21:5

A hymn from Charles Wesley:

Jesus, my Strength, my Hope,
On Thee I cast my care,
With humble confidence look up,
And know Thou hear'st my prayer.

Give me on Thee to wait
Till I can all things do;
On Thee, almighty to create,
Almighty to renew.

I want a true regard,
A single, steady aim,
Unmoved by threat'ning or reward
To Thee and Thy great Name.

I rest upon Thy Word;
The promise is for me;
My comfort and salvation, Lord,
Shall surely come from Thee.
But let me still abide,
Nor from my hope remove,
Till Thou my patient spirit guide
Into Thy perfect love. Amen.

Rev. James A. Harnish

-------- ★ ★ ★ --------

GOD'S GREAT LOVE 1:30 p.m. prayer
Ephesians 3:18-21

*L*oving God, on this important day in the life of our country and in the life of your daughter Hillary pour out your Holy Spirit so that she may be reminded of your presence, filled with your strength, and blessed by your grace. May your love overflow within her heart as she embarks on the journey that lies ahead. Amen.

Bishop Thomas J. Bickerton

* *

GOD'S PROTECTION 2:30 p.m. prayer
Isaiah 43:1b-2

*L*oving God, let your daughter Hillary know that you are with her, a very present help, strength, and shield. Bless and protect her in every circumstance so that she might continue to stand firm in faith, hope, and love as a wise leader and humble servant not only of this nation but of your kingdom. Amen.

Rev. Ginger E. Gaines-Cirelli

------- ★ ★ ★ -------

Senator Tim Kaine
@timkaine

Thinking about my daughter right now. No little girl will ever again have to wonder whether she, too, can be president.

RETWEETS 16,175   LIKES 73,051

5:30 PM - 8 Nov 2016

2.7K   16K   73K

DO NOT BE ANXIOUS 2:45 p.m. prayer
Philippians 4:6-7

Holy God, I am anxious as I wait with hope and expectation. I am anxious as I wait with fear and doubt. Send your spirit of peace as you did with Abraham and Joseph, Ruth, and Mary while they waited to see how your promise would unfold. I give thanks for your grace that covers all fear. I give thanks for your spirit of joy. I give thanks for you, my Creator, who loves me through all things. Amen.

Rev. Janessa Chastain

* *

BELOVED 3:00 p.m. prayer
John 1:12

Above all else today, remember that you are not the first female major party candidate, not a former secretary of state, not a former senator but a child of God. You are beloved. No matter what the outcome is today, you are a child of God. Rejoice that you are born of God and loved by God, a God who loves all of humanity enough to become flesh and walk among us.

Rev. J. Paige Boyer

———— ☆ ————

I AM YOURS, LORD 3:30 p.m. prayer
Romans 8:26-28

Covenant Prayer of John Wesley:

> I am no longer my own but yours.
> Put me to what you will,
> rank me with whom you will;
> put me to doing,
> put me to suffering;
> let me be employed for you,
> or laid aside for you,
> exalted for you,
> or brought low for you;
> let me be full,
> let me be empty,
> let me have all things,
> let me have nothing:
> I freely and wholeheartedly yield all things
> to your pleasure and disposal.
> And now, glorious and blessed God,
> Father, Son and Holy Spirit,
> you are mine and I am yours. So be it.
> And the covenant now made on earth, let it be ratified in heaven.

Rev. Matthew T. Curry

* *

FEAR NOT 4:00 p.m. prayer
Isaiah 41:10

Holy One, I stand in this tense place—embodying both excitement and anxiety. Help me to feel your presence fully as I honor the myriad emotions I am experiencing today. Thank you for this day. Amen.

Rev. Julia Singleton

★ ★ ★

MY STRONGHOLD 4:45 p.m. prayer
Psalm 27:1, 12-14 ESV

*T*he LORD *is my light and my salvation; whom shall I fear? The* LORD *is the stronghold of my life; of whom shall I be afraid? . . . Give me not up to the will of my adversaries, for false witnesses have risen against me, and they breathe out violence. I believe that I shall look upon the goodness of the* LORD *in the land of the living! Wait for the* LORD*; be strong, and let your heart take courage; wait for the* LORD*!*

Rev. Monica Beacham

* *

THE LORD'S PRAYER 5:00 p.m. prayer
Matthew 6:9-13 KJV

*O*ur *Father which art in heaven, Hallowed be thy name. Thy kingdom come, Thy will be done in earth, as it is in heaven. Give us this day our daily bread. And forgive us our debts, as we forgive our debtors. And lead us not into temptation, but deliver us from evil: For thine is the kingdom, and the power, and the glory, forever. Amen.*

Rev. Dr. Bill Shillady

------- * ⭐ * -------

THIS CUP   5:30 p.m. prayer
Isaiah 40:31

G od grant that as we go out and face life with all of its decisions, as we face the bitter cup which we will inevitably face from day to day, God grant that we will learn this one thing and that is, to make the transition from "this cup" to "nevertheless." Amen.[2]

Rev. Dr. Cathy S. Gilliard

* *

HONOR ABOVE ALL ELSE   6:00 p.m. prayer
Isaiah 65:17-18

G od of hope, we give you thanks for your presence and preparations with and for one of your own beloved, one you know intimately by name, Hillary. May she and our nation receive the grace of the Holy Spirit anew. Like prophets past, may she continue the work of leading this nation to honor you and to be a nation of love and hope and not of hatred and fear; in the name of the Almighty One who reigns forever and ever. Amen.

Rev. Wongee Joh

PEACE OF GOD 7:00 p.m. prayer
Philippians 4:7

M ay the peace of God surprise you, Hillary, in the midst of this journey.
Amen.

Jorge Lockward

* *

GOD'S LOVE REMAINS 8:00 p.m. prayer
Psalm 31:24

G racious Lord, surround our sister Hillary Clinton and her family as she
waits, and be with the people of this great nation as they exercise the right
to vote. May we be humble in victory and gracious in defeat. May we recognize
that what make us great does not come from outside ourselves but within. We
thank you that your love for us does not end or begin with the outcome of these
elections. Long after the importance of this day fades away, when our faith has
been tested and our hope torn away, your deep and abiding love will remain.
Amen.

Rev. Leslie Stephens

------ ⭐ ------

It's Official: Clinton Swamps Trump in Popular Vote

More Americans voted for Hillary Clinton than any
other losing presidential candidate in US history.
The Democrat outpaced President-elect Donald Trump
by almost 2.9 million votes, with 65,844,954 (48.2%)
to his 62,979,879 (46.1%), according to revised and
certified final election results from all 50 states and the
District of Columbia.[3]

CNN Politics
December 21, 2016

UNEXPECTED JOURNEY
Exodus 1:17

I t takes strength to stand up to authoritarian power, but it's the kind of strength the world calls weakness. It's strength that's not speaking but listening, mastery that's not rule following but rule breaking, and power that's not killing but birthing.

Shiphrah and Puah embodied this strength. Just two women who refused to do what was wrong, because they had a vocation to bring what was right to life. It's hard being a righteous woman in this world, measured by the standards of our current principalities. But it's a sacred duty—to do what is right, facing any threat. We women know what real strength can bring into being.

Our nation is in a time of transition—of rebirth—that doesn't look like you imagined or hoped that it would. Yet we still need strong, patient, and tender midwives who honor our Creator, whose hearts are guided by your true vocation: the soft cry of freedom signaling God's new path forward toward justice and mercy. How will you continue to live into this call? How will you respond to God's leading on this unexpected journey?

------ ⋆ ⭐ ⋆ ------

Holy One, let me be the midwife of your dream for our neighborhoods, nation, and world. Shine your lamp of truth to show me the way, lend me your strength for the struggle, and fill me with hope for new birth's coming. Amen.

Rev. Julia Nielsen

AS WE WAIT

James 5:7-11

Henri Nouwen writes:

> How do we wait for God? We wait with patience. But patience does not mean passivity. Waiting patiently is not like waiting for the bus to come, the rain to stop, or the sun to rise. It is an active waiting in which we live the present moment to the full in order to find there the signs of the One we are waiting for.
>
> The word patience comes from the Latin verb *patior* which means "to suffer." Waiting patiently is suffering through the present moment, tasting it to the full, and letting the seeds that are sown in the ground on which we stand grow into strong plants. Waiting patiently always means paying attention to what is happening right before our eyes and seeing there the first rays of God's glorious coming.[4]

The Letter of James is filled with good instruction to educate the church community about the rules to follow for a well-lived life. In this passage, James speaks to those not-so-well-off. His message to these strugglers is, "Be patient," patient in the sense of a humble dependence on God's mercy, a dependence on the one who will sort out the mess for us. So James is calling on us to rely patiently on the Lord's promised mercy.

Much of our striving produces mediocre results, but God's ultimate intentions for us in Christ are anything but mediocre. Let us rest on the truth that our momentary limitations will ultimately be transformed by our patient dependence upon God.

------- ★ ★ ★ -------

Lord, I want patience and I want it NOW! This is my desperate prayer at times when my life is so chaotic that I can't seem to move forward. I need to be reminded that, as the spring comes with rain, the harvest will yield results even though I can't see them in the rains. I put my trust in you, O God, for my life to be made whole in your time. Amen.

IN ALL CIRCUMSTANCES
1 Thessalonians 5:16-18

The above words from Paul's Letter to the Thessalonians are among the most challenging words in all of Scripture. Why? Because it's easy to rejoice when things are going well in life, when we're victorious or successful in some venture, great or small. It's also easy to be thankful when we receive a gift, a windfall, or some unexpected good fortune.

Yet when life goes against us, that's when Paul's words challenge us deeply, into our very souls. When we get diagnosed with life-threatening diseases, can we rejoice or give thanks? When we have suffered the loss of loved ones, how is it possible to express joy or thanksgiving? When we've suffered defeats or disappointments in our life's work, how can we possibly rejoice or give thanks?

Paul wrote these words from his own life experiences. He was imprisoned, beaten, shipwrecked, driven out of town, and persecuted for preaching his Christian convictions. Yet he was able to encourage his fellow Christians to always rejoice and always be thankful.

Giving thanks *in* all circumstances is not the same as giving thanks *for* all circumstances. Of course we don't give thanks for cancer, death, defeats, or disappointments. The key is to cultivate a kind of thanksgiving that is not dependent on the circumstances of the moment.

The reason we can rejoice and give thanks in all circumstances is that God is in all circumstances—even in that ultimate circumstance of death. One of the great benedictions in the *United Methodist Book of Worship* is: "In life, in death, in life beyond death, God is with us! We are not alone. Thanks be to God!"

------- ★ ★ ★ -------

God of joy and gratitude, give us the strength and faith to always recognize your presence in good times and difficult times, in victory and defeat. In your presence we find deep joy and deep gratitude. We can always be thankful that you are with us in any and all circumstances. Amen.

Robert Martin Walker

I AM HOPEFUL
Psalm 27:13

I am not an optimist by nature. Thankfully, the psalmist does not call us to be optimists. He simply states what he believes to be true based upon a deep and lasting confidence built upon his community's experience with God. The situation in which he finds himself may be bleak and the evidence around him might speak to the contrary, but the psalmist's faith in the God who will redeem him is unwavering.

The Rev. Dr. Martin Luther King Jr. once said, "I am not optimistic, but I'm hopeful," in regard to the future of the movement toward racial equality for all. Dr. King knew the threats to his life and to the movement presented by bombings, water hoses, and terrorists. Yet, where King's optimism withered, his hope sprung up from the soil of a moral arc stretching across the universe towards justice.

We've spent a year and a half bringing together millions of people from every corner of our country to say with one voice that we believe that the American dream is big enough for everyone.[5]

Hillary Rodham Clinton
November 9, 2016

Our belief that God is not yet done with us or our country rests not on an ignorant optimism but rather in a deep and lasting hope that even when circumstances seem to say otherwise, the goodness of the Lord is yet at hand.

Rev. Kevin K. Wright

------ ★ ★ ★ ------

Lord, as we enter into this season of waiting called Advent, we whisper to our hearts, "Be still. The Lord is coming. Surely the Lord will come." Hear our whispers, Lord. Amen

OUR HOPE MUST REMAIN
Psalm 131

I f we are honest with ourselves, we know that there are many mornings when we wake up, and like the psalmist, our hearts are not lifted up. It seems like more than we can possibly do to get out of bed and be real, functioning people. To have to think about the things facing us and all that we have to do feels like far too much to handle. Even spending time dwelling on the wonderful things of the world weighs down upon us, because our hearts are heavy and hurt and overwhelmed.

Isn't it a liberating thing to be able to recognize this, though? There is healing that comes from being able to own that this is how we are feeling. There is something freeing about saying to the universe, "I am disappointed. My soul is sad. My wounds are real. I ache, and even if I cannot put my finger on what hurts the most, the hurt is real."

Perhaps the fact that the psalmist was able to claim these feelings was precisely the thing that led to the psalmist's soul becoming calmed and quieted, like a child resting upon one who loves him or her so very, very much. Perhaps being able to speak these things to ourselves and to God is the thing that can lead us to finding calmness and quietness in the arms of the One who loves us very, very much.

As the psalmist says in verse three, our hopes must remain in the Lord. There is hope that even when we doubt, even when our hearts are not lifted up, and even when the good things are too much to handle, that God is God, loving us, hearing our cries, and promising to be with us not only right now but forever and ever.

O Great God, help me see that no matter how I feel that you listen to my cries, understand my sadness, and bear my grief with me. Help me to be able to express these things to you and find comfort in your arms. Never let me forget that you created me and love me, now and forever, and that because of you, I can begin to see the hope that only you can bring. Amen.

Rev. Shannon Rodenberg

GOD IS PRESENT
Esther 4:14

Today's Scripture captures the current state of our nation: nothing that has happened within the past month has happened in isolation. There is a history behind today's realities. In the same vein, we also remember that social change—the leaning of communities and cultures towards justice, compassion, and the bringing about of the kingdom of God upon earth—did not just "suddenly happen." The hand of the divine has been present, is present, and will be present in the future. We don't know exactly when "such a time as this" is, but we do know that even if we can't see the entire picture, we are still called to participate in God's co-creation of a new heaven and a new earth.

May we be lifted up by the reminder that change—especially social change—takes time. Many invisible and visible voices whisper truth behind closed doors as groups of people learn about new ways of being. We don't know how our individual and collective service for the greater good will become realized in future days, months, and years. We are simply called to serve and to use our gifts and graces in ways that transform the world in ways great and small. Sometimes our words, our service, our presence—they are utilized by the divine in unexpected ways "for such a time as this."

Our responsibility as citizens is to keep doing our part to build that better, stronger, fairer America we seek. And I know you will.[6]

Hillary Rodham Clinton
November 9, 2016

Holy God, may you continue to transform my life as I seek to follow Christ's call for compassion and justice. May my communities continue to be transformed by individual and collective service in ways more glorious than I ever could have imagined on my own, and may you continue to be at the center of all I do. Amen.

Rev. April Casperson

HOLY WHOLENESS
Luke 13:10-17

When I read this story, it makes me wonder if the leader was really mad about the supposedly Sabbath-breaking nature of the healing or if it was something deeper—maybe that Jesus dared to touch a woman in a society where touch between unrelated men and women was taboo. If you imagine a woman bent over so that she cannot straighten up, how do you picture Jesus facing her? Based on all the stories of Jesus in the Gospels, I believe he sought to look her in the eyes for this interaction. This means he was not standing above this unnamed, physically disabled woman as he placed his hands on her but rather kneeling in front of her, putting himself in a position of humility and connection as he let God's healing power flow into her bound body, allowing her to stand up straight and look other people in the eye for the first time in eighteen years.

When we seek to join in God's work of healing the brokenness of the world, we may be called upon to kneel down before those the world regards as objects of pity, to make eye contact and acknowledge their worth and dignity. We may be criticized—often indirectly—by those whose fragile ego or rigid need for hierarchy and rules cannot abide the possibility that God cares for the poor, the outcast, the foreigner, the differently abled, the least, and the lowly. But we can have confidence in the rightness of our actions when we work to restore to wholeness those who have been bound or are broken.

------ ★ ★ ★ ------

God of holy wholeness, let your healing power flow through me this day. May I recognize the dignity and sacred worth of each person I meet. May I be willing to humble myself to take part in your sacred work in the world. Amen.

Rev. Kerry L. Greenhill

PROCLAIM JOY

Zephaniah 3:14-20

There are tragedies in the world and things that can't be undone. There are scars that remain from the hurts that we've inflicted and that have been inflicted on us. God knows that well, for God still bears the wounds inflicted on the one who came and loved us best. The promise is not that history will be changed; the promise is that the future can be.

God's love, made manifest in Jesus, frees and strengthens us to choose mercy and love and peace and hope again and again—no matter what—and to defiantly claim the life we've been given as a gift. What then should we do in this hot mess of a world? Utter a holy and broken hallelujah and proclaim joy nonetheless.

Lord, help my heart to sing hallelujah in the midst of despair. Help me to love as I have never loved before, with your love as the source of all my being. Amen.

Rev. Ginger E. Gaines-Cirelli

THE FAITHFULNESS OF THE PROPHET
Lamentations 3:22-23 ESV

Jesus said that no prophet is without honor except in his own hometown. Basically, from far away, it's easy to see the courage and bravery that telling the truth takes, but up close, truth telling stings. So we try to take down the truth-teller because she's making us uncomfortable.

This is nothing new, and anyone who is in leadership—whether in a home, a classroom, a boardroom—knows this is how these things work. But the reason so many lose their faith in humanity is because the toll this type of targeting takes on a leader and a truth-teller is intense and tremendous. We all certainly have felt this whenever we have been surrounded by people who live their lives motivated by extreme dysfunction and fear.

If you look to the earlier part of Lamentations, you can read the lament of the prophet and feel the desolation that has settled over his spirit. And, especially in chapter 2, he cries over what seems to him like God's complicity in the devastation he feels. It's funny then that the text takes a sudden and sharp turn in chapter 3 when Jeremiah, the author of Lamentations, stops his lament abruptly and begins the mantra: "The steadfast love of the Lord never ceases, God's mercies never come to an end." That's where he ends up.

And that's where we must end up, so the darkness all around us will not overcome us.

----- ★ ★ ★ -----

God, we know we are not alone. We are not abandoned. We are not without hope. Your steadfast love never ceases, and your mercies never come to an end. Amen.

Rev. Dr. Amy K. Butler

BECOMING A MESSENGER
Luke 24:9-12

An encounter with God is so compelling it pushes those who have experienced it beyond their comfort zones. The women who went to anoint their teacher's body walked away that morning as the first witnesses to the Resurrection. Being in God's story changes the servant into the messenger.

Along your faith journey you have met God and been changed by those experiences. God may have broken into your life through the love and example of a Sunday school teacher or in an earth tilting moment as a volunteer serving those on the margins. As part of God's story in that moment you became the carrier of God's love and truth.

It is daunting to be called as a messenger. There is a risk that the world will not believe your message because of who you are. Hold on to the power of the good news that God sees you as worthy to share in this incredible story. Remember there are always the ones like Peter, who know God at work in the world when they hear it. Through your message they may have a renewed experience of the inbreaking of God. This in turn will lead them to become messengers who carry God's light and love even further.

------ ⋆ ★ ⋆ ------

God, break into this moment and empower me, your servant, to bear witness to you in the world. Help me to trust that I will be heard and believed. May others come to know you through my story. Amen.

Rev. Eilidh Lowery

GO BACK TO THE BEGINNING
Matthew 26:6-13

CeCe Winans's song "Alabaster Box" pictures what it was like for a woman to walk into a room filled with people who were judging her. CeCe helps to humanize this woman. She helps us relate to how she felt coming to anoint her Savior and to pour out her praise on him.

Can you identify with the woman in this Scripture? Most of us have our own box of alabaster as a result of God freeing us from all the times we have fallen short. No one knows what that box contains even though others try to cast judgment on our box.

CeCe sings, "You did not feel what I felt when he wrapped his loving arms around me. And you don't know the cost of the oil in my alabaster box."

Sometimes we need to go back to the moment that Jesus found us and remember how lost we were to be thankful for the gift of love that God has given us. We need to remember where our worth comes from. We are God's beloved, and God calls each of us by name. This woman remembered that her worth was shown through the eyes of Jesus, and that is how she walked into that room. That is how she tuned out what others were saying. That is how she had strength to heap her praise upon God in the midst of what was happening around her.

When was your moment? Can you hear God's voice calling you "beloved"? Do you see your worth in the eyes of Jesus or in the eyes of those in the world? Do you have your own alabaster box to offer back to Christ?

------ ✦ ★ ✦ ------

Dear loving God, help me to find my worth through your eyes. Remind me that you are my strength when my legs are too weak to stand. Help me to remember the cost of my alabaster box so that I might anoint you with my praise today out of the gift of love you have given me. Be my center. When the world around me seems full of hate, remind me that your love will prevail. Continue to walk with me on this journey and guide my steps; in the name of the one who gives me life. Amen.

Rev. Rebecca L. Laird

LET US FOSTER CHANGE

Philippians 4:8-9

Many people are finding it hard to concentrate since the election results were announced; they are having difficulty staying positive amid personal anxiety about the future and concerns for their brothers and sisters who have even more reason to worry. I imagine you are experiencing many of these feelings as well, along with great disappointment.

Paul calls us not to worry but to think on what is true and good. This doesn't mean we ignore the pain. We can't overlook the people who are suffering; we can't disregard the violence and hatred that is present. Instead we can view it as a motivator, as a call to action. When we ponder our concerns, let us turn them around and foster change.

And to all the little girls who are watching this, never doubt that you are valuable and powerful and deserving of every chance and opportunity in the world to pursue and achieve your own dreams.[7]

Hillary Rodham Clinton
November 9, 2016

Paul told the Philippians to look at him as an example—not that he was perfect, but because we find inspiration through the people we look up to. Even as this chapter of your career closes, God will use you. Millions of people are still looking up to you and being inspired by you. Continue to think on what is commendable and you will continue to inspire change.

------ ⋆ ★ ⋆ ------

God of peace, take away my anxiety, ease my disappointment, and work through me to bring change in the world. Show me how I can turn my concerns into action. Help me inspire people to do what is true, honorable, just, pure, commendable, and pleasing to you. Amen.

Rev. Katrina Paxson

THE GOOD NEWS
Mark 16:8

S o ends the original conclusion of Mark's Gospel. It ends not in triumph but in fear and silence. Three women came to the tomb to anoint Jesus's body, and they find Jesus's body gone. They want it to be a sign of hope after the most disappointing death, a death they weren't expecting, a death that turned their worlds upside down. But there still isn't much evidence of life after death, just the emptiness of the tomb. There is emptiness. And so they are silent.

Yet. Yet in spite of the women's initial silence, the church exists today. Our silence will not be silenced. The good news gets out; it always does. We await the birth of Jesus during Advent. He comes not born with parades and acclamations from powerful people. He comes in the silence. He was born in a stable, in the meekest of beginnings. The good news, however, gets out, through angels' proclamations to the unlikely and humble shepherds and through a silent, shining star. Hope broke into the world when it seemed that hopelessness was all there was. Both times—with the birth of Jesus and with his resurrection.

This means that even in moments of deepest disappointment, in moments when hope seems like a specter, in moments when fear and silence overtake us, even in these moments, God is present. Even in these moments, God is whispering the good news of Resurrection that we and the world both are aching to hear. God is lingering in the silence, in the emptiness, preparing a voice to rise out of the depths, saying, "Jesus is coming. Hope is alive. Love is alive."

------ ★ ★ ------

Loving One, when death seems stronger than life, when fear seems stronger than hope, when hate seems stronger than love, give me the courage to believe that you are on your way, that you are already here. Resurrection means love is the strongest thing in the universe. Embolden me again and again to give my voice and my life for love. Amen.

Rev. Alison VanBuskirk Philip

IT IS WELL WITH MY SOUL
Philippians 4:11-13

There is nothing like singing the songs of our tradition, the songs that are often etched into our hearts and souls, surrounded by the voices of a faith-filled congregation. As a hospital chaplain, I am constantly struck by the power of music to cut through painful moments, providing comfort and assurance even in the most difficult situations. One of the songs I often play for families in those moments is "It Is Well with My Soul."

It usually isn't "well" with their souls, but this song has the ability to re-center them, and they cling to the lyrics, singing through their tears, until the words become true, until they feel God's presence and God's peace in the depths of their souls. And I too turn to the songs of my faith when I am faltering. This song in particular comforts me, the simple melody and repetitive words calming both my breath and my soul.

I still believe as deeply as I ever have that if we stand together and work together with respect for our differences, strength in our convictions and love for this nation, our best days are still ahead of us.[8]

Hillary Rodham Clinton
November 9, 2016

In your moments of frustration, loneliness, confusion, or anxiety today may these melodies of our tradition rise from your heart and soul and speak to you of God's faithfulness and unending grace, love, and peace.

------ ★ ★ ★ ------

Holy comforter, may I know you in the melodies of my faith and the lyrics of my tradition. As these songs rise from deep within, enable them to remind me of who you are and who I am in you. Amen.

Rev. Dr. Christina L. Wright

CONTINUE ON

Galatians 4:4-7 ESV

The end of this year has been hard. We can name the reasons. Another year is not always about starting anew. Another year may be continuing forward with a renewed sense of purpose, focus, and zeal for the work God has called you, me, us to do. "The fullness of time had come . . . born of a woman . . . to redeem . . ." From the start, women have been part of God's work. Making possible for new life, new love, new grace, new opportunities, new redemption to be born into this world through our bodies, our hearts, our minds, our forgiveness, and our work. We have and will always be a part of the laboring.

The facts and our reality have been considered. And now. Now is the time for joy as we continue forward with the assurance of a call, the hope of redemption, and the task of divine work to bear grace into the world. The fullness of time had come that Christmas morning long ago. The fullness of time has come. The incarnation of God, born of a woman, makes possible our call, our work, our redemption. May we continue on, easy or not, because we serve alongside the Savior of hope, peace, joy, and love.

Light of life, you came in flesh, born into human pain and joy, and gave us power to be your children. Grant me faith, O Christ, to see your presence among us, so that I can be part of all of creation singing new songs of joy, be grounded in love, plant seeds of hope, and walk in the way of peace. Amen.

Rev. Blair Tolbert

NEW YEAR, NEW BEGINNINGS

Isaiah 43:8-9

Individually and certainly as a nation, I think many of us are just waiting to put the year behind us. Surely, surely the next must be better, right? Deep down though I wonder if we expect the new year really to bring more of the same. We make half-hearted resolutions, not actually believing we can change. We give ourselves permission to fail before we even begin, telling ourselves (and whoever will listen) that resolutions are pointless. We are so full of grief and pain. But do we really want something different?

Throughout the Scriptures, God is unrelenting in hope for the world. Sometimes though I'm a skeptic. God asks, "I am about to do a new thing . . . don't you see it?" And I can't. Not yet. I think that my lack of vision comes from trying to create my own new life instead of remembering that it is God who is in the business of resurrection. I can't make my whole life new, much less make a new world. But I work to increase my faith that God can. It is God who makes all things new, God who transforms our hearts and lives. When we put our hope and trust in God, when we let God work in and through us, when we open our whole lives to God's movement, some incredible things can happen, things we thought were impossible! God can make a way in the wilderness of the world, a river flowing in the desert of our hearts.

I'm back to being an activist citizen—and part of the resistance.[9]

Hillary Rodham Clinton
May 2, 2017

------ ★ ⭐ ★ ------

God of new beginnings, give us strength and hope for these days ahead. Help us see you at work in our world, and help us find our places in your unfolding story. Amen.

Rev. Dr. Elizabeth Quick

WITH YOU
Exodus 1:8-22

I n this Scripture passage, the midwives were given a direct order by the most powerful man in their world, the pharaoh of Egypt, and they ignored it. They didn't refuse him or fight back, but they also didn't follow his orders. The two women spoke with one voice throughout the passage. Scholars have suggested that they were likely leaders, allowing the collective voice of the midwives to be shared. They used their voice to manipulate the Pharaoh, using his biases and assumptions for the well-being of their community. When called to account for the living baby boys they had been told to kill, they responded (in essence), "Because Hebrew women aren't like Egyptian women. They're much stronger and give birth before any midwives can get to them." The Pharaoh wanted to believe them, so he did.

Despite their work, the passage ends with the Pharaoh making things worse for everyone—a precursor to the arrival of Moses and the deliverance of the Hebrew people from Egypt. In justice work, things usually get worse before they get better. I hope the midwives give you courage and hope along your journey, even if it is not the journey you envisioned. Things will get better, there are midwives out here joining you in the challenge of bringing something subversive into the world. And so we shall.

------ ★ ★ ★ ------

God of Love, may the wisdom of the ages continue to inform us today. May those who live in oppression find power in shared voices. May we, united as your children together, find our shared humanity and reconciliation time and time again. Amen.

Rev. Sara E. Baron

ONWARD

Romans 8:38-39

Good Morning on the last day of the year! Today will be the last daily devotional. It has been an unbelievable, sacred privilege to write these devotions and to organize a team of writers to write devotions for you for the last twenty-one months.

Let me say this is not the end. When I am moved by a piece or have a creative moment, I will send you some thoughts. I also will continue to pray for you, Bill, Chelsea, Marc, Charlotte, and Aidan. As I read my own devotionals and offer prayers, you are always there, close to my heart.

There is a sense of grief that I am ending this routine, but I am here for you if you need me. So with all that being said, here is my prayer for us this day.

------- ★ ★ ★ -------

Eternal God, you are the sovereign Lord of all our beginnings and all our endings. Give us courage to face the unknown challenges ahead. Help us learn from the mistakes we have made in the past. Help us forgive ourselves then others so that we may go on to write new chapters with confidence. Strengthen us in every good and worthy resolve, shaping our conduct more and more in the image of Christ's compassion and integrity. Give us the wisdom we need to allow your will to be done.

Be with our nation and our world during this unsettled time of conflict, fear, and anxiety. Keep us secure in your peace; for Jesus's sake. Amen.

FROM: H
SENT: December 31, 2016
TO: Rev. Bill Shillady

Dear Bill,
Thank you so much for your daily messages over such a stressful and challenging time. They lifted me up and often kept me going.
　I wish you and Judy a happy, healthy and productive new year.
Onward into 2017. –H

CONTRIBUTORS

Thomas J. Bickerton
J. Paige Boyer
Amy K. Butler
Matthew T. Curry
Frederick A. Davie
Danyelle Ditmer
Ginger E. Gaines-Cirelli
Cathy S. Gilliard
James A. Harnish
Elaine A. Heath
Wongee Joh

Jorge Lockward
Jane Allen Middleton
Marvin A. Moss
Constance Y. Pak
Emily A. Peck-McClain
Denise Smartt Sears
Shannon E. Sullivan
Jen Tyler
Robert Martin Walker
Kevin K. Wright

We Pray with Her Group

★ ★ ★

Deborah L. Allen
Kris Kraus Androsky
Mara Bailey
Jessica Baldyga
Sara E. Baron*
Monica Beacham*
Amelia Beasley
Katie Black
Lyndsie Blakely
Michelle Bodle
Beth Bostrom
Sarai Case
April Casperson*
Emily Chapman
Janessa Chastain*
Catherine Christman*
Sharon L. S. Cook
Kaleigh Corbett
Katie Z. Dawson*
Mary Dicken
Heather Dorr

Beth Elders*
Melissa Engel
Angela M. Flanagan
Lauren A. Godwin
Jodi Gonzalez
Kerry L. Greenhill*
Anna Guillozet*
Sarah Harrison-McQueen*
Kristin Heiden*
Karen Hernandez
Carol Hill
Brandi Tevebaugh Horton*
Jill Howard
Emily Huyge
Jodie Ihfe
Casey Ann Irwin*
Ashley Fitzpatrick Jenkins
Nicole de Castrique Jones*
Sarah Karber
Meghan S. Kelley
Diane M. Kenaston

* An additional contributor to *Strong for a Moment Like This*.

* *

Laura-Allen Kerlin
Rebecca L. Laird*
Lauren Lobenhofer
Eilidh Lowery*
Melissa Madara
Bromleigh McCleneghan
Sara McManus*
Michelle Mejia
Melissa Meyers
Patricia S. Money
Sara M. Nelson*
Julia Nielsen*
Laura Patterson*
Katrina Paxson*
Katie Goss Pearce*
Olivia Poole
Deborah D. Porras
Colleen Hallagan Preuninger*
Elizabeth Quick*
Lorrin Radzik
Shannon Rodenberg*
Laura Ann Gilbert Rossbert
Stacey Rushing

Elizabeth Ingram Schindler*
Lisa Schubert Nowling*
Allie Scott*
Julia Singleton*
Sarah A. Slack*
Brooke Heerwald Steiner*
Leslie Stephens*
Emily L. Stirewalt*
Megan Stowe
Emily Scales Sutton*
Elizabeth R. Taylor*
Theresa S. Thames*
Megan Elizabeth C. Thompson
Katie Barrett Todd
Blair Tolbert*
Shannon V. Trenton*
Katie Trinter*
Corey Tarreto Turnpenny
Alison VanBuskirk Philip*
Kristen Wall-Love
Megan Walther
Anjie Peek Woodworth*
Christina L. Wright*

NOTES

Accept the Call

1. Amy Chozick, "Hillary Clinton Announces 2016 Presidential Bid," *The New York Times*, April 12, 2015, www.nytimes.com/2015/04/13/us/politics/hillary-clinton-2016-presidential-campaign.html?_r=0.
2. Krishnadev Calamur, "It's Official: Hillary Clinton Announces Presidential Run," NPR, April 12, 2015, www.npr.org/sections/thetwo-way/2015/04/12/397891885/its-official-hillary-clinton-announces-presidential-run.
3. "Worship & Suffering," www.biblesociety.org.uk/explore-the-bible/daily-reflection/worship-suffering-friday-12-june/.
4. "Civil Rights Leader Rev. Dr. Otis Moss Jr. Endorses Hillary Clinton," September 28, 2016, www.hillaryclinton.com/briefing/statements/2016/09/28/civil-rights-leader-rev-dr-otis-moss-jr-endorses-hillary-clinton/.
5. "Full Transcript of Hillary Clinton's June 7 Victory Speech," *Blue Nation Review*, June 8, 2016, bluenationreview.com/full-transcript-of-hillary-clintons-june-7-victory-speech/.
6. Nelson Mandela, *Long Walk to Freedom: The Autobiography of Nelson Mandela* (Boston: Little, Brown and Company, 1995), 625.
7. Eleanor Clift, "Hillary Clinton Vows to Continue the Fight for Women Across the Globe," *The Daily Beast*, April 5, 2013, www.thedailybeast.com/witw/articles/2013/04/05/hillary-clinton-vows-to-continue-the-fight-for-women-across-the-globe.html.
8. "The Liturgical Calendar: The Church Remembers," http://prayer.forwardmovement.org/the_calendar_response.php?id=400717.
9. Clift, "Hillary Clinton Vows to Continue the Fight for Women Across the Globe."
10. Chozick, "Hillary Clinton Announces 2016 Presidential Bid."
11. Nancy L. Roberts, *Dorothy Day and the Catholic Worker* (New York: State University of New York Press, 1985), 22.
12. Heidi M. Przybyla, "Hillary Clinton Says 'Future Is Female' in New Video," *USA Today*, February 7, 2017, www.usatoday.com/story/news/politics/onpolitics/2017/02/07/hillary-clinton-delivers-first-remarks-womens-issues/97577966/.
13. "Hillary Clinton Victory Speech After the Iowa Caucuses," Iowa State University, February 1, 2016, www.womenspeecharchive.org/women/profile/speech/index.cfm?ProfileID=65&SpeechID=5539.
14. "Dance with God," www.infinitejoy.com/ffd/DanceWithGod.htm.
15. Henri Nouwen, *With Open Hands* (Notre Dame, IN: Ave Maria, 1972), 82.
16. Clift, "Hillary Clinton Vows to Continue the Fight for Women Across the Globe."

Have Courage

1. Chelsea Clinton, "3 Reasons to Vote for My Mom," *Us Weekly*, November 3, 2016, www.usmagazine.com/celebrity-news/news/chelsea-clinton-3-reasons-to-vote-for-my-mom-w447256.
2. Hillary Clinton, "We All Have Different Gifts," Hillary for America, September 13,

2015, https://medium.com/hillary-for-america/we-all-have-different-giftsv
-e664ee17ec96.

3. Sam Frizell, "Hillary Clinton Calls for Gun Control in New Ad," *Time*, November 3, 2015, http://time.com/4097904/hillary-clinton-ad-gun-violence/.

4. Hillary Clinton, "We Owe Our Children Better Than This. We Ourselves Better Than This," Hillary for America, July 8, 2016, https://medium.com/hillary-for-america/we-owe-our-children-better-than-this-we-owe-ourselves-better-than-this-7b4f04bf62a1.

5. "American Jewish Congress Bestows Lifetime Achievement Award on Hillary Clinton," *Haaretz*, March 20, 2014, www.haaretz.com/jewish/news/1.580849.

6. Ashley Collman, "'We Need to Nurture Our Girls': Hillary Clinton Surfaces in New York to Collect 'Champion for Girls' Award and Asks Women to Help Each Other," *The Daily Mail*, March 7, 2017, www.dailymail.co.uk/news/article-4291104/Hillary-Clinton-accepts-Girls-award.html.

7. Liz Kreutz, "Clinton: 'There Is No Erasing' Trump's History of Birther Attacks on President Obama," ABC News, September 16, 2016, http://abcnews.go.com/Politics/hillary-clinton-donald-trump-owes-president-obama-apology/story?id=42138137.

8. Lewis Carroll, *Alice's Adventures in Wonderland & Through the Looking-Glass* (New York: Bantam, 2006), 166.

9. Robert D. McFadden, "Dorothy Rodham, Mother and Mentor of Hillary Clinton, Is Dead at 92," *The New York Times*, November 1, 2011, www.nytimes.com/2011/11/02/us/dorothy-rodham-mother-of-hillary-clinton-dies-at-92.html.

10. M. J. Lee and Dan Merica, "The Hero of Clinton's Speech: Her Mother," CNN Politics, June 8, 2016, www.cnn.com/2016/06/08/politics/hillary-clinton-nomination-mother/index.html.

11. Henri Nouwen, "A Courageous Life," Henri Nouwen Society, http://henrinouwen.org/meditation/a-courageous-life/.

12. Randy Ludlow, "'Vote for a Difference,' Bill Clinton Implores Crowd in Ohio," *The Columbus Dispatch*, October 4, 2016, www.dispatch.com/content/stories/local/2016/10/04/bill-clinton-ohio-bus-tour.html.

13. Steven Petrow, "New Cancer Threat Lurks Long After Cure," *The New York Times*, July 16, 2012, https://well.blogs.nytimes.com/2012/07/16/new-cancer-threat-lurks-long-after-cure/?_r=0.

14. Hillary Clinton, "To Young People Who Are Undocumented: This Is Your Country, Too," Hillary for America, August 15, 2016, https://medium.com/hillary-for-america/to-young-people-who-are-undocumented-this-is-your-country-too-e0184e858b40.

15. "Hillary Clinton Statement on the Death of Alton Sterling," Hillary Clinton Speeches, July 6, 2016, https://hillaryspeeches.com/2016/07/06/hillary-clinton-statement-on-the-death-of-alton-sterling/.

16. Katie Bo Williams, "State Releases New Batch of Clinton Emails," *The Hill*, December 1, 2016, http://thehill.com/policy/national-security/308321-state-releases-new-batch-of-clinton-emails.

Do Good

1. Amanda Terkel, "Hillary Clinton: 'There Is Something Profoundly Wrong in Our Criminal Justice System,'" *The Huffington Post*, April 29, 2015, www.huffingtonpost.com/2015/04/29/hillary-clinton-baltimore_n_7170668.html.

2. Adapted from *Adult Bible Studies Teacher*, Fall 2016 (Nashville: Cokesbury, 2016).

3. "United Methodist Women's Assembly," Hillary Clinton Speeches, April 26, 2014, https://hillaryspeeches.com/2014/04/26/united-methodist-womens-assembly/.

4. Hillary Clinton, "My Plan for Helping America's Poor," *The New York Times* online, September 21, 2016, www.nytimes.com/2016/09/21/opinion/hillary-clinton-my -plan-for-helping-americas-poor.html.

5. "Vice President Biden Campaigns for Hillary in Nevada," Hillary Clinton Speeches, https://hillaryspeeches.com/2016/10/29/vice-president-biden-campaigns-for-hillary -in-nevada/.

6. "Transcript of Hillary Clinton's Speech at the Al Smith Dinner," *Time*, October 20, 2016, http://time.com/4539979/read-transcript-hillary-clinton-speech-al-smith -dinner/.

7. Elizabeth Barrett Browning, "From 'Aurora Leigh,'" in *The Oxford Book of English Mystical Verse*, ed. D. H. S. Nicholson and A. H. E. Lee (Oxford: Clarendon, 1917).

8. "Bill Clinton and Senators Sanders and Warren Campaign for Hillary," Hillary Clinton Speeches, https://hillaryspeeches.com/2016/10/04/bill-clinton-and-senators -sanders-and-warren-campaign-for-hillary/.

9. Jack Amick, "Prayer for a New Vision," United Methodist Committee on Relief, September 9, 2015, www.umcor.org/umcor/resources/hotline-news-archives/2015 /september/umcor-hotline-for-september-9.

10. "Hillary Clinton on Using the Golden Rule to Bridge Divides at the 2016 African Methodist Episcopal Church National Convention," July 8, 2016, https://berkleycenter .georgetown.edu/quotes/hillary-clinton-on-using-the-golden-rule-to-bridge-divides -at-the-2016-african-methodist-episcopal-church-national-convention.

11. Henri Nouwen, "Being Given," Henri Nouwen Society, http://henrinouwen.org /meditation/being-given/.

12. Dan Merica, "Chelsea Clinton Gives Birth to a Daughter," CNN, September 27, 2014, www.cnn.com/2014/09/27/us/chelsea-clinton-baby-girl/.

13. "Immigration Reform," www.hillaryclinton.com/issues/immigration-reform/.

14. Liz Kreutz, "In Church, Hillary Clinton Learns to Be 'Nicer to the Press,'" ABC News, September 13, 2015, http://abcnews.go.com/Politics/church-hillary-clinton-learns -nicer-press/story?id=33727039.

15. Henri Nouwen, "Growing Beyond Self-Rejection," Henri Nouwen Society, http:// henrinouwen.org/meditation/growing-beyond-self-rejection/.

16. "John Wesley's Explanatory Notes," Christianity.com, www.christianity.com/bible /commentary.php?com=wes&b=56&c=3.

17. "Clinton Wins 8 of 12 Super Tuesday States," Hillary Clinton Speeches, March 1, 2016, https://hillaryspeeches.com/2016/03/01/super-tuesday-vote/.

18. *The Book of Common Prayer* (New York: Oxford University Press, 1990), 213.

19. "Retirees Strongly Endorse Hillary Clinton for President," Alliance for Retired Americans, June 30, 2016, https://retiredamericans.org/retirees-strongly-endorse -hillary-clinton-president/.

20. Charles J. Chaput, "'Come to Me: Be with Me'—Relationships Have Consequences 2001," *Catholic News Agency*, June 16, 2001, www.catholicnewsagency.com /document/come-to-me-be-with-me-relationships-have-consequences-2001-229/.

21. "Racial Justice," www.hillaryclinton.com/issues/racial-justice/.

22. Jacob Ryan, "Speaking in Louisville, Hillary Clinton Calls for Policies that Advance

Women," WFPL News Louisville, April 26, 2014, http://wfpl.org/speaking-louisville
-hillary-clinton-calls-policies-advance-women/.

Live by Faith

1. Joe Parzlale and Carl Campanile, "Hillary Clinton Touts Free Tuition Program Alongside Cuomo," *New York Post*, April 12, 2017, http://nypost.com/2017/04/12 /hillary-clinton-touts-free-tuition-program-alongside-cuomo/.
2. "Full Transcript of the Democratic National Debate," CNN, March 6, 2016, http:// transcripts.cnn.com/TRANSCRIPTS/1603/06/se.08.html.
3. Henri Nouwen, "The Spirit Will Speak in Us," Henri Nouwen Society, http:// henrinouwen.org/meditation/spirit-will-speak-us/.
4. Melanie Mizenko, "Vice President Joe Biden Speaks at Wilkes University," *Times Leader*, October 21, 2016, http://timesleader.com/news/local/599164/crowd -waiting-for-joe-biden-to-speak-at-wilkes-university.
5. Kyle Balluck, "Clinton Marks March on Washington: 'Something Is Profoundly Wrong,'" *The Hill*, August 28, 2016, http://thehill.com/blogs/ballot-box/presidential -races/293578-clinton-marks-march-on-washington-anniversary-something.
6. Kathleen Gray and Katrease Stafford, "Hillary Clinton: What Happened in Flint Is Immoral," *Detroit Free Press*, February 7, 2016, www.freep.com/story/news/local /michigan/flint-water-crisis/2016/02/07/hillary-clinton-flint-campaign-stop /79902530/.
7. "Full Transcript of the Democratic National Debate."
8. Gray and Stafford, "What Happened in Flint Is Immoral."
9. "Full Transcript of the Democratic National Debate."
10. Anita Snow and Michael Warren, "With Rescue, Miners' Private Lives Come to Light," *The San Diego Union-Tribune*, October 13, 2010, www.sandiegouniontribune.com /sdut-with-rescue-miners-private-lives-come-to-light-2010oct13-story.html.
11. "Full Transcript of the Democratic National Debate."
12. Gray and Stafford, "What Happened in Flint Is Immoral."
13. "Hillary Clinton Statement on Hurricane Matthew Aftermath," Hillary Clinton Speeches, October 11, 2016, https://hillaryspeeches.com/2016/10/11/hillary-clinton -statement-on-hurricane-matthew-aftermath/.
14. Amy Chozick, "Hillary Clinton Emphasizes Importance of Faith to Black Audience," *The New York Times*, September 8, 2016, www.nytimes.com/2016/09/09/us /politics/hillary-clinton-emphasizes-importance-of-faith-to-black-audience .html?_r=0.

Dare to Hope

1. Edward Mote, "My Hope Is Built," *The United Methodist Hymnal* (Nashville: The United Methodist Publishing House, 1989), 368.
2. Vanessa K. De Luca, "What Hillary Clinton Is Promising Black Women", *Essence Magazine*, September 7, 2016. www.essence.com/2016/09/07/hillary-clinton-black -women-vote-2016-election.
3. Lindsey Stanberry, "Chelsea Clinton Tells R29 What Happens Next," Refinery29, January 18, 2017, www.refinery29.com/2017/01/135946/chelsea-clinton-new-days -resolution.

4. Arthur Bennett, *The Valley of Vision: A Collection of Puritan Prayers & Devotions* (Edinburgh, Scotland: The Banner of Truth Trust, 1975).

5. Rachel Gillett, "Hillary Clinton Spoke About the 'Devastating' Election Aftermath and Whether She Expects to Run for Office Again," *Business Insider*, April 7, 2017, www.businessinsider.com/hillary-clinton-election-loss-trump-future-career-plans.

6. "Hillary Clinton Answers *New York Times* Readers' Questions," Hillary Clinton Speeches, October 20, 2016, https://hillaryspeeches.com/2016/10/20/hillary-clinton-answers-new-york-times-readers-questions/.

7. S. A. Miller, "Hillary Clinton Vows to Be Gun-Control President," *Washington Post*, August 26, 2015, www.washingtontimes.com/news/2015/aug/26/hillary-clinton-vows-be-gun-control-president/.

8. "New York City Homelessness: The Basic Facts," Coalition for the Homeless, December 2015, www.coalitionforthehomeless.org/wp-content/uploads/2015/12/NYC-Homelessness-Fact-Sheet-10-2015.pdf.

9. "Remarks Pledging to Fight for Gun Reforms and Protect Communities," May 23, 2016, www.hillaryclinton.com/speeches/remarks-pledging-fight-gun-reforms-and-protect-communities/.

10. "Remarks to the National Action Network," April 13, 2016, www.hillaryclinton.com/post/remarks-national-action-network/.

11. "HFA Memo: The Choice Facing Voters in This Election," Hillary Clinton Speeches, October 31, 2016, https://hillaryspeeches.com/2016/10/31/hfa-memo-the-choice-facing-voters-in-this-election/.

12. "Hillary Clinton Statement on Alleged Plot Against Somali Community," Hillary Clinton Speeches, October 15, 2016, https://hillaryspeeches.com/2016/10/15/hillary-clinton-statement-on-alleged-plot-against-somali-community/.

13. "Remarks Alongside Alicia Machado in Dade City, FL," November 3, 2016, www.hillaryclinton.com/speeches/remarks-alongside-alicia-machado-in-dade-city-fl/.

Overcome Fear

1. "At AME General Conference, Hillary Clinton Calls for Action in Wake of Recent Shootings," www.hillaryclinton.com/briefing/updates/2016/07/08/at-ame-general-conference-hillary-clinton-calls-for-action-in-wake-of-recent-shootings/.

2. Eli Watkins, "Hillary Clinton Blasts Trump on LGBT Rights," CNN Politics, April 21, 2017, www.cnn.com/2017/04/20/politics/hillary-clinton-lgbt-center/.

3. "Climate Change," www.hillaryclinton.com/issues/climate/.

4. Clift, "Hillary Clinton Vows to Continue the Fight for Women Across the Globe."

5. "Hillary Clinton Calls Time Off Campaign Trail for Pneumonia a 'Gift,'" ABC News, September 15, 2016, http://abcnews.go.com/Politics/hillary-clinton-calls-time-off-campaign-trail-pneumonia/story?id=42113292.

6. Rebecca Rozelle-Stone, *Simone Weil and Theology* (New York: Bloomsbury T&T Clark, 2013), 78.

7. Olivia Stacey, "Hillary Clinton's Family: 5 Fast Facts You Need to Know," *Heavy*, August 2, 2016, http://heavy.com/news/2016/08/hillary-clinton-family-husband-bill-clinton-daughter-chelsea-marc-mezvinsky-mother-dorothy-rodham-father-hugh-rodham/.

8. E. M. White, "Hillary Clinton Pens Open Letter to Charleston," Hillary Clinton

Speeches, June 17, 2016, https://hillaryspeeches.com/2016/06/17/hillary-clinton
-pens-open-letter-to-charleston/.

9. Hillary Clinton, "An Open Letter on Charleston," CNN, June 17, 2016, www.cnn
.com/2016/06/17/opinions/charleston-anniversary-letter-clinton/index.html.

10. Henri Nouwen Society, September 12, 2016, www.facebook.com/177672622272908
/photos/a.656757421031090.1073741827.177672622272908/1557808407592649
/?type=3&theater.

11. "Transcript of the Democratic Presidential Debate," CNN, March 6, 2016, www
.cnn.com/TRANSCRIPTS/1603/06/se.05.html.

12. Victor Hugo quotations, www.goodreads.com/quotes/4725-have-courage-for-the
-great-sorrows-of-life-and-patience.

13. Henri Nouwen, "Active Waiting," Henri Nouwen Society, http://henrinouwen.org
/meditation/active-waiting/.

14. Amy Chozick, "Hillary Clinton Gets Personal on Christ and Her Faith," *The New York
Times*, January 25, 2016, www.nytimes.com/politics/first-draft/2016/01/25/hillary
-clinton-gets-personal-on-christ-and-her-faith/.

15. "Remarks at the National Baptist Convention in Kansas City, MO," www.hillaryclinton
.com/speeches/remarks-at-the-national-baptist-convention-in-kansas-city-mo/.

Be Blessed

1. James Merrell, *The Power of One: Men and Women of Faith Who Make a Difference*
(Bloomington, MN: Bethany, 1976).

2. Chozick, "Hillary Clinton Gets Personal on Christ and Her Faith."

3. Hillary Rodham Clinton, *Hard Choices* (New York: Simon & Schuster, 2014).

4. "Matthew and Work," The Theology of Work Project, www.theologyofwork.org
/new-testament/matthew/.

5. Martin Saunders, "The Faith of Hillary Clinton in 7 Quotes," *Christianity Today*, May 20,
2016, www.christiantoday.com/article/the.faith.of.hillary.clinton.in.7.quotes/86481.htm.

6. "Remarks on Working Families in Warren, MI," August 11, 2016, www.hillaryclinton
.com/speeches/remarks-on-working-families-and-her-economic-plan-in-warren-mi/.

7. Suzanne Steinbaum, "Living from the Heart: Demoting Your Brain as CEO," *The
Huffington Post*, January 25, 2013, www.huffingtonpost.com/dr-suzanne-steinbaum
/living-from-the-heart_b_2528372.html.

8. "Hillary Rodham Clinton: By the Book," *The New York Times*, June 11, 2014, www
.nytimes.com/2014/06/15/books/review/hillary-rodham-clinton-by-the-book
.html?_r=1.

9. "Hillary Clinton Fights On," Christian Broadcasting Network, www1.cbn.com/content
/hillary-clinton-fights.

10. "Better Than Bullying: Hillary Clinton's Plan to Create Safer Schools for Our Kids,"
October 27, 2016, www.hillaryclinton.com/briefing/factsheets/2016/10/27/better
-than-bullying-hillary-clintons-plan-to-create-safer-schools-for-our-kids/.

11. Walter Wink, "The Third Way," November 14, 1993, http://web.cerritos.edu/tstolze
/SitePages/Walter%20Wink%20-%20The%20Third%20Way.pdf.

12. "Hillary Clinton Rallies Democrats Via Video," https://hillaryspeeches.com/category
/speeches/page/2/.

13. Wink, "The Third Way."

14. Matthew Henry, *Matthew Henry's Concise Commentary*, An abridgment of the 6-volume *Matthew Henry's Commentary on the Bible*, Christian Classics Ethereal Library, May 16, 2017, www.ccel.org/ccel/henry/mhcc.xxxii.vi.html.

15. Paulina Firozi, "Clinton Thanks Supporters in Year-End Message," *The Hill*, December 26, 2016, http://thehill.com/blogs/blog-briefing-room/news/hillary-clinton-won-the -popular-vote-christmas-message.

16. Chozick, "Hillary Clinton Gets Personal on Christ and Her Faith."

17. Hillary Clinton, "My Plan for Helping America's Poor."

18. Jimmy Carter, *Living Faith* (New York: Broadway Books, 1998).

19. Dan Merica, "New South Carolina Ad Features Reverend Wooed by Clinton's Biblical Knowledge," CNN, January 14, 2016, www.cnn.com/2016/01/14/politics/hillary -clinton-south-carolina-ad-minister/index.html.

20. Thérèse de Lisieux and John Clarke, *Story of a Soul: The Autobiography of St. Therese of Lisieux* (Washington, DC: ICS Publications, 1996), 242.

21. Ed Pilkington and Andrea Bernstein, "9/11 Tapes Reveal Raw and Emotional Hillary Clinton," *The Guardian*, September 9, 2016, www.theguardian.com/us-news/2016 /sep/09/hillary-clinton-9-11-attacks-response.

Call to Love

1. Henri Nouwen, "Unity in the Heart of God," Henri Nouwen Society, http:// henrinouwen.org/meditation/unity-in-the-heart-of-god/.

2. Hillary Clinton, "Commentary: Taking Care of Vets Is 'Sacred Responsibility,'" *Military Times*, November 11, 2015, www.militarytimes.com/story/opinion/2015/11/11 /commentary-taking-care-vets-sacred-responsibility/75525780/.

3. "Love Made Me an Inventor," Faith and Leadership online, September 12, 2011, www .faithandleadership.com/multimedia/love-made-me-inventor.

4. Henri Nouwen, "Doing Love," Henri Nouwen Society, http://henrinouwen.org /meditation/doing-love/.

5. Holley Gerth, "1 Corinthians 13:4 Prayer," Taking It One Step at a Time (blog), February 25, 2011, http://onestep87.blogspot.com/2011/02/1-corinthians-134-prayer .html.

6. David A. Graham, "U.S. Politicians React to the Attacks in Brussels," *The Atlantic*, March 22, 2016, www.theatlantic.com/politics/archive/2016/03/brussels-political -reax-united-states/474825/.

7. Adam Liptak, "Supreme Court Ruling Makes Same-Sex Marriage a Right Nationwide," *New York Times* online, June 26, 2015, www.nytimes.com/2015/06/27/us/supreme -court-same-sex-marriage.html?_r=0.

8. Przybyla, "Hillary Clinton Says 'Future Is Female' in New Video."

9. "U.S. Must Choose Resolve Over Fear: Hillary Clinton Outlines Plan to Defeat ISIS and Global Terrorism," HillaryClinton.com, January 31, 2016, www.hillaryclinton.com /post/us-must-choose-resolve-over-fear-hillary-clinton-outlines-plan-defeat-isis-and -global-terrorism/.

10. "Hillary Clinton Speaks at the Ohio Democratic Party Legacy Dinner," Hillary Clinton Speeches, March 13, 2016, https://hillaryspeeches.com/tag/mount-zion-fellowship/.

11. Henri J. M. Nouwen, *Life of the Beloved: Spiritual Living in a Secular World* (New York: Crossroad, 2002), 106.

12. Henri Nouwen, "Mastering Evil with Good," Henri Nouwen Society, http://
    henrinouwen.org/meditation/mastering-evil-good/.
13. Dan Merica, "10-Year-Old Moves Clinton with Question About Bullying," CNN
    Politics, December 23, 2015, http://www.cnn.com/2015/12/22/politics/hillary
    -clinton-bullying-donald-trump/index.html.
14. Robin Marty, "The Beautiful Message Hillary Clinton Has Been Waiting Decades to
    Proclaim," *Cosmopolitan* online, July 28, 2016, www.cosmopolitan.com/politics/news
    /a62039/hillary-clinton-slogan-message-love-kindness/.
15. Nouwen, "Unity in the Heart of God."
16. Hillary Clinton, "Remarks at Grand Valley State University, Grand Rapids, Michigan,"
    The American Presidency Project, November 7, 2016, www.presidency.ucsb.edu/ws
    /index.php?pid=119690.
17. White, "Hillary Clinton Pens Open Letter to Charleston."
18. "Message of His Holiness Benedict XVI for the Twenty-Eighth World Youth Day
    2013," w2.vatican.va/content/benedict-xvi/en/messages/youth/documents/hf_ben
    -xvi_mes_20121018_youth.html.
19. Chozick, "Hillary Clinton Gets Personal on Christ and Her Faith."
20. Quoted in Brennan Manning, *The Signature of Jesus* (Portland: Multnomah, 2004),
    149–50.

Remember

1. "Democratic Town Hall: Transcript, Video," CNN, February 4, 2016, www.cnn
   .com/2016/02/03/politics/democratic-town-hall-transcript/.
2. "Remarks at the African Methodist Episcopal Church National Convention," July 11,
   2016, www.hillaryclinton.com/speeches/remarks-african-methodist-episcopal-church
   -national-convention/.
3. Daniel Burke, "The Public and Private Faith of Hillary Clinton," CNN Politics, October
   31, 2016. www.cnn.com/2016/10/30/politics/clinton-faith-private/.
4. Daniel Silliman, "Hillary Clinton Showed Up for Church Today. Will Faith Help or
   Hurt Her on the Campaign?" *Washington Post*, September 13, 2015, www
   .washingtonpost.com/news/acts-of-faith/wp/2015/09/13/hillary-clinton-showed
   -up-for-church-today-will-faith-help-or-hurt-her-on-the-campaign/?utm_term=.ce
   7b9c524ebb.
5. St. Patrick, "A Prayer for the Faithful," Catholic Online, www.catholic.org/prayers
   /prayer.php?p=2930.
6. Silliman, "Hillary Clinton Showed Up for Church Today."
7. Marina Fang. "Watch Hillary Clinton Tease Donald Trump at Charity Dinner,"
   Huffington Post, October 20, 2016, www.huffingtonpost.com/entry/hillary-clinton-al
   -smith-dinner_us_58095feae4b0cdea3d869a80.
8. "Earth Day Prayer," Creation Justice Ministries, http://action.creationjustice.
   org/o/50750/t/0/blastContent.jsp?email_blast_KEY=1270057.
9. Evan Real, "Hillary Clinton: Why My Granddaughter Charlotte Inspired My
   Presidential Campaign" *Us Weekly*, April 22, 2016, www.usmagazine.com/celebrity
   -news/news/hillary-clintons-talks-granddaughter-presidential-campaign-w203824.
10. Abby Phillip, "Hillary Clinton Opens Up About Running for President: 'This Is Hard
    for Me,'" *Washington Post*, February 4, 2016, www.washingtonpost.com/news/post

-politics/wp/2016/02/04/hillary-clinton-opens-up-about-running-for-president
-this-is-hard-for-me/?utm_term=.6fee467b18f2.

11. Silliman, "Hillary Clinton Showed Up for Church Today."

12. Henri Nouwen, "Jesus, Our Food and Drink," Henri Nouwen Society, http://
henrinouwen.org/meditation/jesus-food-drink/.

13. J. H. Merle-D'Aubugné, *History of the Great Reformation of the Sixteenth Century in
Germany, Switzerland, Etc.* (Philadelphia: Porter & Coates, 1870), 199. Martin Luther
is said to have prayed this prayer at the time of his appearance before Charles V, the
Holy Roman Emperor, in 1521.

14. Hillary Clinton, "An Open Letter to Latina Millennials," Popsugar, November 8, 2016,
www.popsugar.com/latina/Hillary-Clinton-Open-Letter-Latina-Millennials
-42515985.

15. Adapted from The Diakonia Council of Churches in South Africa. www.diakonia.org
.za/our-history/.

16. "HIV and AIDS," www.hillaryclinton.com/issues/fighting-hiv-and-aids/.

17. Maya T. Prabhu, "Hillary Clinton Continues to Make Case to Black Voters During
Luncheon with Alpha Kappa Alpha Sorority," *The Post and Courier*, February 23, 2016,
www.postandcourier.com/politics/hillary-clinton-continues-to-make-case-to-black
-voters-during/article_b91ca07d-dbe4-50a3-b1a3-083197ffa5c3.html.

18. Adapted from James A. Harnish, *Make a Difference: Following Your Passion and Finding
Your Place to Serve* (Nashville: Abingdon Press, 2017).

19. Julian of Norwich, "All Shall Be Well," Christian History Institute, www.christianhistory
institute.org/incontext/article/julian/.

20. Steve Lieberman, "Clintons Attend Christmas Eve Service at Mount Kisco Methodist
Church," *Lohud*, December 24, 2016, www.lohud.com/story/news/local/2016/12/24
/clintons-christmas-mass-mount-kisco/95836442/.

21. "Remarks at the African Methodist Episcopal Church National Convention."

Make Room for All

1. Chad Livengood, "Hillary Clinton Stumps at Detroit Black Churches," *The Detroit
News*, March 6, 2016, www.detroitnews.com/story/news/politics/elections/2016
/03/06/hillary-clinton-stumps-detroit-black-churches/81407262/.

2. Annie Karni, "Hillary's High Stakes Mission to Charlotte," *Politico*, October 1, 2016,
www.politico.com/story/2016/10/in-charlotte-clinton-claims-obamas-mission
-229009.

3. Paulina Firozi, "Clinton: 'We Don't Need to Be Building Walls,' *The Hill*, April 12,
2017, http://thehill.com/homenews/news/328519-clinton-seems-to-knock-trump-in
-speech-praising-ny-free-tuition-program.

4. George Washington, "Letter to the Jews of Newport," 18 August 1790, Washington
Papers, 6:284-85.

5. Noel Gutierrez-Morfin, "Hillary Clinton Talks Systemic Racism with 'The Breakfast
Club,'" NBC News, October 26, 2016, www.nbcnews.com/news/nbcblk/breakfast
-club-interviews-hillary-clinton-her-69th-birthday-n673291.

6. "Hillary Clinton Delivers Remarks at National Action Network," April 13, 2016, www
.hillaryclinton.com/briefing/updates/2016/04/13/hillary-clinton-delivers-remarks
-at-national-action-network/.

7. Amy Ellis Nutt, Matt Zapotosky, and Mark Berman, "3 Police Officers Killed, 2 Wounded in Baton Rouge; Gunman Dead," The Washington Post, July 18, 2016, www .washingtonpost.com/politics/3-police-officers-killed-3-wounded-in-baton-rouge /2016/07/17/3734a3a6-4c2f-11e6-aa14-e0c1087f7583_story.html?hpid=hp_hp -banner-main_mm-batonrouge-1113am%3Ahomepage%2Fstory&utm_term= .a1f812d1508f.

8. Hillary Clinton, "Statement on Las Vegas Trump Hotel Labor Law Violations," The American Presidency Project, November 4, 2016, www.presidency.ucsb.edu/ws/?pid =119238.

9. Henri Nouwen, "Who Is My Neighbor?" Henri Nouwen Society, http://henrinouwen .org/meditation/who-is-my-neighbor/.

10. David Giambusso, "Clintons Honored at Wildlife Conservation Society Gala," Politico, June 13, 2014, www.politico.com/states/new-york/city-hall/story/2014/06/clintons -honored-at-wildlife-conservation-society-gala-013663.

11. Tom McCarthy, "Hillary Clinton: America Must Confront 'Hard Truths About Race and Justice,'" The Guardian, April 29, 2015, https://www.theguardian.com/us-news/2015 /apr/29/hillary-clinton-criminal-justice-overhaul-baltimore-unrest.

12. "After Orlando Shooting, Muslim Americans Show Support for Victims," USA Today, June 12, 2016. www.usatoday.com/story/news/nation/2016/06/12/orlando -nightclub-muslim-reaction/85790320/.

13. "Fanny Crosby: Prolific and Blind Hymn Writer," www.christianitytoday.com/history /people/poets/fanny-crosby.html.

14. Henri Nouwen, "Jesus Is Merciful," Henri Nouwen Society, http://henrinouwen.org /meditation/jesus-is-merciful/.

15. "Difficult Passages in King Lear," www.shakespeare-online.com/plays/kinglear /learpassages.html.

16. "Interpreting Newspapers from Your Bible," Garrett-Evangelical Theological Seminary, May 28, 2014, www.garrett.edu/interpreting-newspapers-your-bible.

17. Hannah Fraser-Chanpong, "Hillary Clinton Weighs in on Syrian Refugee Crisis," CBS News, November 17, 2015, www.cbsnews.com/news/in-dallas-hillary-clinton-weighs -in-on-syrian-refugee-crisis/.

18. Henri Nouwen, "The Door Open to Anyone," Henri Nouwen Society, http:// henrinouwen.org/meditation/door-open-anyone/.

19. John Wesley, "A Catholic Spirit," Christian Resource Institute, The Voice, www.crivoice .org/cathspirit.html.

20. "Remarks at the Democratic National Convention," July 29, 2016, www.hillaryclinton .com/speeches/remarks-at-the-democratic-national-convention/.

21. "Statement on Assassination of Martin Luther King, Jr., Indianapolis, Indiana, April 4, 1968," Robert F. Kennedy Speeches, www.jfklibrary.org/Research/Research-Aids /Ready-Reference/RFK-Speeches/Statement-on-the-Assassination-of-Martin-Luther -King.aspx.

Pray with Her

1. Madeline Conway, "Hillary Clinton: I Hope a 'Wave of Young Women' Run for Office," Politico, March 7, 2017, www.politico.com/story/2017/03/hillary-clinton-young -women-run-for office-235775.

2. "Hillary Clinton Publishes Op-Ed About Being a Working Mother," Hillary Clinton Speeches, September 29, 2016, https://hillaryspeeches.com/2016/09/29/hillary -clinton-publishes-op-ed-about-being-a-working-mother/.

3. Clift, "Hillary Clinton Vows to Continue the Fight for Women Across the Globe."

4. Hillary Clinton, "What I Learned from Being a Mom Who Works," *Fortune*, September 29, 2016, http://fortune.com/2016/09/29/hillary-clinton-working-mothers -presidential-election/.

5. Dan Graves, "All Shall Be Well," Christian History Institute, www.christianhistory institute.org/incontext/article/julian/.

6. David Weigel, "Hillary Clinton to Democrats: 'Keep Fighting and Keep the Faith,'" *Washington Post*, February 24, 2017, www.washingtonpost.com/news/powerpost /wp/2017/02/24/hillary-clinton-to-democrats-keep-fighting-and-keep-the -faith/?utm_term=.31d551344257.

7. "Clinton Speaks at Children's Defense Fund Event," Hillary Clinton Speeches, November 16, 2016, https://hillaryspeeches.com/2016/11/16/clinton-speaks-at -childrens-defense-fund-event/.

8. Dan Merica, "With Scripture, Hillary Clinton Wins Over a Voter," CNN Politics, May 28, 2015, edition.cnn.com/2015/05/27/politics/hillary-clinton-2016-election-faith/.

9. Przybyla, "Hillary Clinton Says 'Future Is Female' in New Video."

10. "Remarks at the African Methodist Episcopal Church National Convention."

11. Clift, "Hillary Clinton Vows to Continue the Fight for Women Across the Globe."

12. Hillary Clinton, "We All Have Different Gifts."

13. Jared Brey, "In Philly, Clinton Decries 'Senseless' Killings in Dallas, Louisiana, Minnesota," *Philadelphia* magazine, July 8, 2016, www.phillymag.com/news/2016/07 /08/hillary-clinton-dallas-shootings-speech/#mGg6g4ywQA0HfP1Q.99.

14. "Hillary Clinton's Concession Speech, (Full Text)" CNN Politics, November 9, 2016, www.cnn.com/2016/11/09/politics/hillary-clinton-concession-speech/.

Tested by Fire

1. J. Philip Newell, *Sounds of the Eternal, A Celtic Psalter* (Grand Rapids: Eerdmans, 2002).

2. John Dear, "The Prayers of Martin Luther King Jr.," *National Catholic Reporter*, January 15, 2013, www.ncronline.org/blogs/road-peace/prayers-martin-luther-king-jr.

3. Gregory Krieg, "It's Official: Clinton Swamps Trump in Popular Vote," CNN Politics, December 22, 2016, www.cnn.com/2016/12/21/politics/donald-trump-hillary -clinton-popular-vote-final-count/.

4. Henri Nouwen, "Waiting with Patience," Henri Nouwen Society, http://henrinouwen .org/meditation/waiting-with-patience/.

5. "Hillary Clinton's Concession Speech (Full Text)."

6. Ibid.

7. Ibid.

8. Ibid.

9. Philip Rucker, "'I Would Be Your President': Clinton Blames Russia, FBI Chief for 2016 Election Loss," *The Washington Post*, May 3, 2017, www.washingtonpost.com /politics/hillary-clinton-blames-russian-hackers-and-comey-for-2016-election-loss /2017/05/02/e62fef72-2f60-11e7-8674-437ddb6e813e_story.html?hpid=hp_hp -more-top-stories_clinton-250pm%3Ahomepage%2Fstory&utm_term=.75e2418a766a.